ELEMENTARY
SOCIAL
STUDIES

ELEMENTARY SOCIAL STUDIES

A PRACTICAL GUIDE

June R. Chapin
College of Notre Dame

Rosemary G. Messick
San Jose State University

Longman
New York & London

Elementary Social Studies: A Practical Guide

Longman Inc., 95 Church Street, White Plains, N.Y. 10601

Associated companies:
Longman Group Ltd., London
Longman Cheshire Pty., Melbourne
Longman Paul Pty., Auckland
Copp Clark Pitman, Toronto
Pitman Publishing Inc., New York

Executive editor: Raymond T. O'Connell
Development editor: Virginia L. Blanford
Production editor: Louise M. Kahan
Text design: Steven August Krastin
Cover design: Jill Francis Wood
Text art: J&R Art Services
Production supervisor: Pamela Teisler

Library of Congress Cataloging-in-Publication Data
Chapin, June R., 1931–
    Elementary social studies.
    Bibliography: p.
    Includes index.
    1. Social sciences—Study and teaching
(Elementary)—United States.   I. Messick, Rosemary G.
II. Title.
LB1584.C47 1988   372.8′3044   88-553
ISBN 0-8013-0043-6

89 90 91 92 93 94 9 8 7 6 5 4 3 2

Contents

Preface

We have made three assumptions in this book about your teacher-preparation program: first, that you come to the professional sequence of your program with a general background in those disciplines that serve as a foundation for elementary social studies; second, that you, like students in most professional programs, are scheduled for only a one-semester, one- to three-credit course in teaching social studies; and third, that you have other courses in your program that expose you to learning theory, curriculum planning, the teaching of concepts and generalizations, and instructional technology.

You can predict the scope of this text by its title. Our intention is to expose you to what is *basic* and *specific* to teaching the social studies in elementary grades. Although the text focuses on topics essential to elementary-classroom social studies instruction, additional elements have been woven purposefully into the exposition. The vignettes, their analyses, and much of the text itself are meant to augment your knowledge about classroom instruction and curriculum in general. Chapter introductions and definitions of terms provide you with links to your other professional courses in the areas of curriculum and learning. Exercises, lesson plans, and other activities suggest instructional resources to pursue in your own teaching.

Some topics in this text are common to any basic social studies methods textbook. Some, however, are distinctive. They include Chapter 4 ("Social Studies in the Primary Grades"), Chapter 5 ("Social Studies in the Fourth through Eighth Grades"), Chapter 6 ("Elementary Citizenship Education"), and Chapter 8 ("Communication Skills in the Social Studies"). Other chapters include basic and essential definitions and structures for social studies instructional organization, planning, matching instructional strategies to topics, learning about cultures, teaching special skills, and evaluation.

The social studies typically receives little attention in elementary school, especially in the primary grades. Our hope is that you will come to see the social studies as a vital part of the school day at all levels, not only as an application area for basic skills and values but also and, more importantly, as a bridge between the school and the experiences your students will have outside the classroom.

We continue to learn from the experiences of our own students, from classroom teachers with whom we work, and from our university colleagues throughout the country. We are grateful for their valuable contributions to this text, although we alone are responsible for any errors in it. Between us, we have taught in the Midwest, overseas, and, for many years, in California. We have seen teachers make a positive difference in the lives of children and feel privileged to watch children gain opportunities through education. We believe that the social studies can help you make dreams a reality for the children you teach, and we invite you to work with us toward that goal.

June R. Chapin
Rosemary G. Messick

CHAPTER

1

The Elementary Social Studies Curriculum

In this chapter we introduce current trends in defining the social studies curriculum. Specifically, we treat the following topics:

1. Images of the Social Studies
2. Why Teach the Social Studies?
3. Definitions of the Social Studies
4. National Curriculum Patterns
5. Importance of Textbook Series
6. Scope and Sequence Issues

IMAGES OF THE SOCIAL STUDIES

Welcome to the world of social studies! What do you remember about your own elementary social studies program? If any of the following activities seem familiar, jot down on a piece of paper whether or not the memory is pleasant.

Clipping out items from a newspaper for Friday current events
Doing a research report on Daniel Boone from your school's encyclopedia
Finding out the latitude and longitude of a long list of cities
Learning about the Pilgrims at Thanksgiving
Visiting a site where your state's Native Americans lived
Writing a contest essay on American government
Answering the questions at the end of a textbook chapter

Writing to foreign consuls and embassies for information about "your" assigned
    country
Reenacting pioneer life
Making a papier-mâché globe
Writing a personal history book
Drawing neighborhood maps
Working on a committee where one person dominated
Learning about the immigrant group from which you came

Exercise 1.1   *WHAT WORKS BEST?*

Now add to this list the activities that you remember experiencing in elementary social
studies. Try to include both pleasant and boring times. Compare your list of what you
liked and didn't like with others in your class. Are there activities that everyone
remembers enjoying? Are there other activities that everyone disliked? Your image of
what elementary social studies is stems mainly from your own experiences.

How do you rank the social studies in importance in the elementary curriculum?
Look at the following list of subjects normally taught in elementary school.

Health/physical education (PE)   Reading
Language arts   Science
Mathematics   Social studies

Exercise 1.2   *HOW IMPORTANT IS SOCIAL STUDIES?*

Now rank these subjects in order of importance to you, 1 through 6. Share your list
with other members of your class. You will probably find that, in common with most
elementary teachers and students, you ranked social studies fourth or lower. What may
have influenced your response?

Elementary teachers often have negative attitudes toward the social studies as a result
of their own school experiences, perhaps because of the following:

Learning about social studies largely emphasized trivial facts.
The dominant instructional tool was the textbook.
Most social studies activities concentrated on large group recitation and lecture.
Emotional or affective objectives were not included as part of the curriculum.

Two other reasons may also account, at least in part, for the less-than-enthusiastic attitude that many elementary teachers have toward the social studies: lack of preparation and lack of interest. Many of you have taken only a few social science or history courses in college. You may feel underqualified or reluctant to tackle the sometimes controversial subject matter of the social studies. Many of you may feel strongly that reading and math programs are basic in elementary education; however, a social studies program is also basic. In fact, a good social studies program can go far toward improving skills in other subjects, including reading, writing, and arithmetic.

A good social studies program can also produce good citizens. The educational reform reports of the 1980s have reaffirmed the importance of the social studies in citizenship education. Citizens must make decisions, and they must make them thoughtfully. The "nation (is) at risk" unless we have the background and skills needed for that difficult task. Attitudes toward authority and government are formed early, in the elementary grades; they do not wait until junior high school years to appear.

We believe in the *vital* importance of social studies instruction, both in providing students with basic skills needed in the real world and in preparing students to become responsible, thoughtful, participating citizens. If we are successful in transmitting this belief to you, social studies teaching, at least in your classrooms, may not suffer the neglect that otherwise often occurs at the primary level.

This text will help you find ways of teaching the social studies that you and your students will both learn from and enjoy. Social studies *can* be taught creatively and thoughtfully. As a result of your efforts, students may find that social studies is their favorite subject. More importantly, through your social studies instruction, your students will acquire the necessary knowledge, skills, and values to participate as active citizens in our society.

WHY TEACH THE SOCIAL STUDIES?

The social studies is about people. No other area of the curriculum is more concerned with human relations than the social studies, which is designed to help us understand both ourselves and others—from our families and neighbors to those who live halfway around the world. Each of us is concerned about self, family, and friends. The social studies therefore builds on an area of inherently high interest.

Children studying the social studies today will live much of their lives in the twenty-first century. They will experience a world rapidly changing as knowledge dramatically expands. Their occupations and the skills they need to function in a modern, information-based society may change rapidly as well. As teachers, we must always be conscious of how we can help our students live successfully in the coming years; we must prepare them *now* for the twenty-first century and not wait until it arrives.

In addition to teaching one about human relations, social studies plays an important role in preparing students to become active citizens. Students need to know their rights and their responsibilities as American citizens. They will have to make intelligent choices within the context of our democratic society about what kind of community and world they wish to inhabit. We want them to care about the quality of life in their own community, in their nation, and in the world.

Achieving peace and justice pose an enormous problem to all people. Students must not only incorporate basic American values such as equality, freedom, and respect for people and property, but they must also be able to put those values into action through effective participation in the classroom, school, community, nation, and world. A goal of the social studies (as well as of schooling in general) is to help students *reflect* on their own experiences and values. Mastery of the social studies ensures that students will be informed and thoughtful when they begin to participate in both American culture and the global community.

Creative social studies instruction offers the possibility of producing humane individuals willing to help one another and to make the best of the world. All elementary teachers want their students to *know* things, but they also want to try to shape what their students will become. They want them to be "good" people—caring, thoughtful, and humane, rather than selfish and cynical. An important goal of the social studies, then, must be to support the growth of humane and thoughtful values in students and to produce informed and participating citizens.

The social studies curriculum can be defined in terms of four major categories:

Knowledge   Skills   Values   Social Participation

The *rationale* for elementary social studies can be summarized in four major goals:

To provide *knowledge* about human experiences in the past, present, and future
To develop *skills* to process information
To develop appropriate democratic *values* and attitudes
To provide opportunities for *social participation*

These four goals are not separate and discrete; rather, they are intertwined and overlapping (see Figure 1.1). You may find that in some state frameworks, the third and fourth goals are treated as one objective; social participation is regarded as a democratic value. In other cases, social participation is defined as a skill (the second goal). Values may sometimes be called *civic* values, to differentiate them from *personal* values. But regardless of how the goals are defined, together they form the basic objectives of a social studies education.

Frequently, the process of learning has emotional values attached to it. Did you *hate* math in school? Did you *love* music? When students study something such as pollution, they usually acquire opinions or attitudes about it. Emotional experiences can have a striking impact on both subject area and skill development. The development of content and skills cannot be divorced from the values that govern their use. Certain skills may be taught in school, but there is no guarantee that students will make use of them. Unless students have a commitment to, a need for, or a willingness to use the skills they have learned, those skills will be of little value either to the students or to society. All of this

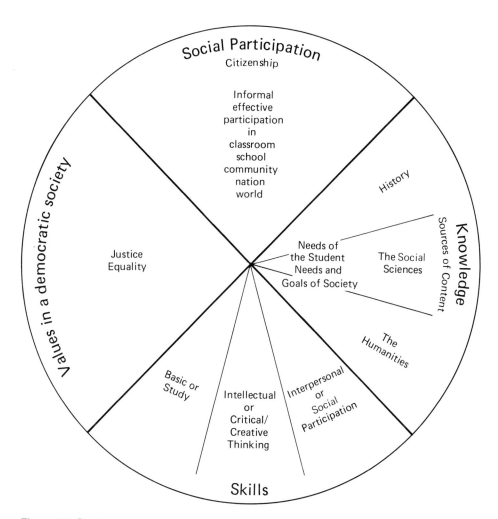

Figure 1.1 Goals of the social studies.

underlines the fact that although we often speak of the four main goals of a social studies education, we must not forget their inherent interrelationships.

DEFINITIONS OF THE SOCIAL STUDIES

Although we have listed four main goals, educators do not always agree on what *content* should be included in the social studies.

Traditionally, the social studies draw upon seven disciplines: history, geography,

TABLE 1.1   DISCIPLINES OF THE SOCIAL STUDIES

The Past	*The Present*	*The Future*
History	Geography	Future science
Geography	The social sciences:	
Anthropology	Economics	Where and how might people
	Political science	live in the future?
How did our	Sociology	
world/nation/community	Anthropology	
come to be the way it is?	Psychology	
	Where and how do people live now?	

economics, political science, sociology, anthropology, and psychology. (See Table 1.1.) We study people in the context of their environment, both past and present. The combination of history, geography, and the social sciences helps explain the events, individuals, and ideas that have produced both continuity and change in our world. Content from the humanities—literature, art, music—and from science can also enliven social studies instruction.

Exercise 1.3   *CONTENT FOR THE SOCIAL STUDIES*

What do *you* think the social studies should include? Write down the topics that you would expect to teach. Would you include subjects such as career education, consumer education, drug-abuse education, family education, or environmental education?

Although definitions of the social studies may vary, the definition that *you* settle on is important. Every elementary teacher should be able to define his or her objectives in teaching the social studies, as well as his or her own decisions about its content.

Here is a definition of three main social studies traditions as outlined by Robert Barr, a social studies educator, and his colleagues.[1]

Social Studies Taught as Citizenship Transmission

Purpose—Citizenship is best promoted by inculcating right values as a framework for making decisions.

---

[1] Robert D. Barr, James L. Barth, and S. Samuel Shermis, *Defining the Social Studies*, Bulletin 51 (Washington, D.C.: National Council for the Social Studies, 1977).

Method—Transmission: Transmission of concepts and values by such techniques as textbook, recitation, lecture, question and answer sessions, and structured problem-solving exercises.

Content—Content is selected by an authority interpreted by the teacher and has the function of illustrating values, beliefs, and attitudes.

Social Studies Taught as Social Science

Purpose—Citizenship is best promoted by decision making based on mastery of social science concepts, processes, and problems.

Method—Discovery: Each of the social sciences has its own method of gathering and verifying knowledge. Students should discover and apply the method that is appropriate to each social science.

Content—Proper content is the structure, concepts, problems, and processes of both the separate and the integrated social science disciplines.

Social Studies Taught as Reflective Inquiry

Purpose—Citizenship is best promoted through a process of inquiry in which knowledge is derived from what citizens need to know to make decisions and solve problems.

Method—Reflective Inquiry: Decision making is structured and disciplined through a reflective inquiry process which aims at identifying problems and responding to conflicts by means of testing insights.

Content—Analysis of individual citizen's values yields needs and interests which in turn form the basis for student self-selection of problems. Problems, therefore, constitute the content for reflection.

Citizenship Transmission

What do you think the tradition of social studies taught as citizenship transmission means? Every nation or group brings up its children to reflect its own values and culture. Primitive groups as well as the most advanced technological societies attempt to socialize their children. The French want their children to appreciate French culture; members of various religious groups want their children to practice their religious beliefs.

In the United States, children must also be prepared to live in our common culture. This means that they must know about and understand our unique American heritage and our political and economic systems. In addition, it means that they must be able to speak English and to participate in community life. Many institutions in our society, including the family and the media, contribute to our children's knowledge about mainstream culture. Our schools also play an important role in this process of teaching about our shared political and social values.

In fact, some social studies authorities like James Shaver argue that the school *must* instill in students a commitment to democratic values. These basic values, which might be called "the American creed," cement the nation together; they include, among other things, due process of law, respect for others, free access to information, freedom of choice (including multiculturalism), and the value of rational thought. According to Shaver, it is crucial that social studies instruction be based on democratic values and that students accept the basic values of our society as givens, not as questions for debate.[2]

But this position does not mean that the teacher has the right to indoctrinate students in every area. *Indoctrination* is the shaping of people's minds by providing information without permitting them to question or examine the information being transmitted. When the purpose of indoctrination is to make citizens dupes of those in power or to influence students to accept a particular solution to a problem, we may well become anxious about it.

We are guilty of using indoctrination as teachers if we base our presentations on biased or incomplete data or if we do not allow students to question ideas to problems. Sometimes a teacher's motivation in such a case may be understandable or even admirable; he or she may not want students to express certain "wrong" ideas or opinions. For example, assume that Ms. Cherez wants the students in her class to collect funds for starving children in Africa. Therefore she may want to show a film or pictures demonstrating the great need that exists. But she probably does *not* want to receive comments from students suggesting that, according to their parents, donated money would be wasted because it would not actually get to the starving people or that developing nations should solve their own problems. If Ms. Cherez manipulates the discussion, then, to cut off such alternative opinions and comments, she is guilty of indoctrination—even if it is indoctrination for a so-called good cause.

However, the citizenship-transmission model of social studies often contains elements of indoctrination. One of your goals is to instill in your students the basic American values—not simply an understanding of those values but the values themselves. In this process of cultural transmission, you will emphasize the positive nature of our society's democratic values.

Many authorities want to teach children to be patriotic and to love their country. They want all students to know about our historical traditions, our nation's great achievements, and our uniquely high ideals. How can this goal be achieved? Traditional methods include starting the school day with the Pledge of Allegiance, singing patriotic songs, and retelling legends and myths like the story that George Washington never told a lie. Celebrating birthdays of our presidents or outstanding citizens also makes children aware of the heros and heroines of our nation's history. In these activities, the teacher is not simply using a textbook or a prepared curriculum guide but is also socializing for the desired value. Good literature or films can also be used to invoke in students good feelings about their heritage.

---

[2]James P. Shaver, "Commitment to Values and the Study of Social Problems in Citizenship Education," *Social Education* 49 (March 1985), pp. 194–197.

As students get older, however, you and they must begin to explore how the basic values of our nation should be interpreted to help solve the problems facing our society. The goal should always be to promote a "good" society.

According to the citizenship-transmission tradition, social studies education has two main purposes: to instill a basic commitment to the values of our society and to provide an ability to *apply* those values to the issues facing our nation. Note that a vital component of our basic values is the use of rationality and critical thinking, or inquiry, especially in older children.

Social Science

What main ideas in the social studies are taught as a social science model? This model became popular in the 1960s, when a wide variety of new social studies curriculum projects were funded by various government agencies. Curriculum planners wanted students to understand how social scientists did their work and to grasp the major concepts of each social science discipline. There were anthropology projects, for instance, in which students were given actual artifacts from a particular culture and were instructed to study the objects and guess their purposes. In the study of history, students were taught the difference between primary and secondary sources. They might, for example, be provided with conflicting eyewitness reports of what happened on Lexington Green at the start of the American Revolution and be asked to compare these reports with the description in their textbook.

Social studies textbooks in the 1960s began to include more short selections from original source documents so that students might learn more about how historians actually go about writing history. Sociological Resources, the American Sociology Association's project for the Social Studies, designed inductive exercises in which students gathered data and then were led to form hypotheses from a more critical point of view. Students might be asked to complete sentences like the following: "Parents are ----------." "Rich people are _____," "Russians are ----------," "Police are ----------." Typically, students filled in the blanks with glib generalizations, often based on inadequate information, limited experience, and prejudiced views. After gathering data on the topics covered, they were made aware of their errors. The goal of this kind of exercise was to show students how easily we all jump to conclusions, rather than treating general statements as hypotheses to be tested. These exercises also demonstrated how sociologists obtain data on stereotypes.

In some cases, the new curriculum projects focused on a single subject area—such as economics or anthropology—but in many cases they used an interdisciplinary approach—such as Asian studies. On the whole, the new social studies curriculum projects included more sociology and anthropology than did more traditional approaches. But in the 1970s, many questioned whether these new curriculum projects with their emphases on the structure of the social sciences were relevant. In many cases, students had difficulty with the reading and conceptual levels of these projects.

Reflective Inquiry

The social studies taught as reflective inquiry emphasizes the importance of getting students to think. The teacher helps students use logical thinking and scientific investigation to decide upon issues and values. One difficulty with this approach is the lack of a clear definition for *inquiry* or *reflective inquiry*. In general, with the *inquiry* approach, one engages students in the process of finding out and thinking for themselves, weighing pros and cons, and interpreting the facts. In other words, students are taught not merely to absorb or memorize materials but to evaluate them critically.

There are many formats for reflective inquiry. To some it means simply answering the questions under an illustration in the textbook. For others, it involves the use of case studies that place individuals in dilemmas (whether or not to support the American Revolution) or force them to examine questions (what should happen to individuals who have broken a law). The new law-related education projects often use this format. In general, this approach is more open ended than the more traditional social-studies-as-citizenship-transmission approach.

Two Other Approaches

Two approaches in addition to those outlined above are sometimes used in social studies education. One suggests that the purpose of social studies and other subjects should be student centered and directed toward personal development. The focus is on development of the student's unique potential by allowing for the fullest pursuit of creativity, personal integrity, love of learning, and self-fulfillment. Students should feel that they are competent and capable of making choices and that they can influence their own behavior as well as that of others. This student-centered approach, which concentrates more on the individual than on the needs of society, encourages students to gain an understanding of their own needs and to work with others to achieve their goals. This approach is sometimes followed by private schoolteachers using the Montessori philosophy.

The final approach might be called social studies as informed social criticism, or the new criticism. This approach, which is based on Marxism, calls for giving students the opportunity to analyze critically the ideological base of their schools and of our society. You would not likely find this approach used in standard teacher-training programs or in school districts, but it has adherents at the graduate university level and can be found in the literature on social science education.

Your Choice

Which of these five approaches do you like the best for teaching elementary social studies? Which model do you think reflects the most common practice in schools today? These questions may be difficult to answer, because most teachers use some combination of all three mainstream approaches. They choose from various positions depending on the topic being taught. They do some indoctrination, especially of American values and patriotism, while also encouraging students to think about social policy issues. They teach one unit on a problem in the community using an inquiry approach and the next unit on local government using a traditional citizenship-transmission approach. Monday's lesson might be on making economic or consumer choices, whereas Tuesday's lesson might return to a structured textbook reading with questions at the end of the chapter.

Probably the approach that is *least* used of the three main traditions is social studies taught as social science. Unless a teacher is willing to do a great deal of preparation and gathering of materials, this approach is difficult to implement. Most elementary textbooks include material from all social sciences but do not devote much time to explaining the methods used by various social scientists and historians.

You can see now that definitions of social studies content will vary depending on the value system or philosophical orientation of the teacher or curriculum planner. The *citizenship, or cultural heritage, approach* tends to emphasize American history and our nation's high ideals and achievements. The *social science approach* uses content from the various social science disciplines and history with a view to understanding both the major concepts and the respective methods of gathering data. The *reflective-inquiry approach* can use almost any content as long as it encourages thinking on the part of students.

Exercise 1.4   *MAKE A CHOICE*

Do you now have a tentative definition of the social studies? Which approach do you think is best for the children? List the strengths and weaknesses of each model on a piece of paper. Which model do you think you would use most often in an elementary classroom?

Exercise 1.5   *PARENT SURVEY*

Interview three parents and then three other adults who do not have children in the schools. Ask them to define the social studies. Ask what they think the social studies should do for children. Bring your responses to class. What concerns does the public have about social studies education?

The public may be more concerned than some elementary teachers about which curriculum is implemented in elementary social studies classrooms. In fact, court cases indicate that many parents are very worried about which values and curriculum approaches the schools are using. Controversies over the adoption of social studies textbooks by districts confirm that indication. Some critics of the schools seem to fear that an approach bordering on Marxism and undermining our whole society is being taught and call for a return to the basic citizenship-transmission approach.

NATIONAL CURRICULUM PATTERNS

The United States has thousands of local school districts. Although each one is autonomous and can organize a curriculum to suit its own needs and state requirements, a national social studies curriculum does in fact exist. There are two reasons for this. First is the dominant role that textbooks have had in social studies instruction. In fifth- and eighth-grade classrooms across the nation, you will find United State history being taught from books published by only a handful of large companies. Eight or ten publishers probably control about 90 percent of the textbook market, which ensures a certain similarity in course offerings throughout the nation.

A second reason for the national curriculum is that most educators follow guidelines produced by the National Council for the Social Studies as well as by their own states. Some state guidelines are very broad, requiring only that history, geography, and the social sciences be taught in some manner from kindergarten through twelfth grade. The trend recently, however, has been toward more state control and guidance, particularly since the reform movements of the early 1980s. Some states require that all students be tested in the social studies before they can graduate. Some state frameworks, such as California's, already provide topics in considerable detail for each grade level. In addition, California tests all eighth graders in the social studies and is moving toward testing sixth and twelfth graders as well. Statewide testing tends to make teachers follow the state frameworks more carefully, since students may suffer if the content taught does not match what is being tested.

Social studies state frameworks in turn influence textbook publishers, who want as broad a market as possible. In particular, the state frameworks of the largest states, particularly California and Texas, help to determine what focus textbooks have. For these interrelated reasons, we see a certain amount of uniformity in elementary social studies programs throughout the nation.

In 1980 Project SPAN (Social Studies: Priorities, Practices, and Needs, funded by the National Science Foundation) found the following social studies curriculum pattern in most United States schools:

Grade	Topics
Kindergarten/Grade 1	Self, Family, School
Grade 2	Neighborhoods
Grade 3	Communities
Grade 4	State History, Geographic Regions
Grade 5	United States History, Culture, and Geography
Grade 6	World Cultures, History, and Geography
Grade 7	World Cultures, History, and Geography
Grade 8	United States History
Grade 9	Civics

Grade 10   World History
Grade 11   United States History
Grade 12   American Government/Problems of Democracy

The National Council for the Social Studies Task Force on Scope and Sequence (1983) recommended the following topics:

Grade   Topics

K   Awareness of self in a social setting
1   The individual in primary social groups: Understanding school and family life
2   Meeting basic needs in nearby social groups: The neighborhood
3   Sharing earth-space with others: The community
4   Human life in varied environments: The region
5   People of the Americas: The United States and its close neighbors
6   People and cultures: The Eastern Hemisphere
7   A changing world of many nations: A global view
8   Building a strong and free nation: The United States
9   Systems that make a democratic society work: Law, justice, and economics
10   Origins of major cultures: A world history
11   The maturing of America: United States history
12   One-year course selection (issues and problems of modern society, introduction to social sciences, arts in human societies, international area studies, elective)

Is it the pattern that you followed when you were in school? The basic pattern of social studies content at both elementary and secondary levels has changed little during the past 50 years. But a careful reading of the above lists reveals some problems in the traditional social studies curriculum.

Notice first that United States history is taught at three grade levels. Too often, all three courses are surveys, covering again and again everything from Columbus to the latest space shot. There is little differentiation of content and little attempt to build from one course to the next.

How did this come about? It happened partially for historical reasons. In the early years of this country as history, children attended only a few years of school. It seemed important to teach them United States history before they ended their school careers. So American history was taught in the fifth grade. Then, as more children stayed on in upper elementary school, the course was taught again in the eighth grade, just before students left school to go to work. Finally, as more students continued on through high school, educators again wanted to make sure that they remembered their United States history. So history was repeated yet again, in the eleventh grade.

Concerns about patriotism continue to favor the inclusion of United States history in both elementary and secondary schools. It would be unpopular for a local district or a state framework committee to suggest dropping a United States history course—how unpatriotic or un-American! Thus the impact of tradition and patriotic concern has led to the entrenchment of three separate United States history courses.

Notice also the problem area in the sixth and seventh grades. Both grades cover the same broad topics, and there is little agreement about what the content should be at these levels. In some schools ancient civilizations is taught in the sixth grade; in others this topic is found at the seventh-grade level.

Some social studies educators believe that the primary-grade topics are not well enough differentiated. One study by Marion Rice of the University of Georgia (1966) showed that second graders' knowledge of content before instruction ranged from 33 to 84 percent: in other words, in some classrooms students knew a third to virtually all of the material *before* it was taught. Topics are stressed in the first, second, and third grades without new material being introduced or higher levels of thinking being required.[3]

But perhaps the heaviest criticism of primary social studies content focuses on the "holiday curriculum." In many schools, holidays like Thanksgiving, Christmas, Presidents' Day, Valentine's Day, Easter, and Mothers' Day dictate what is covered in the primary social studies program. These holidays do offer the opportunity to explain much about our cultural heritage. But the reliance on them suggests that many teachers feel more comfortable teaching these topics than ones that require more thoughtful preparation.

The holiday curriculum, however, need not be narrow. Holidays can be used as springboards for teaching about cultural diversity by showing how they are celebrated (or not celebrated) in this country and throughout the world. In many cases, though, holiday activities are simply repeated grade after grade, with little attention paid to learning beyond parties and entertainment. Valuable social studies time is wasted. Furthermore, teachers are not always sensitive to the feelings of children from different backgrounds who may be offended or excluded by the holiday focus. In the same manner, children may not understand why religious holidays are not mentioned, or are celebrated in ways unrelated to their religious meanings. The separation of church and state in the United States means that children may *learn* about different religions but religious beliefs may not be practiced in the classroom.

As you can see, there *is* a national social studies curriculum pattern. But your state's pattern may vary from this model in several ways. Each state generally requires that its own state history be taught at the fourth-grade level. Check on what your state recommends for the sixth- and seventh-grade levels as well. Information about social studies content guidelines can be obtained from your State Department of Education. Your state may also have *legal requirements*—observance of holidays, positive and accurate

---

[3] Marion J. Rice, *Educational Stimulation in the Social Studies: Analysis and Interpretation of Research*. Athens, GA: Research and Development Center in Educational Stimulation, University of Georgia, 1966.

portrayal of the roles of women and minority groups, or the protection and conservation of the environment—that dictate to some extent what will be taught in the social studies.

IMPORTANCE OF TEXTBOOK SERIES

The adoption of textbooks has had a great influence on what is taught in elementary social studies. Have you recently looked at a social studies textbook series? If you compare a new series to the one that you had in elementary school, you will notice how much more colorful and attractive textbooks are now.

There are other differences as well. Almost all textbook series now show pictures of a wide diversity of ethnic, racial, and religious groups, in response to demands to eliminate racism and sexism. The portrayal of the elderly and the handicapped shows an interest in presenting a more realistic view of American life. The primary social studies textbooks on the family now move beyond a traditional two-parent family; an illustration may show a mother remarrying with her two children looking on or a family headed by a mother, father, or grandmother.

Generally, the large publishers offer a series (often called a *basal series*) of textbooks covering kindergarten through grade six or seven. For the kindergarten level, some publishers issue only a teacher's manual; more frequently, kindergarten-level texts are small booklets containing attractive pictures with no vocabulary. A teacher's guide is essential to the use of such kindergarten booklets.

Even if you follow a basal series closely, you will have some choices about what you teach. One choice occurs at the fourth-grade level, where state history and geography are generally taught. The major publishers issue specially prepared state textbooks for large states, and regional books are available for smaller states. Smaller publishing firms may also offer small state history textbooks.

The next choice occurs at the sixth- and seventh-grade levels. Since there is no standard curriculum pattern at these levels, publishers often offer two or more textbooks that can be used for either grade, thus providing a wider range of topics—the Eastern Hemisphere, the Western Hemisphere, or the world, for example.

Far more supplementary material coordinated with the textbooks is now available than ever before. Publishers have recognized that elementary teachers are busy planners with responsibilities for many subject areas and activities. Along with the traditional student textbook and teacher's manual, the major publishers are now likely to include a workbook for students containing exercises to supplement the textbook, tests for chapter and unit review, and in some cases additional resources for the teacher such as posters for the classroom. Generally, this is all packaged attractively in one large binder. It seems likely that future textbook series will also include computer software to supplement each unit. Teachers now expect assistance from the publisher and would be reluctant to adopt a series that did not have such aids.

CONTENT OF THREE BASIC SOCIAL STUDIES TEXTBOOK SERIES

Scott, Foresman Social Studies (1983)[4]

Kingdergarten *People around Us*
Identity
Choices
Power
Socialization
Interdependence
Diversity
Change

First Grade *Families and Friends*
Who Are You?
You and Others
You Need Rules
Choices You Make
People Need Each Other
All Kinds of People
Changing Through the
  Years

Second Grade *Neighbors Near and Far*
People and Places Close
  By
Your Neighborhood
Needs and Wants
Deciding and Doing
Alike and Different
The Group around You
Making Changes

Third Grade *City, Town, and Country*
What Is a Community?
Communities Bring
  People Together
What Your Community
  Means to You
Communities Needs
  Government

---

[4] *Scott, Foresman Social Studies Series.* Glenview, IL: Scott, Foresman and Company, 1983.

Different Communities,
 Different Choices
Communities Need One
 Another
Changing Communities

Fourth Grade   *Regions of Our Country
  and Our World*
Our Country Then and
 Now
Our Country Grows
Our Country Today
Governing Our Country
Regions of Our World
Our Ties to Other Places,
 Other Times
Living in a Changing
 World

Fifth Grade   *America Past and Present*
These United States
Settling North America
Winning Independence
The Nation Changes
New Beginnings
New Directions
Neighbors Near and Far

Sixth and   *Our World: Land and
Seventh   Cultures*
Grades   How Societies Are
  Similar and Different
How People Learn to
 Live Together
Who We Are
How People Use Their
 Resources
Leadership in
 Government
International
 Interdependence
Cultures Change

Eastern Hemisphere:
   Europe, Asia, Africa,
   and Oceania
People and the Land
People of Long Ago
Turning Points to the
   Present
Western Europe Today
Eastern Europe and the
   Soviet Union Today
Africa Today
Asia and Oceania Today

Western Hemisphere:
   Latin America and
   Canada
Lands and People of the
   Americas
The First Americans
The Road to
   Independence
Canada
Mexico and the Nations
   of Central America
The Andean Countries,
   Venezuela, and the
   West Indies
Brazil and the Silver
   River Countries

Silver Burdett Company Social Studies (1986)[5]

Kindergarten   *My World and Me*
               You and Me
               Family
               School
               Change
               Needs
               Rules
               Where We Live

---

[5] Silver Burdett Social Studies, *The World and Its People Series*. Morristown, NJ: Silver Burdett Company, 1986.

Grade One   *Families and Neighborhoods*
About Me
About Families
Families Need Food
Families Need Clothes
Families Need Shelter
Families Live in
    Neighborhoods
Living in the United
    States

Grade Two   *Neighborhoods and*
    Communities
Where We Live
Living in Communities
Working in Communities
Communities Make
    Rules
Communities Long Ago
    and Today
Community Celebrate
    Holidays

Grade Three   *Communities and Resources*
Learning about
    Communities
Living in Different
    Communities
Farms and Resources
    Support Our
    Communities
Citizenship in the United
    States

Grade Four   *States and Regions*
The Earth—Our Home
Forest Regions
Desert Regions
Plains Regions
Mountain Regions
Regions Working
    Together

Grade Five   *The United States and Its*
              Neighbors
              Tools for Learning about
                  Your Country
              An Age of Adventure
              A New and Growing
                  Nation
              The United States Comes
                  of Age
              The United States in the
                  Twentieth Century
              The United States: A
                  Land of Great Variety
              Canada and Latin
                  America

Grade Six   *Canada and Latin America*
or Seven   Learning about the
                  World
              Canada: Our Northern
                  Neighbor
              Latin America
              Middle America
              South America

              Europe, Africa, Asia, and
                  Australia
              Knowledge That Helps
                  You Learn
              Beginnings of Western
                  Civilization
              Western Europe
              The Soviet Union and
                  Eastern Europe
              The Middle East and
                  North Africa
              Africa South of the
                  Sahara
              South Asia, East Asia, and
                  Australia

Webster Division, McGraw–Hill (1986)[6]

Kindergarten   *Looking at Me*
Looking at Me
My World
My Story

Grade One   *Meeting People*
Going to School
Looking at You and Me
Families and
    Neighborhoods
Our Country and Our
    World

Grade Two   *Going Places*
Maps and Globes
Earth, People's Home
People in Groups
Groups Help Fill Needs
Where Food Comes
    From
People Live in
    Communities

Grade Three   *Communities*
The Eastern United States
The Middle United States
The Western United
    States
Our Northern Neighbor

Grade Four   *Earth's Regions*
Complete Map and Globe
    Course
North America and Its
    People
South America
Africa
Europe
Asia

---

[6] Social Studies: *Our Nation, Our World Series.* New York: McGraw-Hill Book Company, 1986.

Grade Five   *United States*
              Mapping North America
              Exploring and Settling
                  North America
              The United States Is
                  Born
              The United States
                  Changes
              The United States in the
                  Modern World
              United States Geography
              United States Neighbors

Grade Six   *The World*
              Mastering Map and
                  Globe Skills
              Societies of Long Ago
              Societies in Europe
              Societies in Asia and
                  Oceania
              Societies in Africa
              Societies in Latin America

Exercise 1.6   *COMPARE THE SERIES*

At the library, examine three different social studies textbook series at one particular grade level. Note carefully what content is covered in the textbook. Also look at the teacher's guide for suggestions on how the program is to be taught. How are the series alike? How are they different?

Some critics argue that the basal social studies textbooks are very similar. This concern may stem from the similarity of titles; the word *family*, for example, shows up frequently at the first-grade level. But a careful examination of the textbooks will show more differences. Some textbook series are better for slower learners. Others emphasize global education. Still others, although they bear recent copyright dates, really have changed very little from those of 20 years ago. Map skills are found in all textbooks, but some series emphasize reading skills, information-finding skills, and thinking skills as well.

Educators complain about overreliance on the textbook. Often it has been the only instructional tool used, and this has resulted in narrow, restricted programs. Used creatively, however, the textbook can be a very valuable resource. It is important for teachers and committees concerned with the selection of textbooks to look very carefully at the possible choices. There are many differences among the textbook series. The wide range of activities suggested in a teacher's guide may make a social studies textbook series unique. Teachers stuck with unsuitable textbooks for their classes work at a disadvantage in trying to provide a good social studies program.

SCOPE AND SEQUENCE ISSUES

As you noticed in looking at social studies textbooks and the unit titles found in them, almost all of the textbooks use the *expanding communities pattern* or the *widening world scope and sequence model*. *Scope* is the list of topics covered in a program. *Sequence* is the order in which they are covered. Usually, the two words are used together to indicate what is being taught when in the social studies or in any other area of the curriculum.

Scope and sequence issues are important. You need to know when students are ready for certain difficult concepts, like time or chronology. Most primary students have great difficulty trying to imagine what life was like 2,000 years ago. They may think that we have always had television, airplanes, and cars. B.C. and A.D. pose conceptual difficulty for most primary students. Determining at what grade level you might successfully try to teach time concepts is a scope and sequence issue.

The traditional scope and sequence pattern for the elementary grades—the expanding communities—is based on a consideration of the developmental needs of the child. Children usually learn better about real things and life around them than about abstract topics that they cannot see or feel. Therefore, the expanding communities concept begins with where children are when they enter school. The focus in the primary grades is first the family and then the school, the neighborhood, the larger neighborhood (city, county, etc.), the state, the region, and finally the nation and the world (Figure 1.2).

This pattern of expanding communities made a lot of sense years ago. But at present, with mass media, and especially television, children are exposed to events and issues taking place far from their homes. Primary-grade children are aware of international and domestic crises, the threat of nuclear weapons, and pollution problems in their neighborhoods.

It may seem as though all of the social studies textbooks are following the expanding community concept for scope and sequence, especially if you scan chapter titles. But a more careful examination often shows that even in the first grade, information about families includes families in Israel and Zambia. A second-grade textbook on neighbors may focus on groups both in the United States and in other parts of the world. A topic such as where food comes from is now more likely to expand into farming in other lands, since the United States gets more and more products, including food, from other parts of the world.

So the traditional scope and sequence pattern of expanding communities found at most elementary grades is being supplemented by topics outside the child's immediate

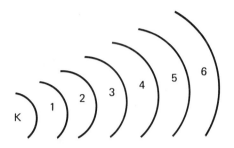

Key:

K Self and Others   4 Regions
1 Families   5 United States and Canada
2 Communities   6 World
3 Cities

Figure 1.2 The expanding horizons curriculum.
Source: Reprinted from *Defining the Social Studies*, Bulletin #51 by Robert D. Barr, James L. Barth, and Samuel Shermis, with permission of the National Council for the Social Studies.

environment. But not all educators are satisfied with this arrangement. Many want to break away even further from the traditional scope and sequence patterns.

One alternative pattern is the *spiral* curriculum advocated by Hilda Taba (Figure 1.3). In this model, basic concepts and processes from the social sciences such as interdependence or cultural change are taught each year on a higher level of abstraction. For example, first-grade students might learn how families depend on institutions like stores to get their food. In the sixth grade, they might study how nations depend on one another for natural resources and manufactured goods. The spiral curriculum is found in one or two textbook series. Care must be taken in using this pattern to ensure that students are truly moving to higher levels and not just repeating topics such as "community workers" or "food."

In a special issue of *Social Education* in 1986, several social studies experts gave their suggestions for alternative scope and sequence patterns.[7] The proposals illustrated a great diversity of opinion, and some differed radically from the typical pattern of expanding communities.

Matthew Downey, a historian, would like the fourth grade to focus on early peoples of the world and on primitive cultures that exist today, the fifth grade to study classical and medieval civilizations, and the sixth grade to focus on United States history with an emphasis on the early period of building a new nation. In the seventh grade the content would be world history and early modern and industrial eras; in the eighth grade, United States history would focus on the years 1789 to 1914. As you can guess, the eleventh grade would study United States history in the twentieth century.

---

[7] *Social Education* 50 (November–December 1986) special issue on alternative scope and sequence patterns.

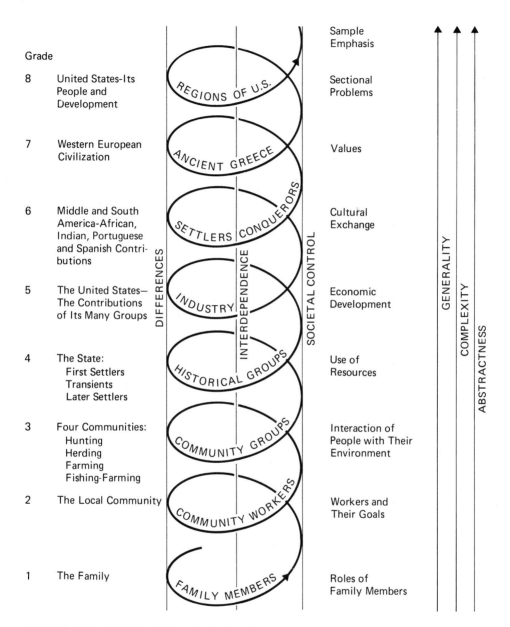

Figure 1.3 The spiral of concept development.

Source: Teacher's Handbook for Elementary Social Studies, by Hilda Taba. Addison-Wesley, 1971. Reprinted with permission of Addison-Wesley.

This historian is trying to bring a chronological coherence to the curriculum and also to improve the teaching of United States history by dividing the three offerings into specific periods. For years authorities have recommended that something be done to distinguish the three United States history courses from one another. More radical is Downey's emphasis on history in the elementary school. In his curriculum, history is the dominant subject from the fourth grade on, and students learn both world and United States history. This emphasis on history reflects a conservative movement in social studies instruction that has some support among the public.

In the same issue of *Social Education*, Shirley Engle and Anna Ochoa proposed a curriculum for democratic citizenship. They suggested moving away from memorization of facts in the social sciences and history and focusing instead on the study of problems—past and present—as the best way to prepare citizens in a democracy. For example, environmental concerns and international problems such as terrorism would be appropriate choices for study.

Other proposals include more emphasis on global education within the social studies and on the simple idea that the content taught be current, accurate, and comprehensive. What all of these proposals suggest is that there is not presently a consensus on scope and sequence in the elementary social studies curriculum. This issue probably will not be settled for some time to come, and we can expect further debate in the coming years.

No matter what material you eventually teach, we would like to point out two important concerns: gender bias and the increasing number of different ethnic or racial minorities in many urban public schools. We must continually try to ensure that our social studies curriculum, as well as all school experiences, include women and minorities. Teachers who wish to improve student attitudes in these two areas should not limit themselves to a special unit taught once a year. The infusion of all assignments and materials with an antibias, projustice concern will have more impact than a once-a-year unit. In addition, you need to be very conscious of your own teaching behavior. Whom do you call upon to answer questions? Who gets the hard thinking questions? Far too often, teachers fall into patterns of reinforcing boys to the detriment of girls and of not expecting high achievement from children of certain ethnic and racial groups.

Exercise 1.7   *CHECK WHERE YOU STAND*

Do you think any changes should be made in what is taught (topics) and when it is taught (specific grade levels)? Should there be more emphasis on certain topics?

SUGGESTED READINGS

Barr, Robert. D.; Barth, James L.; and Shermis, S. Samuel. *Defining the Social Studies.* Bulletin 51. Washington, D.C.: National Council for the Social Studies, 1977.

The two journals of social studies that teachers should become familiar with are *Social*

Education and *The Social Studies*. In addition, publications like *Learning* and *Instructor* may also have social studies materials.

Social Education 48 (April 1984), special issue with responses to preliminary report of Task Force on Scope and Sequence.

Social Education 50 (November–December 1986), special issue on alternative scope and sequence patterns.

Social Education 49 (May 1985), special issue on The New Criticism: Alternative Views of Social Education.

Social Education 49 (March 1985), article by S. Samuel Shermis and James L. Barth followed by response of James Shaver on indoctrination in the social studies.

Social Studies Curriculum Materials Data Book. Vols. 1–X. Boulder, Colo.: Social Science Educational Consortium, 1971–85. Analysis of textbooks, materials, and media.

CHAPTER

2

Planning for Social Studies Teaching

This chapter focuses on planning with the following specific topics:

1. Planning
2. Goals, Long-Range Planning, and Behavioral Objectives
3. Resources for Planning
4. Units
5. Lesson Plans
6. Organizing and Scheduling

PLANNING

The teacher is the key to what the social studies program will be in any classroom. As a teacher, you will make many decisions: What units will I include during the year? How will I teach tomorrow's lesson on the roles of the family? In general, the more decisions you can make in *prior planning*, the better prepared you will be. Your other choice is to make decisions on the spot, with a classroom full of students waiting for your instructions.

How do you go about planning? First, assemble all available planning tools and resources. They include the following:

State and/or district curriculum guide(s)
Your adopted textbook, the teacher's guide, and ancillary materials
Media catalogues for your district and county
Recommendations from your school media specialist (usually your librarian) for stories, trade books, and reference books

Ideas from other teachers in your building
Parent resources
Community resources

When your resources are assembled, begin to make choices. Choose units and activities for which you have appropriate materials and that you think will interest your students. Equally important, choose a program that interests *you*. Any lack of interest on your part will surely be conveyed to your students. Finally, prepare your plans in detail. Write down not only the names of the units you wish to cover but also the specific topics you will include and, if possible, some thoughts about how you will teach them.

Should you, as a beginning teacher, try to create original lesson plans, or should you use plans designed by "experts" like textbook authors and curriculum designers? Some local districts mandate that all teachers cover given units according to specific instructional modes—often the popular Madeline Hunter direct instruction model. Other districts give teachers complete freedom to choose both content and method of instruction. Most districts occupy a middle ground: they outline the general content areas to be taught but allow flexibility for teachers to achieve content goals in any manner they wish.

Most beginners would panic at the thought of total freedom and move quickly to see how they can adapt an existing textbook program or other curriculum project. Many experts would approve of this decision, arguing that often teachers, especially beginners, can best select and modify existing materials and ideas rather than try to create entirely new programs. This alternative makes better use of teacher time and is more likely to bring success. Developing an innovative social studies program on your own is difficult, and it ignores time-tested resources already at hand, including the teacher next door.

"Borrowing" creatively also provides for flexibility in your social studies program. Why, after all, do experienced teachers continue to attend conferences, workshops, and courses if not to get new ideas from other experts? Good teachers are continually modifying their programs, always on the alert for new and useful suggestions. In borrowing, however, you need to make sure that the new ideas and materials you adopt help you to achieve your desired objectives and that their appeal is not *simply* their newness.

Exercise 2.1   *DESCRIBING YOUR ROLE*

Does an effective teacher need to plan? Jot down the reasons you see for planning ahead. Can you think of any arguments against planning? How is an effective teacher different from a parent? From a police officer?

Sometimes elementary schoolteachers resist planning because they are so busy with immediate responsibilities—filling out forms, grading papers, checking homework.

Planning is often a low-priority task. But there is an important psychological benefit to planning and especially to working out and writing down daily lesson plans: confidence. With a plan in front of you, you feel organized and ready to face the class. A plan a day keeps disaster away! Planning can often help you anticipate management problems in the classroom, and it enables you to have better control of the situation.

Sometimes a new teacher will say, "I did a lot of planning for a lesson on our local transportation system, and the whole thing fell flat. But the next day I walked in 'cold' and taught a terrific lesson on neighborhoods. So why plan?" This can happen. Planned lessons do not always go as well as expected. Instead of abandoning planning, however, you should go over an unsuccessful lesson at the end of the day, when you are less emotionally involved. At what points did it go off track? Were the students bored? Unable to keep up? Confused? What actually was wrong with the lesson? Make notes on your lesson plan to help you with future planning.

If a lesson *is* successful, critique your written plan anyway. What would have made the lesson better? Write down proposed changes so that you won't forget them. Having in writing both the original plan and your notes on how to improve it will provide you with an ever-expanding resource file in years to come.

Some teachers argue that planning encourages rigidity. Having a written plan, they suggest, prevents teachers from taking advantage of unexpected instructional opportunities. Serendipity is always welcome! Your lesson plan, however, is meant to be a guide, not a prison sentence. Always be ready to bend it to take advantage of student interest or some recent and unanticipated event.

You may find that you have no choice about writing out lesson plans. Some school districts and/or principals require teachers to submit lesson plans for the coming week throughout the year. Frequently, administrators ask only for brief statements of topics and textbook pages to be covered. Most plans written for administrators show very little detail. The fact that a lesson plan must be turned in, however, acts as an incentive for many elementary teachers to plan ahead, if only to list the subject areas they will cover in a given week. Writing in topics under subject-area headings—science, social studies, math—may suggest areas of potential integration: How can language arts or science work with this week's social studies lesson?

There are often differences between what is listed on the plan handed in to an administrator and what actually goes on in the classroom. Some differences are inevitable, since lesson plans should always allow for flexibility. In a few cases, subjects get listed that are never taught. Frequently, this happens because the teacher has done no planning in detail and so has no real plan to implement.

Successful planning needs to be detailed enough actually to help organize what happens in the classroom. It is inaccurate to suggest that only drudges and drones plan; planning is a vital and basic skill for all effective teachers. Research indicates that teachers who plan are more likely to be satisfied with their teaching and are more likely to remain in the teaching profession. Poorly planned activities are frustrating to both teacher and students; valuable time wasted can never be recovered.

Exercise 2.2 *ANALYZING YOUR FAVORITES*

Jot down what you remember most vividly about your favorite elementary school-teacher. Do you remember what he or she taught you about social studies? Do you think that your teacher planned? What characteristics suggest his or her planning or the lack of it?

GOALS, LONG-RANGE PLANNING, AND BEHAVIORAL OBJECTIVES

Goals

Goals are broad statements of desired outcomes. In education, they provide the pillars for setting up learning experiences. Goals do not define specific achievements to be attained within a specific period; a goal is not necessarily to be reached in an hour, a day, or even a year. Rather, goals are frequently defined in terms of enhancement or of providing foundations. We work on some goals such as improving our reading skills throughout our schooling—even throughout our lives.

Each school district usually has a list of its own goals, which often include some of the following:

Education should provide a basis for good citizenship.
Education should provide a basis for vocational choice.
Education should provide the best of our cultural heritage.
Education should provide each student with a command of fundamental skills such as reading, writing, arithmetic, information finding, problem solving, and computer literacy.
Education should develop each student's ability to think clearly.
Education should develop each student's unique potential.

Other goals may have to do with ethical character, health, or personal behavior. Generally, school-district goals reflect the broad desires of the community. In many districts, parents have helped significantly in defining the district's goals.

Promoting good citizenship, which is often found on district lists of educational goals, is also generally listed as a goal for social studies education. The social studies program does not have sole responsibility for teaching citizenship skills; other areas of the curriculum also contribute. But an elementary social studies program should be designed to do as much as possible to move students toward effective citizenship participation. As an elementary teacher, you will plan the entire day for your students. In looking over the day's program, you should be alert to those activities that best promote both broad educational goals and specific goals of the social studies.

In Chapter 1, we mentioned the four basic social studies goals:

1. To provide knowledge about human experiences in the past, present, and future
2. To develop skills to process information
3. To develop appropriate democratic values and attitudes
4. To provide opportunities for social participation

These goals provide the framework for planning in the social studies and also fit easily into the general goals of many school districts. Since they are so broadly stated, however, almost any social studies activity you propose to teach could be listed under at least one of them. Goals are useful in defining broad objectives, but they lack the specificity necessary for effective day-to-day teaching.

Long-Range Planning

Most elementary teachers begin social studies planning by roughing out an outline of the entire, year-long curriculum. Given the number of weeks in the school year, how will you divide the subject matter normally covered in, say, the second grade? What would make reasonable, manageable sections? You must make some decisions: Will you select only certain units from the textbook, or will you try to cover all of them? Will you use the district's curriculum guidelines, or will some of your units be from specific curriculum packages—an economic simulation perhaps? Once you begin to make these basic determinations—what you will cover and how much time you will devote to each topic—you can focus your attention on the individual chunks of time, frequently called *units*.

Long-range planning is vital, since there is usually far more content (and resource materials) available than there is time to teach it. Your first step should be to examine what must be taught, according to state or local mandate, at your particular grade level. Usually, grade-level mandates are broad.

What other criteria could you use for selecting topics for a year-long curriculum? You should consider all of the following:

The adopted textbook
Tradition
State mandated tests
What other teachers in your building are doing
Pressure from parents
Potential management problems
Need for efficient use of time in planning and developing materials

Of all these considerations, the most important one is probably your textbook. You may have the freedom to choose a textbook series, but most often you must use the one provided by your school or district. Look it over carefully. Examine the teacher's manual and any ancillary materials. If you use the textbook as your main guide in long-range curriculum planning, you should typically follow these steps:

1. Skim the text looking at broad unit titles. Decide which ones you will use. (The author's recommendations about how much time a unit will typically take may be helpful.)
2. Examine the teacher's guide. Look for activities both for you and for your students.
3. Find other activities to supplement the text. The teacher's guide may suggest some; the publisher may also provide other materials, like worksheets.
4. Decide whether or not you will use the tests supplied by the publisher for evaluation.

Since a major part of your long-range planning will be done early in the school year or even before it begins, you probably won't know your students' full range of talents and abilities. Once you begin to learn more about your students, you may need to modify the learning activities in your year-long curriculum to fit your classroom, where abilities may range from special education students to the gifted.

Behavioral Objectives

Whereas a *goal* is a broad statement of purpose, a *behavioral objective* is a specific accomplishment that you want your students to achieve in a specific period. A behavioral objective in education describes what a learner is expected to know, will be able to do, or will demonstrate as a consequence of instruction. A well-written objective specifies the level of acceptable performance and the conditions under which a student must perform. Many teacher-training institutions advise their students to use Bloom's taxonomy for writing objectives in the cognitive domain.

You are no doubt familiar with the general process of curriculum planning. Typically, there are three main questions to answer:

1. What are your objectives?
2. What learning experiences will be used to achieve the desired objectives?
3. What evaluation procedures will be used to see if the objectives have been achieved?

You have probably learned a formula for writing behavioral objectives: "The student will (insert an action verb, such as *write, identify,* or *say*) (insert content, such as *three major roles of a parent*)." An appropriate behavioral objective might be: "The student will identify three major roles of a parent." Objectives should also include any restrictions on time, equipment, or aid. For instance, you might write, "*Given an outline map of Europe,* the student will list the names of all major rivers shown." Let your students know the criteria for an acceptable performance. Must the names be spelled correctly, with proper capitalization? Will a student be considered successful if he or she can identify eight out of ten rivers shown?

Behavioral objectives, often called simply objectives, may be broad or narrow. You may set a few broad social studies objectives for the year, narrower ones for each unit, and specific objectives for each day's lesson. This division into long-range and short-term, broad and narrow, objectives is a reflection of how teachers typically plan a curriculum.

What is your opinion of the behavioral objective approach? There are signs in teachers' lounges that say "Stamp Out Behavioral Objectives." Because of the time necessary to write them out, many teachers strongly resist having to translate broad long-range objectives into more specific ones. In making a choice for yourself, think about the following issues:

1. *Is specifying objectives worthwhile for elementary teachers?* Teachers, even those who have been trained to write out behavioral objectives, frequently think first about learning activities or materials and only then about a suitable purpose or objective. Some teachers believe that they are using behavioral objectives but write them so vaguely that the objectives are virtually useless; others write them at the lowest level of factual information, using content such as memorization of state capitals. Advocates of behavioral objectives believe that some of the negative feelings about their use stem from misuse. They believe that much of the instruction in education is aimless because teachers fail to define objectives clearly. What do you think?

2. *Do your students need to know what the behavioral objectives are to ensure achieving the desired behavioral change?* If you assign a worksheet, do you need to explain the behavioral objective to the students in order for them to understand what they are gaining? There is some research indicating that this does help students to achieve.[1] What about objectives in the affective domain, for example, improved citizenship or respect for people of various ethnic or racial groups? Do students need to be told what your objectives for them are in these areas?

3. *Do students have to know what an adequate performance level is?* Part of the problem in teaching important social studies skills like small-group participation or writing and presenting a report is that students do not always know what a good paper or a good discussion is. Often they do not receive corrective feedback about how to improve. Selecting and writing down objectives can be an important first step; teaching the material in a variety of ways is a second step. The third step, equally important, is evaluation. Typically, evaluation is the weakest area in social studies programs. Do you think students should be told in the beginning what constitutes acceptable performance? Can you think of methods in addition to tests and quizzes through which you can evaluate performance?

In thinking about objectives, you face the questions not only of defining important content in the social studies but also of how you should go about teaching and evaluating students to see if they are in fact achieving your objectives. But many objectives written by

---

[1] Jere E. Brophy, Mary Rohrkemper, Habim Rashid, and Michael Goldberger., "Relationships between Teachers' Presentation of Classroom Tasks and Student Engagement in Those Tasks," *Journal of Educational Psychology* (August 1983): 544–52.

teachers are not precise. Behavioral objectives in the affective or value domain are particularly difficult to write and measure. However, *any* effort made to think about and plan your teaching objectives is probably better than none.

Since teachers often have difficulty writing objectives, many publishers now provide in their teacher's guides objectives for each unit and for each lesson. Often these aids are helpful for teachers to target more clearly where they are going and what they are trying to achieve. Other teachers, professional journals, and instructional objectives exchanges can also offer assistance to teachers in writing objectives.

Exercise 2.3 *EXPLORING POINTS OF VIEW*

Administrators and teachers often view behavioral objectives in a different manner. List three reasons why administrators more than teachers might favor the behavioral objectives approach.

RESOURCES FOR PLANNING

In thinking about objectives, can you identify any factors unique to the field of social studies that should be considered in planning? Students' families, the community, and other resources may help you better plan your social studies program.

Parent and Family Resources

Since the social studies are about people, members of the students' families can often be used as resources. A grandmother may be able to tell what it was like to live on a farm 50 years ago. A parent may be able to describe his or her job when the class is studying community workers or the job market. There may be artifacts from different nations in the homes of students that would be of interest to the class. Many teachers find that these resources add sparkle to the class. Try writing notes or newsletters to parents outlining what is going to be covered in the coming social studies unit and asking if they can help in any way. Use the opportunity to provide information on community resources such as zoos and libraries that may be helpful to busy parents. Use special events such as open house and media presentations by the class to talk to and ask for help from parents.

Community Resources

The community is the neighborhood beyond just family. There are two important community resources: field trips and guest speakers. Use the community as a resource for field trips, especially if the students are able to walk to see something such as the local bakery or police station. If this is not feasible, resource people from the community such as probation officers or park rangers can come to the classroom. Community resources can also include free local newspapers or materials from the local bank or other institutions in the community.

In addition, students can serve the community in projects ranging from helping senior citizens to cleaning up local parks. Community service provides a bridge between students and the community and can be an important resource in building toward the goal of citizenship. (Be certain to clear such projects with your school principal.)

Media and Inexpensive Resources

You need to look carefully at the films, filmstrips, photographs, slides, television series, and so on that can be obtained in your district. Typically, the sooner your order is placed, the better, since other teachers also may want to use these resources about the same time. These media, especially with visual components, can add meaning to otherwise abstract ideas that a teacher's voice cannot provide.

Free or inexpensive posters and other materials may be obtained from the consulates of foreign nations in large U.S. cities. Order the materials as early as possible to allow time for shipment, and make arrangements for speakers, especially those on tight schedules such as government officials, well in advance.

Current Events/Current Affairs

The social studies are unique among elementary subjects because events are continually happening in both the local community and the wider world that have an impact upon the students and their families. Often these events are directly relevant to what you are trying to achieve in your social studies program. The goal of encouraging social participation in community affairs should lead you to consider how current events can be used to enrich the social studies program.

Weekly papers, prepared by publishers at the appropriate reading levels for students in different grades, can be helpful. But in real life, newspapers and magazines are not as neatly balanced and objective, and students eventually need to become familiar with "regular" news reports. In addition, students living in an environment dominated by television must understand what the news reporters on television are talking about. Discussions on television are often incomplete, and students need more background to understand the issues. Also, television news is frequently weak on analysis. Teachers must teach students to understand how all elements of the mass media are important and how they can analyze what messages are being given.

All of these things make the social studies unique among subject areas and should be part of your consideration in planning.

UNITS

A *unit* is time allocated to teaching, but it is more than that. It is a plan that organizes a sequential progression of lessons that are related in theme. Typically, a social studies unit covers the main concepts of a particular subject area. In addition, the unit has provisions for the teaching of skills, values, and, if possible, social participation.

You have seen examples of units, such as *Africa Today* or *Our New Nation Develops*, in the list of texts from three major publishers. Social studies units might be on computers, the nation, local Native Americans, or an industry such as textiles or housing; they might be on very broad topics such as the media or focus more narrowly such as on one American like George Washington.

Why do experts recommend teaching in units? It is better to have a progression and develop a theme than to teach isolated lessons. Students learn less if on Monday they have a map exercise on latitude and longitude, on Tuesday they have a value exercise on twenty things they love to do, on Wednesday they visit their local fire department, on Thursday they read their social studies textbook on Native Americans in the northeastern part of the United States, and on Friday they study current events. Each lesson may be worthwhile by itself, but the lessons do not build sequentially. A unit should tie skills and knowledge together under a theme so that learning is not isolated and fragmented.

A unit can also be rewarding to you as the teacher. Building a unit provides a sense of achievement. You can be creative and design something to help your own class.

Beginners often ask how long a unit should last. There is no fixed answer to this question, but younger students probably profit more from shorter units, perhaps a few weeks, and older students gain more from units that are longer, up to six weeks. If the unit goes on too long, students may lose interest. Some teachers, however, find that students beg for more after interesting units, such as the economic simulation called *Mini-Society*, which lasts a full six weeks. The ideal time depends both on the age of the students and the material being taught.

Units may vary in length depending on how many other areas of the curriculum are included in them. A social studies unit that incorporates art, music, literature, and science may last longer than one that includes no other disciplines. In planning a unit, try to incorporate as many relevant curriculum areas and skills as possible.

SAMPLE UNIT PLAN 2.1
Travel Day to Hawaii

The following unit is planned to last one week and is prepared for the primary grades. Usually, such a unit has both a broad objective and specific daily objectives. Although it might be inappropriate to use verbs such as *know*, *value*, and *understand* in behavioral objectives for individual lessons, such words are appropriate at the beginning of a unit where they provide overall guidance and organization to the instructional process.

Unit Objectives

1. Students will understand the geography, history, and traditional culture of Hawaii.
2. Students will identify different types of transportation.

Day 1.

Objective: To learn and experience the culture, history, geography, art, and foods of Hawaii.

1. Introduce the vocabulary term *island*. Brainstorm with the class: What is an island? Looking at a map of the United States, have the children find a state that is a group of islands.
2. Discuss the history of Hawaii. Share past experiences of children or their parents who have visited there.
3. Tell the children that the class will go on a "pretend" trip to Hawaii in five days. Discuss different modes of transportation.
4. Draw the islands on brown butcher paper and label them according to shape. Have the children pin up the product on the bulletin board with a blue background for water.

Day 2.

Objective: To introduce different types of transportation and calculate distances from their own state to Hawaii.

1. Brainstorm with the children as to the different ways the class could travel to Hawaii (airplane, ship, sailboat, etc.)
2. Design an airplane ticket. Include the date, time of departure, and so on.

Day 3.

Objective: To expose the students to the traditional culture and history of Hawaii.

1. Read "Palm Tree" from *Young Folks Hawaiian Time.*
2. Discuss the term *luau*, as well as foods usually eaten, dances, and so on.
3. Have children make drawings of Hawaiian traditions for a mural.
4. Learn the "hula" dance from a community member.

Day 4.

Objective: To learn about the geography of Hawaii and how islands are formed.

1. Brainstorm the term *volcano*. Discuss how volcanoes formed the islands.
2. Have the children divide paper into four squares. Illustrate an eruption of a volcano in sequence.

Day 5.

Objective: To simulate a travel day to Hawaii. This lesson plan is part of a full day's activity; a "pretend" in-classroom flight to another state. Hawaii is used as an example in this lesson, but other states or nations could be used as well.

This travel day combines all subjects in a *fun* educational setting. The following is an example of such a day.

Morning Lesson

1. "Takeoff"
   a. Collect children-made airplane tickets at the door.
   b. Review the flight route (ocean to be flown over etc.).
2. Math-Macaroni Leis
   a. Pattern lesson with dyed macaroni and construction-paper flowers. Save for the luau.
3. Language/Letter-Writing Skills
   a. Write and design a postcard to a friend or family member. Discuss how to address a postcard, the purpose of a stamp, and how to use descriptive language.
4. Reading/Vocabulary Skills
   a. Share "Hawaiian Alphabet" from *Young Folks Hawaiian Time*.
   b. Worksheet on Hawaiian terms.
   c. Write in alphabetical order.
5. Science: Parts of Flowers
   a. Label a hibiscus flower. Discuss the climate needed for it to grow and the stages of plant growth in general.
6. Art and Music
   a. Learn the hula and Hawaiian folk tales.
   b. Design a scrapbook of the day's events. Draw scenes of Hawaii with short written descriptions.
7. Social Studies: Culture and Foods of Hawaii
   a. Finish with a luau in Hawaii. Poi, coconut, and pineapple juice are a few suggested foods to share. The children should eat with their fingers.
   b. "Reboard" for the return flight home.

Elizabeth A. Gelbart reported about this unit, which she had designed at a social studies conference. In addition to the outline given above, she provided 10 pages describing in more detail worksheets with topics such as "A Hawaiian Volcano Erupts."[2]

Exercise 2.4   *ANALYZE THE UNIT*

In the Sample Unit Plan 2.1, is the theme and content appropriate for the age group? Are there provisions for teaching skills and values? Is there a variety of activities for the

---

[2] Elizabeth A. Gelbart, "Travel Day to Hawaii," Presented at California Council for the Social Studies Conference (Los Angeles, 1986).

children? Is there integration with other subjects areas of the curriculum? Do you think the class would enjoy the unit? Is there a progression of experiences and activities that leads to a cumulation in the unit?

Sample Unit Plan 2.1 has many strengths; many classes would learn from and enjoy it. But there is one serious concern: Is the unit reinforcing stereotypes about Hawaii? Will students learn about the large city of Honolulu with its wide diversity of peoples? The unit focuses on the tourist world of Hawaii. Attractive as that may be, it is not the whole picture. Note that the basic plan of this unit could be used for other nations or even states within the United States. But a teacher must be certain that students understand there is more to a region than the tourist view.

SAMPLE UNIT PLAN 2.2
Understanding Prejudice

The following excerpts are from another unit developed by San Mateo Elementary School Districct (San Mateo, Cal.) that emphasizes the affective domain. This unit is designed for the sixth grade and is intended to last almost four weeks. Notice the difficulties in writing objectives in the affective domain.

Unit Objective:

The students will demonstrate an acceptance of human differences while engaged in activities in the classroom and in other situations.

Specific Unit Objectives:

1. The students will define prejudice and give examples.
2. The students will distinguish between dislike and prejudice.
3. The students will recognize stereotyping, including male and female roles.
4. The students will recognize prejudgment against persons who are handicapped, either physically or mentally.
5. The students will understand the physical differences of ethnic minorities.
6. The students will describe differences related to socioeconomic, religious, and emotional factors.

Lesson: The Stranger

Objective: The students will define prejudice and give examples of it.
Procedure: Ask a visitor to come to the room dressed entirely in paper bags. The visitor should come in and sit down with no introduction or other attention directed toward him or her. After the visitor has spent about 15 minutes in the room, he or she may leave and a discussion should follow.

Possible questions: What did you think about the stranger when he or she first came into the room? Who can tell us about the stranger? Record answers since they may bring out fears and stereotypes. How did you feel with a stranger in the room? Would someone tell us about a time when you were a stranger in a group of new people? How did you feel? What did you think of the other people? Why? How do you react to words such as *beggars*, *Arabs*, and other groups?

Lesson: Stereotyping

Objective: Students will be able to give an example of stereotyping.
Procedure: Review the meaning of prejudice. Ask the students how they think children learn prejudice. Then do the following:
Instruct the students to close their eyes and imagine an American Indian. Have them draw their idea on paper. Show some of the pictures to the class. Next show them some pictures of American Indians without feathers, war paint, and so on. Ask them where they learned about Indians.
Discuss with the students how they might expect a typical person of another race, nationality, and so on to look. Discuss why they might expect these things because of stereotypes. Ask if stereotypes are good to have. Ask if stereotypes can make us treat people unfairly.

Lesson: Stereotyped Attitudes

Objective: Student will recognize and give examples of stereotyping attitudes.
Procedure: Discuss with the class the fact that some people think that most children are terrible. Have them give examples of things they have heard people say about their age group.
Then ask the students what they think about these things. Are they fair? Why? Why do some people feel that way? Do they have reason to be upset?
Stress that ideas are formed by our experiences, but we should try not to group all people by the actions of a few. Ask them to write a description of a teacher. When they are finished, read the descriptions and explain that teachers are not all exactly alike just because they are teachers.

Exercise 2.5   *ANALYZE A UNIT*

Look at the questions in Exercise 2.4. What are the strengths of the sample unit plan "Understanding Prejudice"? From the lessons provided, do you see any weaknesses in this unit? What skills might a teacher need to make this unit work properly?

Elements of a Unit

What does a unit usually contain? The following elements are typically found in a unit:

Unit title.

Description of the grade level, target student population, and general rationale for the unit.

Goals or major objective(s) for the unit.

Series of lesson plans, normally, each with the objective and purpose. The lesson plan should give enough detail on procedures so that the teaching strategies and activities are clear. Worksheets and similar handouts should be included.

List of resources. This could include the list of resource people, media, library books, and so on.

Evaluation. Tests and other evaluation procedures should be included.

No set format exists for writing units. Some teachers prefer to divide a page into three columns, the first one for objectives, the middle one for teaching procedures, and the third one for materials. Others like to put each lesson plan on a separate page so that they can eliminate or modify the lesson plans more easily.

What is the difference between units (sometimes called teaching units), and resource units? *Resource units* are units designed commercially (for instance, by the Census Bureau to help teachers teach about the census) for use by a great many teachers. Districts may design a resource unit for a given topic. Usually, resource units contain more ideas and activities than any one teacher can use.

SAMPLE UNIT PLAN 2.3
Food

The following resource unit, designed to promote global education, is from the *Indiana in the World Teaching Activities Packet:*

Activities:

The pupils may:

Draw a two-column chart. Head one column "Animals" and one "Plants." List in the columns the foods they eat that come from plants and animals.

Make a list of their favorite foods.

Make a collage of their favorite foods.

Make a list of junk foods.

From a list of favorite foods, separate the junk food from the basic four food groups.

Discuss the nutritional value of the food they eat.

List and discuss health problems that can be prevented through adequate nutrition.

Describe and discuss their individual family eating patterns and compare them with other members of the class.

Divide into groups, each group choosing a foreign country; research and list the foods of their chosen country.

Find pictures and make a picture chart of the foods of their chosen country.

Discuss the eating utensils of a country (e.g., chopsticks in the Orient).

Visit a supermarket that features foods of many countries. List the foods that are featured from the country they are studying.

Take a field trip to a restaurant featuring food of a chosen country.

Research and make a picture story chart on the influence religion may have on the food intake of a country.

Plan a balanced diet from the foods of their chosen country.

List five or more foods eaten by people of other countries and state the countries (e.g., octopus, Italy).

Research and report on the history of some foods eaten in the United States.

List some of the foods eaten in the United States that were brought here from other countries. Name the countries.

Find pictures of overweight people in the United States. Explain why overeating is a dangerous habit.

Find pictures of children in other countries suffering from malnutrition. Research and report on the diseases prevalent in these countries due to malnutrition.

Write two story paragraphs, one explaining *plankton* and the other *hydroponic*.

Exercise 2.6   *WHAT ARE THE STRENGTHS OF THESE ACTIVITIES?*

In many cases, teachers incorporate the ideas from resource units or guides into their own teaching. Do you think any of these ideas on foods are helpful? Might you incorporate them into a unit of your own?

What are some special considerations that teachers should be aware of in designing and implementing units in the social studies? One is *variety*. Look at your lesson plans. Are you using the same techniques, worksheets for instance, every day? Are you showing three films three days in a row? Is content emphasized without consideration to the importance of skills, values, and social participation?

To spot these problems more easily, some teachers like to jot in broad outline what they are doing throughout the course of a week. (See Table 2.1.) Seeing a whole week's schedule often points out the need for more variety in teaching strategies and more attention to skills and values.

TABLE 2.1   LESSON PLANS FOR THE WEEK—SOCIAL STUDIES

Monday	*Tuesday*	*Wednesday*	*Thursday*	*Friday*
Introduction of community images	Map of Community	Telephone book used to locate businesses	Librarian to visit	Post office counter used

Subject Area _____   Date _____
Objectives:

Procedures:

Materials:

Evaluation:

Figure 2.1 Lesson plan form.

After you have completed a unit, evaluate it from the point of view of your students. What was their favorite activity? What did they like least about the unit? Most important, what did they learn from it?

LESSON PLANS

A *lesson plan* is an outline of what you expect to teach in a given day's lesson. (See the daily plans in Sample Unit Plan 2.1, a "Travel Day to Hawaii," for examples.) Many teachers begin by making up and photocopying a blank form with several headings (Figure 2.1). This form can be filled in at the beginning of each week or each unit. This is a typical outline, but it neglects some important areas of lesson planning, as we shall see later.

Lesson plans are constructed within the general framework of a unit and should reflect the goals of that unit. You need to be alert, in constructing daily plans, to how activities can move your students toward an understanding of the unit's general goals—how daily activities can make those goals more meaningful. This requires a careful match between student readiness and interest and the activities you plan.

The first consideration in making a lesson plan is the objective or purpose. Is there a special concept that you hope students will acquire? The next step is motivation. What can you do to "tease" the learner to listen? This may involve relating the experiences of students to your objectives. Student interest and involvement in the lesson may be triggered by an artifact, a learning game, or a planned classroom experience.

Beginnings are important. They help to shape the motivation of students. Teachers should try to effect a smooth transition from what students already know to the new material. In general, sequence your instruction from the simple to the complex. Sometimes a brief review by a student of what was done in yesterday's social studies lesson is helpful. Try to create an organizational framework for ideas or information so that students know where things are going. Many times it is valuable simply to state the purpose of the lesson. Some teachers turn lessons into guessing games for their students, who must figure out where they're going and why. This generally does not help the learning process, especially for slower students.

In writing out procedures, teachers are often not detailed enough. What does "read and discuss the textbook" mean? Read aloud? Read silently? Read one paragraph silently and then discuss? Will students discuss questions in small groups? You can see that "read and discuss the textbook" is open to a wide variety of interpretation.

During the lesson, be attentive to the responses of the students. Is there a sense of accomplishment among them? Finally, think about closure, or ending the lesson. Will you depend upon the bell to close the lesson? That can leave students dangling in midthought. A better way is to draw attention to the end of the lesson, to help students organize their learning, and to reinforce what they have learned. Have a student summarize the lesson for the class, or do so yourself.

A good lesson, then, usually consists of the following areas:

Objective to be achieved
Concept or major idea(s) to be taught
Teaching strategies to be used
Motivation for the lesson
Materials and resources needed for the lesson
Closure for the lesson, including independent work and follow-up
Evaluation to see if objective(s) are achieved

A typical outline that lists objectives, procedures, materials, and evaluation (Figure 2.1) therefore neglects motivation, concepts to be taught, closure for the lesson, independent work, and follow-up. Sloppiness in these areas sometimes makes for dull lessons when just a little more planning could turn the lesson into an exciting and useful learning experience for the students.

Exercise 2.7   *LOCATE INTERESTING LESSON PLANS*

It would be exhausting to plan to develop all of your lesson plans by yourself in the area of the social studies. Look at teacher's guides and resources units for ideas for lesson plans. Find three lesson plans that you like. Explain why you like them.

ORGANIZING AND SCHEDULING

Time for teaching is a valuable resource. Many elementary students attend school for more than five hours a day. The trend in the reform movement is to increase the number of minutes that elementary students spend in school. But when you subtract lunch time and recesses, most teachers probably have only about four hours a day actually to teach.

How much time should be spent on teaching the social studies? Many school districts give recommendations. The minimum usually is 15 minutes for the first grade with an increasing time allotment each year. By the fourth grade, around 35 minutes a day is usually recommended, and by the sixth grade, social studies usually occupies a full period of around 40 to 45 minutes.

But these time allocations presume that subjects are not integrated. Typically, first-grade language arts (reading, writing, listening, speaking, spelling, handwriting) are allotted *two to three hours* each day. This means that if you integrate different areas, such as language arts (reading stories about the culture you are studying, writing a thank-you note to a community worker who spoke to your class), you can greatly increase the number of minutes devoted to social studies instruction. Integrating science and social studies is also worthwhile; studying the geography of a given area lends itself easily to the study of that area's plants, animals, climate, and the like. Integrating social studies with music, art, dance, and drama is natural, especially when you are studying a particular culture.

When is social studies typically taught during the school day? In many schools the basic subjects, reading and math, are taught in the morning "prime-time" hours. Social studies is typically relegated to the afternoon in such programs. By integrating subject matters, however, you can bring social studies content into the morning hours, when students are fresher and better able to learn.

You may not have complete control over scheduling block time and subject areas. In most schools, physical education, music, art, and other such subjects are taught by specialists, whose schedules will dictate part of your own scheduling. In addition, students are often grouped for reading and/or math and may go to different rooms for these subjects; again, you may have to follow prescribed time allocations for such classes.

Most teachers, however, can make some decisions on how to use the time available. You will probably want to set up a more or less "normal" daily and weekly schedule. You may decide that you would rather teach social studies on Monday, Wednesday, and Friday for a longer block of time than every day for a shorter period. Time allocations may change depending upon the activities. A field trip or a local guest may dictate changes in the "normal" schedule. However, most classrooms eventually move into more or less routine scheduled times for different subject areas, or learning periods. Teachers differ on how to schedule and organize their class time. As long as time is used wisely, these differences are probably not important.

SUGGESTED READINGS

Allen, Jack, Ed. *Education in the 80's: Social Studies.* Washington, D.C.: National Education Association, 1981. An overview of the Social Studies.

Beyer, Barry K., and Gilstrap, Robert. *Writing in Elementary School Social Studies.* Boulder, Colo.: Social Science Education Consortium, 1982. How to use writing as a resource in the teaching of social studies.

Brophy, Jere E.; Rohrkemper, Mary; Rashid, Habim; and Goldberger, Michael. "Relationships between Teachers' Presentation of Classroom Tasks and Student Engagement in Those Tasks." *Journal of Educational Psychology* 75:544–52.

Dick, Walter, and Carey, Lou. *The Systematic Design of Instruction*, 2d ed. Glenview, Ill.: Scott-Foresman, 1985. Organizing learning and instruction effectively.

CHAPTER

3

Instructional Strategies

This chapter focuses on methods of teaching, or teaching strategies. The following areas are highlighted:

1. General Consideration of Methods
2. Direct Teaching
3. Inquiry Modes and Critical Thinking
4. Cooperative Learning
5. Role Playing
6. Simulations

GENERAL CONSIDERATION OF METHODS

What methods, or instructional strategies, should be used to teach elementary social studies? Planning instruction is like planning a trip; several elements have to be considered (Table 3.1).

In instructional planning, specific elements must be considered as well (Table 3.2).

In actual practice, you should have a wide repertoire of teaching methods. Using a variety of strategies is more likely to be effective in meeting the varying needs of students, who have different styles of thinking and learning. Of particular interest here is the research on right-, left-, or whole-brain dominance.[1] Those who are left-brain dominant

---

[1] Thomas R. Blakeslee, *The Right Brain* (New York: Anchor Press, Doubleday, 1980).

TABLE 3.1   ELEMENTS IN PLANNING

Planning a Trip	*Planning for Choice of Method*
What is my goal(s)?	What is your goal(s)?
What transportation will be used? Various forms?	What method will be used? Various types?
How much time is available?	How much time is available?
What will I do?	What activities will be used?
What shall I pack? How much?	What materials or resources are needed?
What information do I need?	What background do the students need?
What if there are delays?	What adjustments may need to be made?

TABLE 3.2   ELEMENTS IN PLANNING FOR METHODS

Student Characteristics	+	*Content Characteristics*	+
Reading abilities		Significance	
Other basic skills		Available materials/resources	
Cooperative abilities		Survey versus in-depth coverage	
Attention span			
Motivation needed			

Environmental Characteristics	+	*Instructional Possibilities*	=
Schedule		Exposure: story, film, text, guest	
Space/room arrangement		Skills to be taught: library, coop. learning	
Size of class		Creative: role play, research	

Possible Instructional Sequence
Introduction-overview
Motivation
Development
Student reproduction of knowledge
Culmination, summary, conclusions

tend to be able to remember names, respond to verbal instructions and explanations, and like planned and structured assignments. Left-brain-dominant students primarily rely on language in thinking and remembering. Right-brain-dominant students prefer a more fluid and spontaneous situation. They prefer their work and studies to be more open ended. Right-brain-dominant students rely primarily on images in thinking and remembering. They respond best to illustrated or symbolic instructions. However, some individuals are equally facile with both modes.

Exercise 3.1 *FINDING YOUR STYLE*

What learning style are you most comfortable with? Does your style of learning have any relationship to the methods you feel most comfortable using in teaching? Have you consciously adopted one or more methods in your own teaching experience? Jot down the strengths and weaknesses of your "style."

To meet the wide diversity in student background and learning styles, then, it is wise to use a wide range of teaching methods. For example, with a fifth-grade class studying the history of the United States West, you could start off with an exercise on planning a trip to the West before the Civil War. Have the students, organized in small groups, make decisions about how much they should spend on various supplies and what articles they should put in the covered wagon. (There are computer programs such as *The Oregon Trail* that work on a similar theme, but if you do not have a computer in your classroom, the small-group exercise can work very well.)

Have the students analyze their findings. In a whole-class discussion, they can gain insights from other groups' experiences about what is important for making the trip, and the class can rank the priority items for moving West. (Discussion and list making favor left-dominant students.)

Introduce literature and songs about the pioneers to enhance the students' understanding of the settlement of the West. Have students learn or listen to songs like "Oh Susannah" or "Sweet Betsy from Pike"; talk about the *Little House* books or television shows. Using another strategy, give a short lecture on abstract concepts such as freedom and lawlessness on the frontier. Have students read the appropriate textbook pages and do workbook assignments. Involve the nonverbal students in a range of projects to make or do: putting together a short play on the West, making maps of wagon-train routes, and so on. More verbal students might write "pretend" diaries, songs, or poetry on the West. Finally, have students evaluate their own projects to see how they could serve as stepping-stones for future learning.

The variety of activities in this unit on the West provides channels for a wide range of learners and their abilities. Students start with a concrete experience (planning a trip to the West) and move into concept development (lawlessness, freedom, etc.). Furthermore, the students find applications for the materials and concepts as they develop their own projects. In the process of evaluating their projects, the students engage in analysis and also move into the affective domain by sharing their projects with other members of the class. You will meet many needs in this series of lessons.

In addition to the learning needs of students, certain environmental factors may also influence your choice of teaching methods. Large class size might make some methods inappropriate. The physical environment of the school or the social climate of a given class may not be conducive to certain methods. Simulations, for example, may be noisy. If the walls are thin and a simulation would bother other classes, it might not be politically wise to use it. In addition, each class has its own personality. Often you hear experienced teachers say, "No group reports this year. My kids just don't mesh well enough."

Thus many factors need to be considered when thinking about teaching methods. Each method represents one possible route to more successful learning for your students, and one method may be more appropriate for certain topics and skills, another for other topics and skills.

All teaching methods, however, have some common elements. Each one involves teacher direction of student-thinking processes. All require preparation, concern with motivation, setting up of the learning experience, and the creation of some evaluative technique to assess whether or not students have gained in knowledge, skills, values, or social participation—the four goals of the social studies.

DIRECT TEACHING

Much attention has been focused in recent years on an instructional method known as *direct teaching* or *direct instruction*. The main purpose of direct teaching is to present knowledge and skills so as to enable *all* students to *master* the material being taught.

The most popular direct-teaching model, also known as Clinical Teaching, Target Teaching, Instructional Theory into Practice (ITIP), was developed by Madeline Hunter. What response do you have to these various titles? Do they suggest that Hunter is interested in having teachers sharpen and target their teaching skills so that students can gain higher levels of achievement? Direct-teaching advocates argue that this approach— which includes structured content, the carefully explained introduction of new material, considerable student practice, and frequent recall and comprehension questions—can improve achievement, especially for lower socioeconomic status students.

The Hunter model has been successful in part because it begins from a realistic assessment of what goes on in many classrooms, including social studies classrooms. It recognizes that the textbook is still the major vehicle for social studies instruction. Too often teachers simply assign sections of text and worksheets without much explanation of the material covered. The Hunter model, which is a specific form of direct teaching or lecturing, can be used to help teachers convey content more effectively. A second reason for the popularity of the Hunter model is that it was developed at a time when some educators were questioning the value of the looser, less direct, or less structured teaching strategies, such as role playing, simulations, and value exercises, which relate more closely to the affective domain.

Here are the steps in a direct-teaching model, although district guidelines may vary somewhat, including more or fewer steps:

1. *Anticipatory Set:* Get the students focused on the lesson. Use material relevant to the objective and related to students' past experience or interests. Use when introducing new learning, after an interruption, or at a point of change to a new subject.

2. *Objective*: Tell the students what they are going to learn.
3. *Purpose*: Tell the students the benefit of the learning. Explain why you are teaching the lesson. (Objective and purpose are sometimes combined.)
4. *Input*: Analyze what knowledge and skills need to be learned. Present the material.
5. *Modeling*: Tell the students what to look for. Provide a perfect model. Demonstrate what the end product of the learning will look like.
6. *Check for understanding*: Monitor the learning. Adjust your instruction to accommodate where the students are.
7. *Guided practice*: Actively involve all students. Monitor their activity. (Understanding and practice are sometimes combined.)
8. *Closure*: Tie the learning together. Recapitulate. Summarize.
9. *Independent practice*: Assign classroom work and homework, to be done independently.

What are the key elements of direct teaching? *Pacing* and *learning for mastery* are important. Students spend a high percentage of their time on tasks that they will successfully complete. In contrast, regular instruction too frequently skips many of the elements of direct teaching and leaves students frustrated, either because they are not sure *what* they are supposed to have learned, or because they don't know *why* they are learning it.

The direct-teaching model may remind you of what a public speaking instructor would say: Tell them what you're going to say, say it, and then tell them what you've said. That is, in fact, a large part of direct instruction. In addition, however, the emphasis on "set" is an attempt to relate actual student experiences to the objectives—to bring students into a more active participation in learning. Direct teaching attempts to stimulate student interest and involvement in the lesson by explaining the importance of what they are learning and by doing a good job of explaining the content. Furthermore, the lesson is planned in detail, so the teacher avoids meandering along trivial or personal paths. Finally, direct teaching gives students an opportunity to practice what they have heard and then to reinforce it with further assignments.

When is it appropriate to use direct teaching in the social studies? Certainly, teachers need to explain ideas and concepts to students whenever they begin a new unit of work, a new concept, or a new project, and direct teaching methods can help. Here is how direct teaching using a textbook might work:

A teacher, Mr. Smithy, wants to explain the concept of *organization*—a group that has at least two members who have common interests and rules. To *set* the lesson, Mr. Smithy points out that many members of the class belong to organizations: José is a Cub Scout and Maria is a Brownie. What other students, he asks, belong to these or other organizations? Mr. Smithy explains that religious or after-school-sports groups are also organizations.

Then Mr. Smithy tells the students that they are going to learn about organizations, which form important parts of our modern society, because it is useful for the students to be able to identify them. In other words, he explains the *objective* and *purpose*. In the *input* stage, he may give examples of organizations. The City Council is an organization—it has more than two members, rules, and common interests. The local IBM personal computer club is also an organization. Members have common interests, pay dues, and come to meetings to find out more about how to use their computers. The PTA is an organization; a stamp club or after-school soccer teams are organizations.

Mr. Smithy then gives examples of *non*organizations. The local shoe repair store employs only one person. It is not an organization. A group of individual shoppers in a shopping center is not an organization, even though it includes more than two people, because the shoppers do not meet regularly or follow common rules.

In *modeling*, Mr. Smithy tells his students the main characteristics of an organization. He has provided examples of organizations and nonorganizations. Then he has the class read the pages in their textbooks about organizations.

After the class finishes reading, Mr. Smithy *checks their comprehension* by asking questions about what is and what is not an organization. Then he gives a worksheet to the class and has students check on a list which items are organizations and which are not. The list may include *people at a movie theater, the Sierra Club,* or *people walking in the park.* Mr. Smithy supervises this activity, providing *guided practice.*

After allowing time for this exercise, Mr. Smithy and the class go over the correct answers on the list. In *closure,* the students summarize again the main characteristics of an organization.

Finally, for homework, Mr. Smithy has students ask their parents what organizations they belong to (unions, churches, clubs, etc.). Students then make up, independently, lists of organizations to which their parents belong. This provides *independent practice.* Mr. Smithy may check these lists to make sure that students have an accurate understanding at this point of what an organization really is. (Also see sample lesson plan 8.1, Chapter 8.)

In the above example, Mr. Smithy assumed that all students could read a textbook, which is not necessarily true of all members of every class. By identifying the key ideas before giving students the reading assignment, however, he ensured that even students who were not good readers would find the assignment easier. In effect, he had built in "readiness" for the reading experience. He used the textbook to reinforce his own teaching and to help students understand a concept.

It is not enough simply to create all of the elements of a good direct-teaching lesson. You must *communicate* those elements to your students. Breakdowns can occur in direct teaching as well as in any other teaching method. Because much of the instruction in this method depends on you speaking to your class, your vocal delivery is important. Poor diction, mannerisms, digressions, or lack of clarity may interfere. The level of abstraction may be too great for a particular group, and students may simply "tune out." Students may also ignore what is being said if the lesson goes on too long. Their attention may be diverted by physical distractions in the room or by other students. Concrete examples will always help maintain student interest, as will having students use other senses by employing visual aids or requesting a written response. Too often lecturing is a passive activity for students, who remember little of what they have heard. If you follow the Hunter model carefully, however, step by step, you won't fall into this trap.

In some districts and states, administrators have gone overboard on direct teaching and expect all teachers to use it almost all of the time. Madeline Hunter would not encourage this rigid dependence on her model. Used exclusively, direct teaching can stifle creativity in teachers and prevent them from exploring different teaching strategies in different situations.

Direct teaching obviously has many good points. Whenever you explain or lecture to a class, you would do well to check the steps of the direct-teaching model. Introducing lessons with clear goals and making ideas logical and cogent are helpful principles in conveying knowledge and skills. As with any teaching strategy, however, direct teaching should not be employed day after day in the social studies program. Repeating the same process every day is dull for both student and teacher, unless you are an exceptionally enthusiastic advocate of this method. Direct instruction may be particularly effective for teaching facts and skills to low-ability classes, but the teaching of higher-level thinking skills may best be done by other methods.

Exercise 3.2 *EXPLORE THE PROS AND CONS*

Would you like to teach in a school or district in which direct teaching is emphasized? List the advantages and disadvantages of this situation. (You may want to read criticisms on the Hunter model, which has not yet produced research to support the claim for improved learning.)

INQUIRY MODES AND CRITICAL THINKING

What do the words *inquiry, problem solving, inductive thinking, critical thinking, discovery learning,* and *thinking skills* have in common? They all refer to the processes that everyday citizens as well as scientists and scholars use to discover knowledge, make decisions, and solve problems. The schools have always claimed to do more than just teach the three R's. One goal of education has always been to foster the thinking skills that are desperately needed outside of the classroom. Many believe, however, that thinking is a process rarely encouraged or manifested in most classrooms.

When thinking skills are not taught, many students (and, as a result, many adults) lack confidence in their own abilities as thinkers. For most, critical thinking is a *learned*, not an *innate*, skill. Those without it feel unsure of themselves and believe that they cannot generate good ideas. This lack of confidence is true even of those students who receive high grades in all subjects on their report cards.

In the 1960s a reform movement recognizing the need to teach thinking skills began. Many of the more than 50 new social studies projects created then had some emphasis on teaching thinking, most commonly at that time called inquiry. Although educators in the 1970s showed more concern with values and relevance of materials to students, an interest in teaching thinking skills has manifested itself again in the 1980s. Many reasons account for the increased emphasis in reform reports on thinking skills. Our society in general is more concerned about being able to compete in a worldwide market. Only if its youth are educated to think, this argument goes, can the United States survive as a leading industrialized nation with a high standard of living. In addition, citizenship goals have always emphasized the need for teaching all children to think.

Although in practice thought processes differ from one person to the next, the following steps outlined by John Dewey are a good starting point for "thinking about thinking." [2]

1. Define the problem.
2. Suggest alternative solutions to the problem; formulate hypotheses for testing.
3. Gather data to support or negate hypotheses.
4. Select supportive hypothesis or reject unsupported ones.

These steps translate into the following steps for teaching thinking skills.

1. Introduction—problem, question, or dilemma posed
    Example of activities:
        What are our images about Mexico?
            Brainstorm by small groups.
            Chairpersons report back to the class.
            Items on Mexico presented from media.
2. Development of a hypothesis (tentative answer)
    Example of activities:
        Teacher leads a discussion of ideas generated from brainstorming and teacher/class selects the best one; hypothesis could be that our images of Mexico are not accurate or it could be the more specific hypothesis that Mexico is facing serious financial (or political or social) problems.
3. Gathering data
    Example of activities:
        Data presented by teacher in charts.
        Data from the textbook.
        Data collected by students (group or individual research).
        Data classified and interpreted by the students.
4. Hypothesis accepted or rejected
    Example of activities:
        Class/teacher evaluates data and methods of research.
        Class/teacher states a conclusion.
        Students suggest further questions for investigation.

---

[2]John Dewey, *How We Think* (Boston: D.C. Heath, 1933), p. 72.

We use these processes of problem solving in our everyday lives. For example, assume that you go to your car in the morning and it does not start. Definitely a problem! You listen and it seems to be making a funny noise as you try to start it. You form a hypothesis: the battery is dead. Then you get help from a friend or neighbor who charges the battery. It works! Your hypothesis (that the cause of the problem was a dead battery) has been supported.

Students also face decision making or problem solving on many different levels in their own lives. They may make plans for a birthday party and have to decide whom to invite or what activities to plan. They need to decide how to use their leisure time. Should they watch television, read a book, or play soccer? They may face problems in getting along with classmates or siblings that need to be resolved. They may need to figure out a way to earn money. Students may also have grave concerns about how they should behave in school or outside the classroom.

Problem-solving skills, then, have universal value. Anything that the schools can do to sharpen thinking skills now will have a big payoff in the future. Certainly, both individuals and our society face many problems that can be solved only through informed and logical thinking. But developmental stages are important, and there are limits to what children can do in thinking and problem solving. Many students at younger ages, for example, cannot think abstractly. In addition, children who are impulsive and not motivated toward intellectual tasks may not show much interest in thinking activities in school. In teaching students to think, you need to consider both the formal process and the specific needs of your students.

Defining the Problem

To resolve any problem, we must first be able to recognize it and define it; this is the first thinking ability that you should encourage in your students. A good way to approach this first step at the elementary level is through *inductive reasoning*. In inductive thinking, an individual perceives a particular pattern of relationships based upon a finite number of items or events. It is a way of generalizing from experience or data.

To encourage inductive thinking in helping students recognize that culture influences art, you might bring in pictures or show filmstrips on the art and architecture of a particular society such as that of the Mayans or the ancient Greeks. After they have seen a series of art "products" from that culture, have the children try to state something about that culture's beliefs. How are women depicted? Men? Does most of the art represent gods and goddesses? What does that suggest about the importance of religion? By beginning with the concrete objects and encouraging students to generalize from them, you will make the concept of culture's influence on art easier for children to grasp. In contrast, simply asking your students how cultural beliefs affect a society's art will provide a far more difficult problem for them.

Many forms of problem solving begin with inductive reasoning. Teachers often try to trigger student thinking by presenting a discrepancy between what students *think* they know and some new data. Ask your students what images they have about a given nation.

Contrast this with actual data. Or raise a controversial question such as what a community should do about housing the homeless or controlling pollution. Contrast the students' solutions with what is actually being done.

Generating Ideas

The second step in thinking is to generate ideas or hypotheses (tentative answers) to help explain why a problem is occurring. Try to draw forth as many ideas as possible without making any judgments. Even silly ideas should be accepted.

You might ask students individually to jot down as many different ways as they can think of to improve the common bathtub or, for more of a social studies flavor, their local transportation system. We recommend that each student work by himself or herself for a minute or two before moving into small groups to share ideas. Always have a student do some of his or her own thinking first; students should not get into the habit of believing that they can only think when they are part of a group.

In the group each student will usually find out that the others have different ideas. Some might think that public transportation should be increased, whereas others might think that workers need to arrive at their places of work at different times to avoid commuter congestion. It is good for students to learn that not everybody perceives the world and solves problems in the same way. In some exercises, especially at the beginning, you may not want to focus on determining the *best* ideas. In fact, students should be encouraged to brainstorm and generate ideas without making judgments about which ones are best. Students used to questions with only one right answer (what is the capital of Chile?) may find the notion of many right answers both confusing and exciting.

Class activities can help students learn to select good ideas, decisions, or solutions. In the following example, students take the role of an explorer and try to determine solutions to particular problems. The exercise encourages cooperation rather than competition. Notice also that the exercise tries to break down the steps of thinking. It does not simply pose the problem but first provides background information. Too frequently, teachers pose problems too broadly. In this exercise, the student is led step by step through the process to see what ideas will work best in the particular situation.

SAMPLE LESSON PLAN 3.1
Deciding Which Ideas Are Best

In 1542 the Spanish had a claim, or right to the land, in California. This was a land in which about 300,000 Native American lived. However, California was not settled by Europeans. But in the 1700s the Russians were moving down from Alaska. They wanted the rich otter fur trade. The British were also coming closer to "Spanish" land.

Around 1700 the Spanish had settlements in Baja California (now part of Mexico). To protect their claim, the Spanish government decided to send soldiers and missionaries to California to teach the Indians and to create a permanent Spanish settlement.

The military leader of the group sent to California was Captain Gaspar de Portola, the governor of Baja California. The religious leader was Father Junipero Serra, a Spanish priest and missionary.

Captain Portola had to decide how to move his group to San Diego, 640 kilometers (400 miles) north of Baja California. He had two choices: water or land.

1. Put yourself in Captain Portola's place. List the one most important consideration he should think of in making his journey. _____

_____

Ships at that time were small, about 30 meters (100 feet) long. A crew might number 20. The winds might blow the small ship off course. The captain had poor maps. The crew and passengers might get ill from not eating the proper amount of fruits and vegetables, especially when away from land for a long time.

By land there was possible danger from the Indians. The group had to bring enough food since they could not depend on living off the land. Water had to be found. The trip was also slow since most people walked only a few miles (kilometers) each day. There were only a few mules and horses available.

2. Captain Portola has to consider an additional problem. In 1769, the year the trip was to start, Father Serra was 55 years old. He was short and walked with a limp. How do you think Father Serra should travel? Why? _____

_____

3. Captain Portola also wanted to bring some cattle and horses with him to California. The animals would be useful in the new settlement. What would be the best way for them to travel?_____

_____

4. Now, with these considerations, what choice do you think Captain Portola should make on how to travel to California? Why? _____

_____

Captain Portola decided to "hedge his bets." He would use both three ships and two land groups, one land group going ahead of the other land group.

5. Was this the best plan? Why? _____

_____

6. Captain Portola had to decide whether he himself, the leader, should go by land or by the sea route. Portola was a skilled army leader. Which way would his talents be best used? _____

_____

Captain Portola and, surprisingly, Father Serra went by land. Limping and riding, Father Serra, with great determination, made it to San Diego. There they met the group who had gone by sea. One of the three ships was lost at sea, and many from the voyage were sick and died. The land party also had sick men who died. But even with these hardships, Captain Portola was successful in establishing the first permanent European settlement in California. Had he used the best ideas in his decision making? What would you have done differently?

Exercise 3.3   *TAKE THE STUDENT ROLE*

Pretend that you are a student. Work out the exercise on Captain Portola. Then share your responses with a small group or with the class. Do you think the above exercise helps students to think? What if a student decides that Portola should do something other than what he actually did? Should the student's idea be accepted? How would you respond?

Students need a lot of practice in generating ideas and then in deciding which ones are best. Usually, if a student's explanation of events or situations takes into account all of the relevant facts, it is an idea worthy of consideration and should not be rejected. Ask your students to make sense or to generate ideas out of puzzling things, such as why Stonehenge in England was built or why Indians, called Mound Builders, built their large structures in certain parts of the United States. Most students will enjoy thinking and looking at data about the Loch Ness Monster or, in the United States, Big Foot and drawing conclusions about whether these "monsters" exist. Or students can be given more formal social studies exercises, such as trying to account for the growth of large cities in their state. All of these examples can serve as springboards for thinking and for generating ideas (hypotheses) to be tested.

Gathering Data

After identifying the problem and coming up with promising ideas to explain or solve it, the third important step in problem solving is gathering data to support or reject the hypothesis. It is important for students to get data from a variety of sources, and finding information often involves skills best taught directly via the Hunter Model. Thus, in teaching the more creative thinking skills, you may find yourself using direct-teaching methods.

Information Skills

1. Finding information in a book
   Using a table of contents
   Using an index
   Using a glossary
   Using an appendix
2. Finding information in a library/media center
   Using a card catalog

Using the Dewey Decimal System
Using encyclopedias
Using an atlas
Using an almanac
Using other reference books
Using a telephone directory

In many cases, before students can find information and data to support their hypotheses, they must be able to use books and the library appropriately. Usually, your school librarian will be helpful in explaining how to use the library and how to gain information from printed resources. Worksheets (on how to find encyclopedia information about the Mongols, the Suez Canal, or the growth of railroads, for instance) can be helpful.

Here are other examples of activities that encourage information skills. Photocopy for each student the one-page Quick Reference Index of *The World Almanac and Book of Facts*. Then ask students to give the *category* in which you would look to find out about major earthquakes, the population of Canada's provinces, where nuclear reactors are located in the United States, and so on. Similarly, prepare an abbreviated ditto on the telephone numbers of government offices. (In real life, people often need to telephone government agencies about things such as how to fill out an income tax form or how to go about getting a dog license.) Then explain how to find government office telephone numbers in the pages of the telephone directory. Finally, ask students to find and write down the telephone number for offices such as Animal Control, Birth Records, Boating, or Building Permits.

Students may also assemble their own data from interviews and questionnaires, but they must be taught to ask questions in an objective manner and to communicate clearly what is being asked. Most students will need your assistance in designing an interview sheet or questionnaire to gather data, for example, on how local residents view traffic problems in their neighborhood. Poorly designed interview forms and questionnaires may yield misleading information that is of little value in proving or disproving a hypothesis. Such questionnaires also may reflect unfavorably upon the school and the teacher.

Accepting or Rejecting a Hypothesis

After students gather data, they need to classify and organize the information. It requires skill to find relationships and classify facts under main headings. Students must be able to see, for example, that data on immigrants might belong in several categories such as the problems immigrants face and successes they have had. In addition, students will often have to analyze and interpret their information to see what it really means. Only then are they in a position to accept or reject their hypothesis, the final step in the thinking process. Do the data support the hypothesis?

We have tried to show that you will probably have to use a variety of methods to teach problem solving or thinking. Sometimes students will work in small groups; other times, they will work alone. In some cases, your role will be indirect as you try to encourage students to generate as many promising ideas as possible. In these cases, your role is not to judge but to encourage an atmosphere in the class where ideas are welcome and not subjected to ridicule by other students. On the other hand, direct teaching of specific skills, such as how to find information in an atlas, may work best. But it is not enough just to drill these skills into the students. Worksheets or other teaching tools should be as entertaining as possible so that students will want to use the skills after they do the required assignments. Skills that are not used in the future are not a good payoff for either the students or the school.

In teaching thinking skills, then, present a variety of problems for the students to think about. Make sure that they become interested in the problems, and don't pursue a problem if most students seem bored. Also, don't foster dependency in students by giving them too much help. Be positive about their ideas, and remember that many students have not had much experience in thinking and will not become creative thinkers in merely three weeks. Finally, make the encouragement of critical thinking a goal in everything you do and every lesson you teach, throughout the year.

Exercise 3.4   *JUST THE FACTS!*

How much thinking do you believe goes on in a typical social studies classroom? Does it occur during the whole day? If you believe that not much thinking takes place in most classrooms, list three reasons that many teachers concentrate on having students recall facts instead of emphasizing thinking.

COOPERATIVE LEARNING

Cooperative learning, the "new" name for small-group instruction, is getting increasing attention in education. There are many reasons for its growing popularity, but the primary one is that research, an area usually filled with conflicting findings, consistently shows that cooperative learning results in both academic gains by students and better attitudes toward fellow students. Indeed, these are powerful reasons to use cooperative learning or small-group instruction. Although not necessarily the best or the only way to teach, cooperative learning is one more strategy to deliver content and to teach skills.

There are many different definitions of cooperative learning. Some educators include peer teaching and cross-age tutoring as examples of cooperative learning. But the most accepted definitions stress the size of the group. *Cooperative learning* consists of three or more students who are united by a common purpose to complete a task and to include every group member. Not all educators, agree on the best size of a group for a given task, but Robert Slavin suggested the following:[3]

---

[3] Robert E. Slavin, "Synthesis of Research on Cooperative Learning," *Educational Leadership* 38 (May 1981): 660. Reprinted with permission of the Association for Supervision and Curriculum Development. Copyright © by ASCD. All rights reserved.

Student–Teams–Achievement Divisions (STAD)

Teams of four or five members complete worksheets provided by teacher, followed by a quiz.

Teams's overall score is determined by each student's improvement over past performance.

Team with greatest improvement is recognized in weekly class newsletter.

Teams–Games–Tournament (TGT)

Similar to STAD, except no quizzes. Instead, students play academic games with other class members with similar past performance.

Team score is based on individual improvement.

Jigsaw

Teams of five or six members. Teacher gives each student an informational item to "teach" the team.

Students are tested individually.

Learning Together

After teacher presentation, students work in small groups on a single worksheet.

Team as a whole receives recognition and praise for mastering worksheet.

Group Investigation

More complex grouping, requiring students to:
Accept greater responsibility in deciding what to learn
Organize themselves in how to master the material
Decide how to communicate their learnings to the remainder of the class

Why do experts recommend cooperative learning? In the real classroom, the average student during a discussion has only 1 chance out of 25 (or whatever the class size may be) of getting a chance to speak at a given moment. But if he or she is put into a small group of four, the probability of speaking goes up to 1 in 4. This means that there is a lot more interaction among students, a valuable asset in the classroom.

Furthermore, students can help one another learn. In small groups, students can assist those who are having difficulties by acting as tutors. But even the bright students gain from small-group work. In the real world, adults spend a lot of time in small groups. Most of us interact with our families and friends. In community affairs, organizations, and clubs, a task is frequently assigned to a small committee. For teachers, it is almost impossible to avoid being put on a committee to work on some project to help improve the school.

To function in our society, everyone needs the skills to participate in small groups. Usually, it is very pleasant; most of us enjoy the socialization and companionship. But this is not always true. Have you ever been in a three-person group in which the other two members "ganged up" on you and tried to impose their views? In real life, three-member groups are often unstable regardless of the setting—three persons sharing a dorm apartment or three friends. Or have you been in a small group that was unpleasant because one person knew all the right answers and would not listen to others? Just putting individuals or students into a small group is no guarantee that work on the task will proceed or that the contributions of all members will be valued.

Therefore it is necessary for all students to *learn* to work in small groups. In the beginning, small-group exercises may last only a few minutes. Later you can carefully consider the personalities of individual class members and organize the class to work on a longer project. At first the students may float from group to group, but later in the year the same group may stay together for the duration of a project unless you have to make individual adjustments in the assignments.

The literature on cooperative learning advocates that, at the beginning of the year, you set up a number of small-group learning experiences in which students can get to know one another better. Have the students make collages, illustrating things they like to do, or have them share information about themselves with other members of the group.

As the year progresses, have groups work cooperatively on projects. Small groups might make poems on topics such as Thanksgiving or birthdays. Have individual students first jot down ideas or short phrases on the topic. These ideas can be incorporated into the group poem, which one member of the group might then read to the class. You might also want to post a copy of the poem, signed by all members of the group. The purpose of these activities is to teach students to use the ideas of *everyone* in the group and to take pride in *the group's final product.*

In the beginning month or two of school, small groups provide an opportunity for students to get to know one another in a relaxed and unthreatening manner. You can also use small groups during these first months to create a positive feeling among your students for the class as a whole—perhaps by having them find a special name for the classroom or creating a class logo or slogan.

In assigning groups, especially early in the year, you need to look carefully at the personalities of the class members. Generally, there should be a fairly equal distribution of girls and boys and of minority students. In addition, more-verbal and less-verbal students should be dispersed evenly. If you know that two students don't get along, do not, at least initially, place them together. However, later in the year, after their small-group skills improve, you might *want* to assign them together.

Consider size in setting up small groups. Size is a very important characteristic of cooperative learning. The National Aeronautics and Space Administration (NASA) has given a great deal of attention to the "right" size of the group in assembling space-shot teams. For NASA, as for any other productive group, size must depend to some extent on the number of tasks to be performed. Aside from task assignments, however, NASA found that the optimal number of adults for a space team is five.

In many classrooms, the whole class is divided into three more or less equal groups—

typically with 7 to 10 members. This is far too large for effective small-group work. In general, younger children profit more from smaller groups. In fact, 2 children is the proper group size for many primary children. Groups of 3, 4 or 5 are appropriate for more mature children. Group members must be able to see the nonverbal clues that other group members give as well as hear what is being said. If the group is too large, members cannot monitor what is happening.

Some educators recommend one-half hour of small-group work each day by the end of the year. Although cooperative learning can be done in various areas, the social studies lends itself naturally to some small-group work. Textbook chapters can often be used for cooperative learning; each group, for instance, may study one Latin American nation. There are many social studies topics on which students may have a variety of opinions. This makes them ideal springboards for small-group discussion.

If groups can be unproductive for adults, it is not surprising that schoolchildren, too, may have difficulty working together. There may be personality clashes, ranging from minor bickering to insults that end in tears. What causes some of these conflicts in the small group? Often it is the recognized stable hierarchies of "smart" and "slow" students. Most students in most classes within a short time categorize every member of the class as smart, average, or dumb, usually based on a verbal ability such as reading. These attitudes about ability can carry over into their small groups. Groups frequently take less advantage of contributions and skills of students who are labeled dumb, despite your plea that everyone participate and that all work together.

Students may quarrel about who is to do what and who should make decisions. In effect, they play power games, just as adults do. Higher-status students want to have leadership roles, and lower-status students resist being in a group that does not seem to appreciate their talents. In many cases, "slower" students withdraw by physically moving away from the group or by disrupting it.

To avoid these problems, some teachers assign roles to each member of the group. Thus one student is the chairperson, another is the secretary, a third is responsible for getting the supplies to the group, and a fourth is charged with seeing that the group stays on task. You might even prepare cards with the title "chairperson" or "secretary" to emphasize that each member of the group is to perform a certain role.

Here are some roles that students can play in small groups:

Facilitator

Organizes the group's work
Makes sure the group understands its job
Takes the group's questions to the teacher *after* trying to get answers from the group

Checker

Checks with the group to be sure that everyone understands the task
Checks to be sure that everyone can explain and agrees with the group's answer

Reader

Reads the problem or directions to the group

Recorder

Writes down the group's answers on the group answer sheet

Encourager (eventually all members should be this)

Keeps people feeling good about working together
Shows interest and excitement about the group's work

Reporter

Reports the group's answers during the processing discussion

These roles can be rotated throughout the group so that each student has a chance to assume each of the roles. But you need to monitor what is going on. Occasionally, students do not take their roles and thus allow leadership, for example, to pass on to another student who has not been assigned that role.

What content or subject matter is best taught through small-group activities? Almost anything. But one error that teachers often make with small groups is not giving students enough background information for a good group discussion. In these cases, the teacher frequently has put students into a group to discuss an important or controversial current event. The teacher might say, "Discuss in your groups what should be done in striving for world peace," or "What should be done about pollution in our community?" These topics are fine for "brainstorming." But the assignment to the group is too broad, and students may not have enough background to have a fruitful discussion. It is no wonder that they cannot stay on the topic and end up discussing something else such as sports.

Writing out a paragraph or two of information for the small groups may be more effective than simply giving them a problem to discuss. For example, you might summarize data for the class on the amount of air pollution in their community in recent months and also provide a list of major factors contributing to air pollution. Then the students can base their discussion of pollution on relevant information.

In some long-term cooperative learning projects, finding information is part of the assignment. In these cases, your job (with the help of your school librarian) is to make the appropriate resources available to the groups. Perhaps you have made a determination that to "cover" all of the material in the textbook on Latin America or on Native Americans with the whole class would take too much time. Instead, you decide to divide the students into groups, assign each group a single nation or tribe to study in depth, and then direct them to the appropriate sources of information. Finally, the groups can share what they have discovered with the rest of the class.

One problem with cooperative learning is grading. How will the group be graded?

Unfortunately, what often happens in small-group projects is that the "smart" students overparticipate, and the less-able students contribute less (or find their contributions undervalued by the group). Often students see as unfair the teacher's insistence that all members of the group be given the same grade. If you explicitly require that all students in some way participate in the presentation of the group's efforts, however, the "able" students will be more likely to make sure that everyone is included, since otherwise their grades may be lowered. As Slavin suggested, the group's score for improvement in achievement can also be used.

While pointing out possible pitfalls of cooperative or small-group learning, we also want to emphasize that this can be a very productive method. The class spirit and atmosphere may improve as students get to know one another better and learn to work together. Everyone enjoys the class more. Furthermore, the academic achievement level of the class may increase.

But cooperative learning does require special attention and planning on the part of the teacher. Make your assignments and instructions clear, so that the group does not take too much time trying to determine what has to be done. In addition, you must monitor carefully what is going on. Is there one group that is constantly bickering? Is there one student who is always ordering the other members of the group around? If these problems persist, you may have to make changes or, in an indirect way, show the students how to make improvements in the group. Discussing afterwards how the small group is progressing often offers opportunities for students to think about their behavior. Role playing at "being bossy" or other problems can also provide a rewarding opportunity for students to become aware of how to improve their small-group skills. For more about cooperative learning, see Chapter 7.

Exercise 3.5 *TRYING OUT SMALL-GROUP TASKS*

The best way to learn how to use small-group or cooperative learning is to do it yourself. Experience firsthand what it is like to be a member of a small group. Try the following formats and see how you like the experience. First, brainstorm in a group for a few minutes on the advantages and disadvantages of small-group work. The rule here is that no one is allowed to discourage any ideas. Then write down a few ideas on how you think small-group work could be used in the teaching of the social studies. Now convene a second group and try to move toward consensus by choosing the three best contributions. How were the experiences different?

ROLE PLAYING

What is role playing and how does it work? *Role playing* is a method of problem solving that enables participants to explore alternative solutions to a given problem. It is an *unrehearsed* dramatic presentation, usually more appropriate for children of ages nine or older. Role playing is especially useful for dealing with controversial issues.

The impetus for role playing can be provided by reading a story or a law case or by viewing an open-ended film or filmstrip or a photograph showing conflict. Classroom problems such as lack of sharing or breaking school or class rules can also be used for role playing. When using problems in your own class such as dealing with the class bully, however, do not use actual names, and disguise the incident on which the group is focusing.

The basic steps in role playing are the following:

1. Present the open-ended problem. Set the stage by asking, "Have you ever . . ." or "How did you feel when you were . . ." Then say, "Today we're going to hear a story about Jose (or any name other than that of a member of your class) who got into a similar jam. Think about how you would feel if you were in such a situation." Next, read the story up to the conflict point. Encourage students to identify the problem and talk about how the people in the story feel.
2. Select the participants or role players. Ask for volunteers to play the various roles. The rest of the class serves as observers.
3. Begin the role play. Enact how the story might end. Have students pretend to be characters with the feelings and ideas of the people in the specific situation.
4. Discuss the solution, especially in terms of its realism. Ask the observers if there are other alternative ways of solving the problem.
5. Explore the alternative possibilities in further role playing.
6. Discuss the several role-playing experiences and, if possible, summarize what has been learned.

Role playing can be a safe way of exploring alternative behavior. We can express feelings or opinions without risking disapproval. How many of us, while driving on the freeway or sitting at our desk at the end of the day, have said, "If only I had said this or that, the situation would have been better." Students need to know that sometimes alternative ways of acting lead to better solutions. Role playing offers a safe opportunity to explore.

Role playing also can help prepare students to cope with conflict resolution and problem solving. Role playing is used, for instance, to help students "say no to drugs." Proponents of this approach in drug-abuse education believe that it is not enough just to tell a student to say no to drugs. It is better to act out situations, such as a party at which one student offers another student drugs. Showing different ways in which a student can refuse the drugs while still remaining "friends" with the offerer may be important to students. In addition, this approach can suggest to the "straight" student that it is possible to find activities other than drug use to share with the user—a step to help the drug user.

Using role playing in drug-abuse education also illustrates another value of role playing. Role playing can deal directly with issues on which students might be reluctant to bring up their opinions in other formats, such as what to do if you see two children fighting or if you meet a friend after you have heard that this friend has told lies about you. By providing a situation in which students are and yet are not themselves, you give them a chance to bring out feelings and opinions that they might otherwise not be willing to express.

Most students enjoy participating in and watching role playing. It provides an opportunity for more active involvement than many other learning experiences in the classroom, and it is more personalized. Acting out the dilemma of a pioneer child who must decide if he will report to his Indian friend that the Indian camp will be raided the next day involves the students in what has happened in the past. Many teachers say they are using role playing to play out historical events, such as the Constitutional Convention of 1787, exactly as they occurred. Technically, when students act in a prescribed fashion and merely duplicate the historical event, they are doing *dramatic play* and not role playing. The focus of role playing is the concept of *alternatives*, or other ways the story or historical event might have ended.

You may encounter students who are reluctant to volunteer to role play, especially at first. Others are often born "hams" who want to play roles every time. Do not let these "actors" take over the stage completely. Start with less controversial or emotional issues so that students become more at ease in role playing. Continue to encourage the shy students to volunteer, and as students get used to the format of role playing, they will become more eager to play a role. However, be careful not to cast students in the roles they occupy in the minds of their classmates. Do not put the class clown in a role in which he or she plays the class clown. Instead, put each student in someone else's shoes. The class bully should play the role of the weaker student who wants a turn in a game. Continually emphasize the role that the student is playing and avoid calling the student by his or her real name. Refer to the police officer or the landlady rather than to the specific student.

Sometimes students have a difficult time maintaining their roles. They start to giggle and often are distracted by the response of their audience. Members of the audience, too, must play their role appropriately. You may want to comment on this before or after the exercise. Usually, with time and practice, students are better able to maintain their roles.

Initially, you may find that many students want to play the enactment as it "should" be. In other words, they will play a role in a kind and loving manner and do all of the right things. You need to ask if this is how it really happens. Some teachers are bothered if students enact negative, although realistic, behavior. They think that the class may model the wrong pattern. This is especially true, for example, if a student role involves pretending to take drugs or acting according to some other behavior that the community strongly opposes. But this should not be a major concern if an appropriate discussion and debriefing on what was going on takes place. You can ask students who acted in negative roles how they felt. Often they will say that they were uncomfortable about how they acted. Thus the debriefing stage is one of the most important parts of role playing. By sharing feelings and answering questions at the end of the enactment, students may see further alternative ways to act.

Teachers sometimes believe that they must force a generalization from the role-playing experience. They want the group to come to a conclusion, for example, "If you are not hostile in a situation, there is more chance of solving a problem." But sometimes students are not yet ready to reach that conclusion. In those cases, it is best to drop the matter. Perhaps in a further experience, the group will come to that or a similar conclusion.

Role playing in the social studies offers the possibility of moving into the affective domain. It can help teach children to empathize with others by showing them how it feels to be in someone else's place. It can tap the emotional responses of students to certain situations while still moving toward a rational solution to a problem. In fact, this is really one of the values of role playing. Often role playing can be a springboard for further study on a given topic. For this reason, it can be a successful method for the teacher of the social studies.

Exercise 3.6   *DEVELOP A ROLE PLAY*

Try role playing in your class. You might use the scenario of a principal walking into a class when everything is confused and out of order. Assign roles of the principal, student teacher or teacher, and a few students in the class.

SIMULATIONS

Simulations are learning activities that present an artificial problem or event. The situation described tries to duplicate reality but removes the possibility of inquiry or risk. Pilots, for example, learn to fly by using a simulator, while both the military and business worlds may use simulations to learn where to locate a new factory or how to win a military campaign. In many cases, a computer records the responses of the trainee or participants in the simulation.

Like role playing, a simulation allows the trainee or the player to try out a role and make decisions in a safe environment. But unlike role playing, which focuses on problem solving, simulations have a game-like quality in which there are players, roles, and an end-goal like winning. Because of this, many students think that simulations are fun, and they are motivated to do their best. Often they are put in a conflict or crisis situation, such as a political situation in the Middle East or South Africa, and are asked to play high-ranking political and military leaders or other important roles. Usually, they compete with others. One simulation, "Seal Hunt," tries to encourage cooperative behavior, but most simulations are based on competition.

In education, simulations were used initially without a computer. Students played simulations such as "Star Power," which set up an unequal division of power and resources, and were supposed to learn what it was like to be a member of certain power groups. In another social studies simulation, "Farming," set in western Kansas at three different years, students acting in teams of two made economic decisions on what to invest in—hogs, wheat, livestock, and so on. The simulation tried to duplicate the reality of farming in the 1880s, and at the end of the simulation, many of the couples (students) found that they had lost their money. Part of the purpose of this simulation was to bring to life the problems that farmers were facing after the Civil War. One of the advantages of well-designed simulations is that they can make abstract concepts such as oversupply or power more meaningful for students. In addition, simulations provide almost immediate feedback to the students on how they are doing, which is a key to motivation.

We are now seeing more computer-based social studies simulations. In most of them, the individual student interacts with the computer program, playing the role of the king-priest of an ancient city making economic decisions, for instance, or trying to win a political campaign in the United States. In a few games, such as "Geography Search," students act in teams to try to locate valuable resources. In these cases, there is often competition between different teams in the same classroom.

Neither computer nor noncomputer simulations in the social studies are usually designed commercially for the primary-grade levels; they start in the middle grades and beyond. However, primary teachers may design their own simulations, setting up, for instance, a post office, hospital, or other community institution.

Along with many promises, there are also some pitfalls in using simulations in the classroom:

1. In some cases, especially at the junior high level, students may have to learn complex rules in order to play. They may be unable or unwilling to listen to a long explanation, and you may find it best to have students learn by doing, even if some encounter frustration.

2. Some students are motivated in simulations only when they have important roles to play. They find it unfair that they have to play poor people or members of a group that is discriminated against. You may find that students are reluctant to accept these roles, although they are necessary to the simulation.

3. Simulations can have management problems. They are often noisy. Occasionally, students get so involved in playing the simulation that they actually become hostile and even start fights. You must constantly scan the classroom to monitor what is going on.

4. Teachers sometimes believe that simulations misinform students by oversimplifying. If a student plays the role of a United Nations delegate, for instance, the student may then believe that he or she knows all about the United Nations. Some teachers also worry that simulations encourage unethical or immoral behavior, as when students choose to drop bombs and start wars or to take resources from poorer players.

As you can see, some of these concerns are similar to those associated with role playing. As with that approach, discussion and debriefing are essential to clarify what actions players chose to take and what effects those actions had on other players. Thus in "Seal Hunt," students must realize that their decision not to share resources may have forced other students to starve. In the "Mercantilism" simulation, which is set in colonial

America, students, eager to make money, find they are often wheeling and dealing in both slavery and smuggling. It is important in debriefing to clarify what the students were actually doing and to explore the consequences of such behavior.

The strong advantage of a simulation is that students are often highly enthusiastic and motivated. There is a minority of students, however, who would rather read the textbook and answer the questions at the end of the chapter; not all students are the same. You must therefore determine whether a simulation has achieved the desired objectives. Do the students now know more about understanding different cultural groups? Do they feel more empathy for disadvantaged people or developing nations? Like any other method, a simulation is worthwhile only if it conveys knowledge, skills, or changed values.

Exercise 3.7 *RESEARCH BY DOING*

Acquire a simulation. Your library may have one, or a recent catalogue from Social Studies School Services (10000 Culver Boulevard, Culver City, CA 90230) is a good source. Secure the teacher's manual. Go through the simulation, step by step, to see how it works. Do you see possible difficulties? What does it seem to teach? Secure reviews, if possible, from teachers or from computer journals on how the simulation is rated.

Other methods do exist for teaching the social studies. Some teachers individualize instruction and set up learning centers. Others may use supervised study as their main activity for teaching the social studies. Sometimes questioning is listed as a distinct method, although questioning is part of almost all methods. Different methods are more appropriate for certain students and for achieving certain objectives; no method will work all of the time for all teachers and all students. Since you are the decision maker, you must decide what combination of methods is best suited to achieving your objectives.

SUGGESTED READINGS

Chance, Paul. *Thinking in the Classroom.* New York: Teachers College Press, 1986. Excellent overview of several types of current thinking programs.

Horn, Robert E., and Cleaves, Anne, eds. *The Guide to Simulations/Games for Education and Training,* 4th ed. Beverly Hills, Calif.: Sage, 1980. Older but good list of simulations and games.

Johnson, David W., and Johnson, Roger T. *Learning Together and Alone,* 2d ed. Englewood Cliffs, N.J.: Prentice-Hall, 1987. Good on cooperative learning techniques.

Shaftel, Fannie R., and Shaftel, George. *Role Playing in the Curriculum,* 2d ed. Englewood Cliffs, N.J.: Prentice-Hall, 1982. Best text available on role playing.

CHAPTER

4

Social Studies in the Primary Grades

Curriculum considerations for primary-grade social studies are divided into the following sections in this chapter:[1]

1. Children in the Primary Grades
2. Primary Social Studies Curriculum
3. Guidelines for Primary Social Studies
4. Classroom Environment and Scheduling

CHILDREN IN THE PRIMARY GRADES

Although the goals and strategies outlined in the previous chapters apply, you will want to focus specifically on the particular needs and competencies of the younger child when you consider social studies issues to be presented in the primary grades. Children's statements such as, "The moon was at my house last night, not yours." "I'm going to be a ballerina when I grow up because I have a tutu!" "My bike is going faster than that airplane!" reveal the many ways in which young children commonly invent prelogical explanations as a means of coping with the complexity of our world. Children from ages five to eight are just beginning to accumulate the information and experience that we take for granted in the intermediate-age child. They are just becoming aware of their individuality. They are exploring interaction and cooperation with others. They are grasping for explanations of their vast, challenging physical environment.

An effective social studies curriculum for the early years is rooted in an awareness of

---

[1] This chapter was coauthored by Kathleen Burson, DeAnza College, Cupertino, California.

the cognitive, psychological, and social tasks specific to the five- to eight-year-old child. A review of these three areas of development provides a foundation for the selection of social studies activities and teaching methods.

Cognitive Development

Cognitively, most primary-grade children have intuitive rather than logical explanations for social and natural events. The sun "shines" to make us warm. Conceptions of social relations are primarily egocentric, and conceptions of the structure of society may be concentric, with home and family firmly at the center of the universe. One's own family's habits and life-style are often seen as the standard by which other behaviors are measured.

Three cognitive skills are being developed during these early years that help to break down the egocentric and concentric orientations.

1. *Perspective taking*—the ability to recognize that other people may have experiences and feelings that give them a different view of an object or situation. Most children are able to recall how big some familiar object seemed to them when they were younger. They may remember disliking foods that they now like. As they begin to acknowledge internal changes in perspective, children become more aware of options and alternatives. Taking classroom surveys and opinion polls are ways that you can help children see that each person's perspective is unique.

2. *Decentering*—the ability to comprehend that one person may have multiple roles. Most primary-grade teachers have noted the confusion created when they meet one of their students in a supermarket or neighborhood setting outside the classroom. Can a teacher also be someone's mother? Can a mother also be someone's daughter? The understanding of the multiple attributes of a person or object is critical to the later understanding of multiple perspectives and the inadequacy of stereotypes.

3. *Classification*—the ability to make comparisons and to organize objects into groups and subgroups based on similarities and differences. What are the properties that make an island an island? Does every society use "money"? What is the same and what is different about music throughout the world? How does American clothing in the past differ from American clothing in the present? Many opportunities exist within the typical classroom to group and regroup based on a variety of criteria. Contrasting family descriptions and life-styles with others in the class, in the community, and in the world helps children to see their family's way of working, playing, and eating as simply one of many ways of performing universal activities.

Concrete experiences, actual "hands-on" multisensory participation, is the key to the development of each of these cognitive skills. Your role as a primary-grade teacher is to provide your students with direct exposure to new experiences and to create opportunities to act upon and experiment with new concepts as they are forming. Bringing an infant into the classroom rather than talking about growth and change, raising a classroom garden rather than talking about nutrition, preparing and eating ethnic foods rather than seeing pictures of them—these are necessary activities in the primary grades if information is to be assimilated fully as part of a child's knowledge base.

Psychological Development

Psychologically, young children are less introspective than intermediate-aged children. Although preadolescents can readily describe "how I feel," six-year-olds are more likely to give a physical description of themselves. As a teacher you can often be the supportive adult who helps to identify feelings and to find appropriate ways of expression. Many young children continue to be physical rather than verbal in their expressions of anger or excitement, for example.

The self-esteem of each child is always a consideration of the primary-grade teacher. Children interacting in large groups for, perhaps, the first time may find competition paralyzing. They may be reluctant to share personal information and to "be themselves." They may need encouragement to develop their unique talents and interests. The teacher who models respect for each individual prepares children to respect themselves and others.

A final consideration is the Eriksonian concept that this stage is characterized by "industry versus inferiority." In other words, primary-aged children are shifting in interest from learning processes to creating products. Putting on a show, weaving a belt, learning all the rules of a game and using adult tools are all activities that meet psychological as well as informational needs. They help a child feel productive and, therefore, competent and worthwhile.

Social Development

Socially, young children are rapidly shifting awareness from the strictly personal to the group. In four major areas—gender and gender stereotyping, friendship and ways to maintain friendships through conflict, cultural diversity mostly within the classroom, and requirements of "rules" for group living—children are absorbing their social world.

Each of these areas is central to a child's experience. If the curriculum does not address these areas, children will learn attitudes and habits in these areas from their peers, the media, or their own prelogical store of conclusions rather than face uncertainty. Therefore, it is crucial to apply our best judgment to these issues. Zick Rubin's survey of research suggests that social relationships have stages of development paralleling their psychological growth from egocentrism.[2] When we form cooperative learning groups, lead discussions on playground conflicts, and contemplate a particular child's lack of participation, we need to keep in mind this process.

In sum, there is considerable documentation of the early childhood years as a critical period for attitude formation about self and others. Prosocial behavior can be effectively

---

[2] Zick Rubin, *Children's Friendships* (Cambridge: Harvard University Press, 1980).

encouraged during this period. Mary Ellen Goodman's studies document the formation of attitudes toward one's own race and other racial groups in young children.[3] Robert Havighurst cited this period as crucial in the development of attitudes toward groups and institutions.[4] Much evidence exists to demonstrate the difficulty of reversing negative feelings formed about the self or others in this period. Clearly, the social studies curriculum in the primary grades has long-range effects that warrant giving it high priority in classroom planning.

PRIMARY SOCIAL STUDIES CURRICULUM

To explore the elements of a social studies curriculum for young children, we will examine two versions of topical guides around which primary grades' social studies activities are organized, review the various kinds of skills and competencies young children are expected to develop, discuss guidelines for considering the various materials for implementing the curriculum, and outline the specifics of organizing the classroom environment and scheduling social studies activities.

Topical Guides

As we saw in Chapter 1, content guides for primary grades generally elaborate on the developmental needs of children. Topics are sequenced in an *expanding-horizons* model extending gradually from the individual to wider social circles. Notice that each level of the 1981 state guide from California includes topics that represent various social sciences. Which are the geography topics? Anthropology topics? Psychology topics? Sociology topics?

SAMPLE TOPICAL GUIDE 4.1
1981 California History–Social Science Framework[5]

Kindergarten—Myself and Others in My World

> Finding my way in my world
> The uniqueness of me: My similarities and differences
> My needs and the needs of others: How people grow and change
> Self-awareness and the employment of my five senses

---

[3] Mary Ellen Goodman, *Race Awareness in Young Children* (New York: Collier Books, 1964).
[4] Robert J. Havighurst, *Developmental Tasks and Education* (New York: McKay, 1972).
[5] *California State Framework for History-Social Science* (Sacramento: State Department of Instruction, 1981).

My parents—their jobs and jobs that I can do
Special occasions in my life
Cooperation and conflict between friends and classmates in work and play
Songs, stories, games, and dances my friends and I like
Rules and why we need them
Learning to listen and listening to learn

Grade One—People at Home and at School

Relationship of home to school
Getting from home to school safely
Time and my life
Roles people play in my family and at my school
Families—my own and others in the community and the world
Meeting needs at home and at school
Cooperation, conflict, and communication at home and school

Grade Two—People as Members of Groups

Getting around in my neighborhood
Groups to which I belong
American ethnic groups; their roles and contributions
People and the groups they form or join
Roles within groups (e.g., leaders, followers, innovators)
How groups use resources
Rules, responsibilities, and group norms
Communication, problem solving, and decision making in groups
Cooperation and conflict within or between groups
How art, music, and dance influence and enrich group life
People who have contributed to the groups to which I belong

Grade Three—People as Members of Communities

My community—where is it?
What is a community?
Our community—its past, present, and future
How community groups rely upon and influence one another
The diverse cultures and peoples who make up and contribute to our community
How our community is governed
Cooperation, conflict, and communication within our community
Appreciating and preserving the beauty of our community and improving the
    quality of life in it
Comparing our community to other communities in the United States and the world

To separate this list into its academic-discipline components is an adult exercise with no significance for children. As teachers, however, we need to be aware that the various social sciences are interwoven to form a larger set of topics that take the child's perspective into account. Starting with himself or herself, the child is led to explore the names and functions of elements in everyday life. Children come to school with an intuitive knowledge of how their world works. The significance of the formal social studies curriculum is that it contributes, and sometimes substitutes, a more factual understanding and that it makes them more conscious of their social lives. As children begin to express themselves at school, you can facilitate the ongoing reorganization and reintegration of what they know with what they are learning.

SAMPLE TOPICAL GUIDE 4.2
History—Social Science Framework[6]

Kindergarten—Learning and Working Now and Long Ago

Learning to work together
Working together: Exploring, creating, communicating
Reaching out to times past

Grade One—A Child's Place in Time and Space

Developing social skills and responsibility
Expanding children's geographic and economic worlds
Developing awareness of cutural diversity, now and long ago

Grade Two—People Who Make a Difference

People who supply our needs
Our parents, grandparents, and ancestors from long ago
People from many cultures, now and long ago

Grade Three—Understanding Continuity and Change

Our local history: Discovering our past and our traditions
Our nation's history: Meeting people, ordinary and extraordinary, through biography, story, folk tale, and legend

---

[6]*California State Framework for History—Social Sciences* (Sacramento: State Department of Instruction, 1987).

How does this guide differ from the first one? Notice the continuous interplay between past and present. The first topical outline did not contain this historical emphasis. One question we should consider is whether younger children can assimilate the historical perspective. The first content outline is a more traditional, child developmentalist view. The second outline represents a tradition that places greater emphasis on the academic disciplines of history and geography and literature. This recent emphasis in the field of social studies may be expected to increase with the renewal of concern about citizenship and values.

Skills and Competencies

In addition to the topical grade-level outlines, curriculum guides usually list skills and competencies that children should acquire while studying the suggested topics. Typically, social studies skills are divided into research and/or basic study skills, citizenship and/or social participation skills, problem solving and/or critical thinking skills, map or globe skills, and time and/or chronology skills.

Some of these skill areas are also developed in other subjects. Lists of reading competencies include research and study skills. Math lists include problem solving, critical thinking, telling time, and locational skills involving work with grids. In fact, one way to conceptualize the social studies is as a theme that prompts children to practice and grow in their basic skills. Children are gaining study skills when they gather information for a report by observing how groups solve conflicts at recess or by interviewing a parent on the tools that a parent uses in his or her work. They are growing in decision-making skills when they compare several solutions to the issue of how to distribute the play-ground equipment during recess. They are growing in problem solving when they test their prediction about which is the most productive way to get classroom jobs done.

Citizenship Skills.   Some of the skill areas are pertinent to the social studies but are necessary to teach throughout the day. Citizenship is such a skill area. Younger children need special guidance in citizenship skills. They are dealing with the idea of authority in their lives. Their parents, teachers, the traffic patrol guard, the school yard aide, and older children give them orders and rules to follow. Unless you highlight the need for rules and order, children may believe that authority is magical or capricious, not to be questioned, and resides with whoever has the most power and size.

Discuss why we have specific rules. Once the reasons for the rule are clarified, you should play the Devil's advocate role to help the children learn to question authority using a principle or reason. For example, if the children agree that the traffic patrol guard lets us cross after he or she has checked that traffic is stopped, ask them what they should do if they are told to cross while the patrol guard is laughing and joking with someone and has not checked the traffic, or if a friend crosses against the wishes of the guard, or if the guard keeps the children waiting when there is no visible reason.

Posing dilemmas, such as what to do if a baby-sitter exceeds his or her authority, is a natural prelude to role playing alternative solutions. (See Chapter 3 for a basic explanation of role playing.) Teachers find that young children are more easily involved in trying out ideas when simple stick puppets are used. The puppet serves to move the direct focus of the audience from the performing child, which seems to free the child's expression.

Steps in Role Play

1. Teacher sets stage with "Have you ever . . ." question about dilemma to be presented.
2. Teacher asks, "How did you feel in this situation?"
3. Teacher presents the situation stopping at the conflict point. "What is the problem here?"
4. Teacher asks how each person in the situation feels and why.
5. Teacher calls on volunteers to assume roles and play out a solution.
6. Teacher asks, "Could this really happen? Does anyone else have another solution?" Ask for other interpretations until alternatives are exhausted.
7. Teacher asks, "What can we conclude about the problem we have been studying?"

Making up rules and practicing the use of authority are keys that open a child's understanding of justice and fairness. When children have real experience in rule making, they should be led to discuss how rule making and enforcement happen in the adult world. You can promote these exploratory conversations by bringing a newspaper to class and talking about what the president, or other public figure with power, is doing.

To extend the exploration of the idea of authority and power beyond the immediate experience of the children, you should find out what children know about figures in authority. In this diagnostic phase teachers need to interview the children: Who is the president? How does a person get to be president? What does the president do? Why is the president important to us? Can a president make a rule by himself or herself? Is his or her power limited?

Children's answers can help us to know where to start our current events discussions. Typically, teachers will need to "go with the flow." That is, the next step is to build upon the information gained by bringing in pictures and stories that illuminate some of the children's information. Take the information children offer at face value and with seriousness. Laughing or finding fault with what a child offers will guarantee that the child will be less genuine the next time you initiate an interview.

Our ultimate goal is to help children see as real people those who have power in our system because they were elected. They retain this power by following established rules. Bringing such discussions into the classroom will help children make better sense of the bits and pieces they gather from television. We are helping them build a background for interpreting events, which is a vital citizenship skill.

Map and Globe Skills.   Map- and globe-reading skills are among the skill areas specific to the social studies. Younger children need concrete experiences in spacial awareness before they are presented with maps. They need to practice, as is done on "Sesame Street," the locational prepositions of, for example, *under, around,* and *beside.* Songs and games such as "Simon Says" or "Mother May I?" can help them learn *down, up, over, under, through, around, behind, between, left,* and *right.* These concepts must be firmly in place before they can learn about cardinal directions. Learning about the cardinal directions is best done outside at varying times of the day with the sun as a guide to connect to local landmarks. Once they have learned that they can orient themselves using the sun as it relates to morning or afternoon, they are ready to transfer the skill anywhere. Once they learn, for example, that the swings are to their east as they stand outside their classroom door, they are ready to name the direction of other landmarks from that point. After a series of varied, real experiences with finding direction, children are ready to transfer the idea of cardinal direction to the pictures they make of their classroom, school, route from home to school, and neighborhood.

Time and Chronology Skills.   Time and chronology are, in part, social studies skill areas. Math programs usually introduce "telling time" using a clock. Calendar time is usually listed under social studies. Telling time in periods longer than 12 or 24 hours is also important. Beyond the usual calendar routine of most primary classrooms, teachers can help children in stretching their notions of time by keeping a year-long timeline or journal of class events as enrichments to the daily routine. One of the classroom jobs is to record children-selected significant events from yesterday on the class timeline or journal. This practice builds a sense of continuity and recall for children. Another way to stretch the sense of chronology is a personal timeline that has children research and portray their own timelines on learning tasks such as walking, talking, eating alone, dressing, and tricycle riding on note cards that can be sorted and sequenced.

Studies have found that many young children are unaware of and fear change. Teachers need to involve children in activities that call attention to change as a natural part of living that they experience as they grow. Here are key questions that you can use to focus children on changes: Is something different? What is changing? What is causing the change? What do you think might happen because of the change?[7]

Observing change in height and weight by keeping individual charts helps children see change in themselves. Collecting weather and season data on temperature, rainfall, snowfall, the length of the days and nights, the changes in the moon, and the changes in vegetation and animal habits helps children see the cyclical nature of some changes.

Change in the human life cycle also needs to be illustrated. Contact with older people as classroom helpers or storytellers as well as books about growing, changing, and dying assist children in becoming more confortable with the idea that, even with change, there is a continuity of life through our families and that change, including the loss that comes with it, is necessary for us to grow.

---

[7] C. Sunal, "The Child and the Concept of Change," *Social Education,* October 1981, pp. 438–41.

GUIDELINES FOR PRIMARY SOCIAL STUDIES

Developmental psychologists tell us that materials used with young children should promote their interaction, creation, and manipulation. When we look at the kinds of topics suggested for the primary grades, we sense a dilemma between the learning-mode prescriptions and the nature of the topics. How, for example, can we help children learn about families in other parts of the world, or about how groups use resources? Books and film or video best portray these topics. Yet they require the young child to sit and listen or read. To resolve this apparent dilemma, we must learn to use print or visual information in ways compatible with the young child.

There are some guidelines for using "passive medium" materials with young children so that interaction occurs between the children and the material.

Keep input session short—10 to 20 minutes.
Use explicit objectives—"Let's read to find . . ."
Explain new or important vocabulary.
Insert interaction by asking children to answer questions, demonstrate, predict, and so on.
Provide visuals to accompany print information.
Conclude with discussion, chart making, predicting, summarizing.
Follow with related activity that prompts child's expression of topic read or viewed.

These are instructional steps in reading, or viewing, for comprehension. Teacher's editions of social studies texts usually point out these guidelines. We need to follow them when using library, or trade, books and visual media.

Having surveyed the general guidelines, we can look more specifically now at the various sources—textbooks, unit materials, equipment, trade books, holidays—of the social studies curriculum for young children.

Textbooks

The principal element of primary social studies programs should not be the textbook. Texts can be used as a resource. Distributing the books and finding the page robs precious minutes from instructional and attending time. In addition, there will probably be children who cannot read the textbook passages. Teachers have developed several ways to handle this management issue. For example, you need not pass out individual copies of the texts; instead, you can use the text as a storybook and read or storytell essential passages to the children who are seated in close proximity so that they can see the illustrations as you show your copy. You can also set up a listening-post center that children rotate through. Record the text passage including management directions and questions or comments you want children to reflect upon as they follow along in their books.

Diversifying Unit Materials

Textbooks and curriculum guides may present excellent content. To bring that content to life for most young children, you will need to collect and present materials that help children act upon it. Units of instruction are vehicles for the internalizing of ideas through manipulation and creative expression. They involve children in a multidisciplinary exploration of a topic. You should seek activity variety ranging from listening, viewing, painting, writing, and constructing models to classifying, touring, community action, and dramatic expression.

A unit outline on the hospital is presented here without listing the objectives. The "story line" is presented by the teacher using a curriculum guide supplemented with trade books and photographs. Note what materials for children would be needed to carry out this unit.

SAMPLE UNIT PLAN 4.1
The Hospital—Second Grade

Story line	Activities	Skills
Feeling sick	Poem	Describing words
	Sick faces on wet pastel	Painting
How do we know when we are sick?	Drama in pairs: mother/child, doctor/child, Nurse visits	Problem-solving discussion using descriptive words and medical instruments: thermometer, light, stethoscope, etc.
	Medicine precautions	Labeling; poetry writing
Accidents	Collage figures of accidents.	Painting
	List preventable, nonpreventable accidents	Discussion; classifying; list cause–effect
	Design working body	cutouts fastened with brads
Serious illness	Design ambulance	Cut-paste model
	Admission	Fill-in form; writing
	Hospital layout	Draw floor plan
	Dialogue nurse/patient	Role playing

Hospital life	Ward pictures	Labeling
	List hygiene rules	Discussion
	Patient's diary	Sequence drawings
	Diets	Classification
Hospital workers	Collage figures	Painting
	Job descriptions	Classification
People going home	How people get better, worse	Discussion
	Healthy faces	Compare sick-well
	Rules	Creative writing

In this unit the children's materials were chosen to foster artistic and written expression and provide a positive, open-ended forum for discussion of AIDS fears appearing in young children. The teacher used storybooks, pictures, some medical instruments, and a visiting nurse in addition to the curriculum guide. The teacher would have to gather a lot of pictures and storybooks and arrange for the nurse to visit to carry out this unit. The materials resulting from this unit would be voluminous. They would include word cards and lists of pertinent vocabulary, chart stories, a collage of figures representing kinds of accidents and kinds of hospital workers, model ambulances, drawings of hospital interiors, paintings of healthy and sick faces, poems about feeling well, and stories about the hospital. Each visual product of the unit topic can be used to help children discuss what they are learning and thereby organize their thoughts.

Exercise 4.1   *DEVELOP AN ACTIVITY-BASED UNIT OUTLINE*

Here is another possible story line for a first-grade unit on transportation. Without gathering specific materials, develop a hypothetical activity sequence on this topic. You need not elaborate the skills that relate to these activities. Your goal is to provide activity variety that assists children in understanding the story line, or subtopics. Compare your list with that of a colleague.

Story line	**Activities**
My favorite way of travel	
Wheels that move things	
Wings that move things	
Moving big and little things	
People who work in transportation	

Permanent Equipment

Social studies teaching in the primary grades involves only three permanent materials: a globe, a picture of Earth taken from space, and a map of the world. Textbooks and workbooks may also be part of the materials. The vast majority of materials in vibrant social studies programs are materials the teacher has located and selected. As unit topics and seasons change, different materials are needed. Build files from year to year that assist you in bringing new stimulation to your classrooms throughout the school year.

Trade Books

The extensive use of trade books for primary children can be a natural strength for social studies topics. Children love to listen to stories. They empathize with stories more easily than with video or film. Stories are an easy and malleable way for you to deliver social studies content. Stories are more accessible and personalized than most text and video treatments. Selecting trade or storybooks that illustrate social studies topics for young children is a continuing challenge. Recent analyses of popular children's trade books have pointed out the care teachers must exercise when choosing library books to read to children. For example, Patrick Shannon found that popular children's books rarely, if ever, portray characters who work together for collective goals.[8] A prevailing theme is the protagionist who accomplishes a goal alone and against all odds.

Less stereotyping is done in newer books. Wilma Dougherty and Rosalind Engle reported that Caldecott and Honor Books, published in the 1980s for young children, have markedly reduced the portrayal of men and women in traditional sex roles.[9] However, age stereotyping is still portrayed in many trade books for children. Sister Regina Alfonso alerted teachers to stereotypes of age—elderly are senile, elderly must be grandparents, elderly are all alike, elderly depend on their children—to look for in children's books.[10] Sunal listed books that offer sensitive views of different kinds of change that confront children.[11] The Association for Childhood Education International and the Children's Book Council Joint Committee published a bibliography of books focusing on "positive values in a threatening world." Here is a composite list selected from these two sources on the topic of change.

Books to Read to Children for Dealing Positively with Change[12]

> Aliki. *The Two of Them.* Greenwillow, 1979. Child shares grandfather's last days.
> Bunting, Eve. *The Man Who Could Call Down Owls.* Macmillan, 1984. Powerful fantasy about good and evil.

---

[8] Patrick Shannon, "Hidden within the Pages: A Study of Social Perspective in Young Children's Favorite Books," *The Reading Teacher* 39, no. 7 (March 1986): 656–63.

[9] Wilma Holden Dougherty and Rosalind E. Engel, "An 80's Look for Sex Equality in Caldecott Winners and Honor Books," *The Reading Teacher* 40, no. 4 (January 1987): 394–98.

[10] Sister Regina Alfonso, "Modules for Teaching about Young People's Literature: Module 2: How Do the Elderly Fare in Children's Books?" *Journal of Reading* 30, no. 3 (December 1986): 201–5.

[11] C. Sunol, "The Child and the Concept of Change," p. 438–41. See also C. S. Sunol and B. A. Hatcher, "A Changing World: Books Can Help Children Adapt," *Day Care and Early Education* 13 (Winter 1985): 16–19.

[12] Association for Childhood Education International and Children's Book Council, "Positive Values in a Threatening World," *Childhood Education* 62 (January–February 1986): 195–98.

Cazet, Denys. *Christmas Moon.* Bradbury, 1984. Animal character remembers loving ways of grandfather to handle grief.

Cook, Ann; Gittell, Marilyn; and Mack, Herb. *What Was It Like When Your Grandparents Were Your Age?* Pantheon, 1986. The United States in photographs between 1920 and 1930.

Cohen, Miriam. *Jim's Dog Muffins.* Greenwillow, 1983. Child learns to accept loss of pet dog.

Delton, Judy. *The New Girl at School.* E. P. Dutton, 1979. Sensitive, realistic treatment of making friends at new school.

da Paola, Tomie. *Now One Foot, Now the Other.* Putnam, 1981. Grandfather's stroke frightens child.

McGovern, Ann. *If You Lived in Colonial Times.* Four Winds, 1964. Describes daily life—clothes, food, school.

Power, Barbara. *I Wish Laura's Mommy Was My Mommy.* Lippincott, 1979. Child adapts to mother working.

Singer, Marilyn. *Archer Armadillo's Secret Room.* Macmillan, 1985. Grandfather and grandson unite to oppose family move.

As social attitudes change, children's literature attempts to portray these changes. We as teachers need to be alert to these changes. One easy technique to use in evaluating a book that presents social issues is to check the publication date. This is not to suggest that all older books should be ignored. That would force us to abandon some excellent literature. However, when reading pre-1970s books, call the children's attention to any change that has occurred. Ask them to think of ways in which something is different now. Looking at literature from the perspective of period helps children to develop their powers of critical thinking.

Several sources will help you select antibiased children's literature. Publications of The Council for Interracial Books for Children are invaluable guides. That group's book *Human Values in Children's Books,* published in 1976, is continuously updated in the council's periodical *Interracial Books for Children Bulletin.*[13] Recent issues of this periodical have focused on topics such as these:

Teaching preschoolers about work
Martin Luther King
Counteracting bias in early childhood education
Homophobia and education
Children of interracial families
Children's books and economic issues

In addition, *Social Education* publishes an annual listing of notable books in children's literature. Both *Social Education* and *The Reading Teacher* frequently publish articles and studies that analyze children's literature from the perspective of social issues.

---

[13] *Interracial Books for Children Bulletin.* Published eight times a year by the Council for Interracial Books for Children, 1841 Broadway, New York, NY 10023. Subscription: $20 institution, $14 individual.

Exercise 4.2 *BUILD A BIBLIOGRAPHY*

Follow up on one of these sources in your library. Develop a read-aloud bibliography for a topic of your choice. If you and your colleagues work on different topics and share your results, you can develop a rich set of teaching resources. You should read the actual books before you begin reading them to a group of children.

Holiday-Related Materials

These activities are often a major component of social studies for young children. Decorating classrooms using holiday themes is a tradition in many primary classrooms. Children learn to associate symbols such as cupids, shamrocks, turkeys, and pumpkins with certain months of the year. Too often, however, they receive little or no meaning for these symbols. They may be read a poem or story about the folklore of the holiday followed by an art project replicating the holiday's symbols. They may not gain any substantive information about the symbols they are reproducing. They do not know that the shamrock represents the Christian trinity of the Father, Son, and Holy Ghost or that the rabbit and the egg have been associated since pre-Christian times in Europe with the coming of spring and fertility. Using holiday materials that explain these symbols and their lore is part of cultural literacy that children deserve to have.

Young children can understand the significance of Martin Luther King with few materials beyond a photograph and a record. Barbara Green of Olinder School, San Jose, California, began by asking her racially mixed class of second and third graders how they would feel if some of them could not come to this class because of the color of their skins, because of their religion, because of how much money their parents have. After the children responded, Mrs. Green introduced a photograph of King. She told them his name and the story of his fight to end racial discrimination by allowing blacks to have the same access to public places and jobs as whites. Following recess Mrs. Green played a recording of King's "I Have a Dream" speech, and the children discussed King's dream. Mrs. Green asked if they had dreams of their own that they would like to see happen to make this a better country for everyone.

The floodgates opened! Children expressed dreams about eradicating poverty, unemployment, violence, and war that were far beyond Mrs. Green's expectations. This led to a writing assignment in which the children expressed their dreams of social justice. The results were read and discussed with another classroom group. (See Figure 4.1.) This four-part experience gave these second and third graders a personalized, age-appropriate understanding of why King is honored with a national holiday.

CLASSROOM ENVIRONMENT AND SCHEDULING

Implementing the social studies in the primary classroom involves more than thinking about the subject matter itself. Ideally, the goals of social studies teaching will be furthered

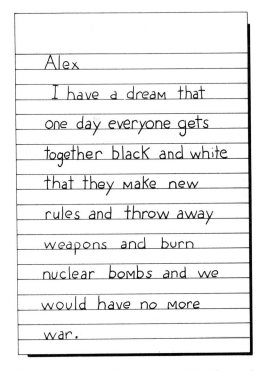

> Alex
> I have a dream that
> one day everyone gets
> together black and white
> that they make new
> rules and throw away
> weapons and burn
> nuclear bombs and we
> would have no more
> war.

Figure 4.1 The content of this writing sample may be suprising; it reveals that young children, in their own way, do think about our most crucial issues.

by the way in which teachers arrange their classrooms and schedule social studies experiences.

Classroom Environments

To organize your classroom space for optimal learning, take into account the variety of activities and positive social groupings young children need. Children need spaces to call their own. Designate a "cubby" or locker-like space for each child to keep snacks, lunches, clothes, and personal supplies to remove the need of assigning a permanent table space or desk for each child, and arrange tables to serve a variety of purposes that children can rotate around throughout the day.

Teacher-led large-group activities usually take place in an area near a chalkboard that has floor-sitting space for the children and a teacher chair. Teacher-led small-group activities often have a special corner with chalkboard, pocket charts, teacher chair, and semicircular arrangement of children's tables and chairs. Seat-work groupings are usually in the middle of the room. Other activity sites include an easel or art area, a listening-post center, a dramatic play area with clothing and props, a writing-reading center with books

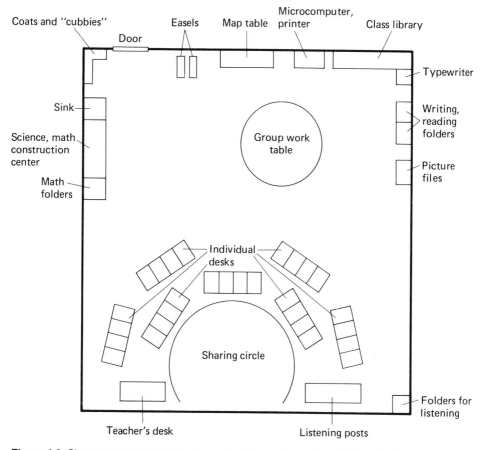

Figure 4.2 Classroom arrangement shows structured choices for children. Children keep their work portfolios near the appropriate activity centers.

displayed and perhaps a typewriter or computer available, and a construction area with art and model-building supplies. Folders for accumulating children's work and boxes for keeping workbooks and text materials are arranged within children's reach near the areas where they will be used (see Figure 4.2).

Materials related to social studies topics can be placed in any of the activity areas—the globe and maps and the class daily journal can be in the reading-writing area, textbooks and related tapes can be in the listening area, community helper or other theme props supply the dramatic play area—and renewed as topics change. Classroom-display areas such as bulletin boards can be used to build collages and murals of social studies topics as children produce them. Teachers who provide a background for murals and collages or work displays find that children can be put in charge of arranging the rest of the displays.

Scheduling

Teachers express their values about what is important for a young child to learn and how that learning takes place in the way they schedule the school day. Some teachers follow a more traditional early childhood schedule by breaking the day into work periods. Each period is separated by a snack, recess, physical education, or other large-group activity, and children rotate from one activity center to the next during different work periods. Thus while you work with a small group on something such as reading, other groups of children might be engaged in seat work or might be at the listening center or in the easel area. Each day begins with planning that suggests what each child must accomplish that day and what options each child has in choosing activities. Children manage their own movement by placing their names in pocket charts for particular option centers at the beginning of each work period. Then as a child finishes, he or she makes a place for the next child in line.

Another pattern designates periods for each subject throughout the day and week. Social studies may be scheduled three days a week after lunch until the afternoon recess. There are benefits and disadvantages to this pattern. Designating a specific time for social studies guarantees that each child will receive some exposure to the subject. For younger children especially, however, that kind of exposure may seem unrelated to other areas of the curriculum and other times of the day. Also, you may find yourself limiting strategies of instruction to large-group intake of reading or visual information and limiting responses to filling out worksheets. Young children need to be engaged actively. For learning to be significant, listening or viewing needs to be followed by building, dramatizing, or some other expressive activity.

Ideally, from our point of view, social studies for young children should be seen as part of an integrated day in which a social studies or science theme provides the informational focus for activities in reading, writing, drama, and art. Basic programs in reading and math skills would continue to be part of the child's daily experience. But language arts, music, art, and physical education would be organized around the current topic under study in the social studies or science. Film and videos would continue to be shown. They would be part of an ongoing study. That is, they would be preceded and followed by intake and expressive activities and would not be an afternoon filler or mere reinforcement of a reading assignment.

Informal Teaching

Topics come up when children are asked to participate in sharing that may influence instructional plans and scheduling. Through the informal method of capitalizing on children's interests, try to construct social studies-related experiences. For example, if a child shares that his pet got hit by a car, you might turn the discussion to the general theme of what we do when we lose someone we love. The following day you could bring in Judith Viorst's *The Tenth Good Thing about Barney*, a story about a boy's grief when his cat dies, to read to the class and discuss. Sensitive teachers attempt to respond to these teachable moments.

Developing an extended instructional sequence based on such a teachable moment requires great flexibility in planning and scheduling. Certainly, organizing instruction based on children's interests is an honored early-childhood ideal.

There are several issues to consider in deciding if the teachable moment merits further class time and attention. First is the issue of attention span. Sometimes when children ask questions, they want only a "yes" or "no" answer, not an elaborated response. We must develop a sixth sense for determining which questions and issues children can sustain with a more detailed exploration. Even when we believe the topic is within the children's attention span, our judgment about which topics really will add to the growth and development of the group is essential.

A second factor in determining how far to pursue a child-initiated topic is the issue of dignity or trust. Children may reveal confidences or home situations such as abuse within families. Teachers, by law in many states, must follow up such confidences and suspicions by reporting them to the school or legally authorized personnel charged with defending children's safety and health. However, to elaborate a miniunit on child abuse based on an individual child's or group of children's concerns would most probably abuse that child's or group of children's dignity within the classroom and damage the children's trust in the teacher.

On the other side of the argument is the need to provide children with proactive models rather than perhaps leaving them helpless by ignoring a topic or denying the appropriateness of a topic for young children. Issues concerning unfairness should not be ignored. Exploring ways to seek justice through discussion and role playing that probes different sides of an issue offer valuable, enduring experience and insight to children. Seeking justice through group action such as requesting to speak to the principal or writing letters to the editorial section of the newspaper or to an organization or to a politician are indelibly instructive to all children.

Adding social studies-related explorations to the daily schedule that spring from children's interests is a laudable practice. The same is true of holiday-related social studies schedules. Both types of scheduling are enriching. Such informal instruction cannot, however, substitute for a teacher-planned curriculum that systematically engages young children in learning more about who and where they are.

SUMMARY

The content and processes associated with the social studies are as essential to the growth and development of the young child as any curricular area. Effective instruction in the social studies for children in the primary grades is experiential and integrative. Concepts are presented in ways that involve children in exploring who they are and where they are. Materials and strategies expose children to a variety of peoples and cultures and problem-solving possibilities. Informal teaching that capitalizes on children's concerns is an enrichment to the basic social studies program that intentionally involves children in exploring facets of their world.

SUGGESTED READINGS

Alfonso, Sister Regina. "Modules for Teaching about Young People's Literature: Module 2: How Do the Elderly Fare in Children's Books?" *Journal of Reading* 30, no. 3 (December 1986): 201–5. 1986. Annotated review.

Association for Childhood Education International and Children's Book Council. "Positive Values in a Threatening World." *Childhood Education 62* (January–February 1986): 195–98. Reviews books that try to handle major issues such as terrorism, environmental disaster, and nuclear destruction in positive, active ways.

Dougherty, Wilma Holden, and Engel, Rosalind E. "An 80's Look for Sex Equality in Caldecott Winners and Honor Books." *The Reading Teacher* 40, no. 4 (January 1987): 394–98.

Shannon, Patrick. "Hidden within the Pages: A Study of Social Perspective in Young Children's Favorite Books." *The Reading Teacher* 39, no. 7 (March 1986): 656–63. Surveys individualist versus collectivist perspectives in children's literature.

Schreiber, Joan. *Using Children's Books in Social Studies.* Bulletin 71. Washington, D.C.: National Council for the Social Studies, 1984.

Sunol, C. "The Child and the Concept of Change." *Social Education*, October 1981, pp. 438–41. Surveys books that portray children dealing with family and individual changes.

Tway, Eileen. *Reading Ladders for Human Relations.* Washington, D.C.: American Council on Education; Urbana, Ill.: National Council of Teachers of English, 1981.

5

Social Studies in the Fourth through Eighth Grades

In this chapter we discuss the teaching of social studies from grades four through eight with special emphasis on strategies and materials that move beyond the basal textbook:

1. Children in the Middle Grades
2. Curriculum: Teaching the Social Studies
3. Current Events Programs
4. Teaching Controversial Issues

CHILDREN IN THE MIDDLE GRADES

Teachers who have experience with both the primary and middle grades are very clear about the developmental differences between these age groups: "I love teaching fourth graders. They can think and enjoy discussions." "My first graders are so loving! They still mix me up with their mothers." "Kindergartners are so active. They need to change activities every 20 minutes."

Cognitively, middle-grade children are ready to incorporate a wider span of spatial and temporal relationships in their thinking. Just as middle graders are extending their personal range of familiar space by roaming farther from home on their bikes and skateboards, they are ready to find out about unfamiliar places in social studies. The contrasting ways of rural and urban or desert and rain-forest life interest them. Middle graders are able to see themselves in the context of time. Their curiosity about prehistory and earlier human times grows. They are eager to conjecture about the future.

Psychologically, middle-grade children are focused on personal competency. They like recognition for what they can do whether it be as an outstanding speller or a whiz at drawing or a standout in recess team sports. Middle graders like quick-paced activity and changes in activities. Class or small-group games such as baseball or 20 Questions or trivia contests are appealing as content-review strategies. Projects that involve them in producing concrete products such as graphs, models, and murals gratify their need for variety and evidence of their competency.

Socially, middle-grade children are entering the age of reciprocity in friendship and human relations. They are able to see that their actions have social consequences. When they are in a group, they are eager to seek fairness. They relish opportunities to make rules, establish consequences for breaking them, and carry out enforcement of the rules.

It is well to emphasize that growth and development occur gradually, and there are individual differences in the rate of growth. The areas sketched are, nevertheless, some of the typical changes in the ways that middle-grade children see and interact with the world that should orient our social studies programs. As you examine content, strategies, and materials for middle-grade social studies, keep these general characteristics in mind.

There are two other things to keep in mind when you begin teaching social studies to fourth through eighth graders. The first is that developmental levels may vary dramatically within each grade and, as with any teaching, you need to be aware of the variations and accommodate your content and methods to the readiness of your students. The second point is that at some time in this grade range, probably at the sixth- or seventh-grade level, students will enter a middle school or junior high school where, typically, schedules will be divided into specific periods for each subject. Students may even begin changing classrooms for different subjects, as they do in high school.

The advantage of this environment is that the teacher will often be a specialist in his or her field and therefore will have more background and interest in the subject matter. The disadvantage, however, is that subject matters tend to be even more compartmentalized, with less and less integration between them. The continued emphasis, particularly in middle schools, on a "core" curriculum means that many schools still schedule large blocks of time and encourage the integration of social studies and language arts, for instance. But in practice, even in these schools, teachers tend to split the period in two.

Almost all experts recommend some degree of integration and particularly the integration of language arts into the social studies. We strongly encourage you to include language-arts content and methods in your social studies teaching, no matter what the organizational structure of your classroom time, since the two areas both complement and reinforce each other. See Chapter 8 for specific tips on using language arts in teaching social studies.

CURRICULUM: TEACHING THE SOCIAL STUDIES

What is currently taught in a typical fourth- through eighth-grade social studies program?

Grade 4: State history, geographic regions
Grade 5: United States history

Grade 6: World cultures, history, and geography
Grade 7: World cultures, history, and geography
Grade 8: United States history

History and geography have traditionally been emphasized at these grade levels, although there has been an attempt in the past 20 years to include more of the social sciences—political science, sociology, economics, and anthropology. This broadening of the social studies framework reflects a similar broadening in research in history. Historical research now emphasizes analysis over narration, a thematic or topical approach over a strictly chronological one, and more statistics, oral history, sociological models, and psychoanalytic theories. The "new" history focuses on everyday family life—patterns of recreation, for instance—rather than on the lives of political, military, and social leaders and their institutions. We are seeing much more research about women, minority groups, and community groups in history. Similar trends have occurred in other disciplines of the social studies as well, and all of this is reflected in what students are taught about social studies. Teachers have attempted to move beyond the basal textbooks in teaching elementary and middle-grade social studies.

Let's look more closely at what can be done in the specific disciplines.

History

History is people's story of the past. There is no single correct method of teaching history; direct teaching, inquiry, cooperative learning, role playing, and simulations all have their places. But there are some difficulties in teaching history to young children. Their ability to comprehend complex ideas like time and change develops at different rates. Generally, as explained in the preceding chapter, children are ready to learn specific *skills* related to history in the primary grades. They can begin to locate places on maps, compose personal timelines, and recognize how authority and rules work for the benefit of society. By the fourth grade, most students have some notion of the relationship of past, present, and future and some idea of geographic space. They are ready to learn *concepts*.

History gives a perspective on what has happened in the past. It is valuable in teaching us our cultural heritage; indeed, that is part of why United States history is taught in the elementary grades. Research indicates, however, that children do not develop much of a real chronological sense until they are about 10 years old.

How do children acquire the concept of *time*? Most children gradually recognize that events fall into patterns. From their homelife children learn that, typically, there is a time to get up, to eat, to play, and to go to bed. Through the use of language and experience, they begin to distinguish among past, present, and future. The present is now, and it becomes past almost as soon as we think about it. The future is what will happen next. Yesterday and tomorrow are early and important concepts.

A more mature time sense allows us to move away from personal experience and to extend our understanding of time both backward and forward. Dates become orientation points, and events fall in chronological order. We begin to be able to visualize how events a hundred or even a million years ago are related to the present. This perspective obviously involves more than simply memorizing dates. We begin to understand the concepts of cause and effect and of continuity. We begin to see that history is constantly in flux, that change is taking place all the time. Individuals change, families change, social institutions change, nations change, the whole world changes. Most changes occur gradually; a child grows older, and the dynamics of his or her family shift a little each year.

The problem in teaching history to elementary students is how much of all this can they understand? How mature *are* their abilities to comprehend time and change? Can a fourth grader really understand what happened when his own state was settled 200 or 300 years earlier? Can a fifth grader grasp what we mean by *colonial*? Some educators have actually suggested that history be abolished from the elementary curriculum, since elementary students cannot comprehend the concepts on which it is based.

Recently, however, there has been a renewed movement to *increase* the amount of history taught in the early grades, especially in grades four through eight. These educators often suggest that history be taught as a separate subject rather than as part of the social studies. They argue that the teaching of history has been diluted during the past 20 years by the addition of other social sciences and that students no longer learn history per se.

Exercise 5.1 *VIEWS OF HISTORY*

Do you think history should be taught as a separate discipline in the middle grades? Do you think the time devoted to history per se should be increased in grades four through eight? Or should the social studies in these grades continue to emphasize an integrated curriculum, including history, geography, and the social sciences? Give three reasons for your point of view.

We can never be certain that every fourth through eighth grader has a fully developed, mature sense of time and change. Therefore, your teaching of these abstract concepts should include as much specific, concrete material as possible. Specific help in teaching chronological skills is included in Chapter 9. There are several other practical possibilities that can lead you beyond reliance on a textbook, however. Texts are important; they provide basic information and are an important resource. But part of the problem in teaching history is that students cannot see how the material relates to them— to their daily lives and their own relationships with the larger world. You can help them change that by using the following techniques.

Oral History.   Students enjoy exploring the past through creating oral histories, a method that historians are using increasingly, especially with groups like immigrants who might not leave traditional written records. Historians obtain oral data not simply from famous or powerful people but also from citizens of a given community (an Indian pueblo), from a given period or national background, or from people who observed or participated in a specific activity (a strike or a protest march). These kinds of firsthand accounts fascinate children.

How can you use oral history in your classroom? First, determine a topic that is relatively narrow—what life was like in an elementary school 20, 30, or 50 years earlier, for example. Don't expect students to question people about their whole lives; instead, define the topic clearly. Together with your students, make up a short list of questions. They might ask, for instance, what subjects were taught, how large the classes were, if students in a single classroom were all the same age or different ages, how long the day lasted, what games were played, and how the teacher enforced discipline. The questions should be clear, and each child should write out a copy.

Practicing interviews in the classroom often helps. Have your students role play. Often students simply go down their list of questions, ignoring any possibilities of interchange that might arise during the interview. You can encourage them in the role playing to take advantage of loose ends to move beyond the interview questions while still making sure that they gather the required material.

You need to determine if students will tape the interview or take notes. In either case, role playing in the classroom will help them develop their skills. Taping requires good equipment that should be tested before use. If they will take notes, students must know that they cannot expect to take down every word; you will need to work with them on listening skills. A form with the questions and spaces provided for answers is very helpful to many students. They can take notes directly on the form, or if they tape the interview, they can transfer the information onto the form later.

Children can interview anyone who fits the category for the information required—parents, grandparents, community members, even the school principal. When the data are all gathered, you can use the information not only to help your students understand history—what went on in elementary schools in past years—but also to help your students understand the work of *historians*. How do historians weigh the information provided in oral histories? Did the respondent, for example, stretch the truth? Did he or she *really* walk three miles to school every winter through three feet of snow? Does he or she remember only the pleasant things? By compiling *all* oral histories that the class has gathered and comparing them, your students should be able to determine those areas on which most respondents agree. If there is a local historical society, its members may be able to confirm or disagree with some parts of the material you have collected. Finally, your class will have a valuable picture of what life was like in earlier years—of *history*—and they will have acquired it through active participation in the process of historical research.

Family History.   The same kind of active participation can be achieved through creating family histories. Many teachers use units on immigration, urban life, or other concepts that actually depend on students' family histories for part of their content. Data from student family histories in effect are used to support or disprove generalizations.

Encourage students to make their own histories: When and where were they born? Have they seen their own birth certificates? What do they and other family members remember about them as they were growing up? Are there photographs to analyze? What about written reports? Report cards? Certificates? Have these historical documents been saved along with "artifacts" like baby shoes? Students can make timelines, grade by grade, and the whole class can then correlate them with historical events for each year.

Usually, your job in creating family histories is to structure the data you need. Do you want to record birth dates and addresses of parents and other family members? The various jobs held by all family members, including grandparents? Use prepared worksheets showing the information to be gathered, such as family trees with blanks to be filled in. Determining what data you need and then structuring a way to report it helps students complete their tasks and makes analysis of the data simpler.

Looking at Objects of Historical Significance.   In addition to learning from oral histories and family histories, students in grades four through eight can gain insights from seeing historical objects. Cemeteries can be remarkably useful classrooms. If one is near your school, walk through it with your students. Provide guidelines about the information they should gather; a worksheet can be useful here too. Ask students to list the name and sex of the deceased, age of death, and occupation if it is given. Have one student write down interesting inscriptions. Students may be surprised to note, when the data are collated, that many more infants and children died in the past than today. This may lead to a discussion of mortality rates and the reasons for their change. Did husbands generally survive their wives or vice versa? Did occupation, if it is provided, seem to affect the age of death? How and why?

In addition, a walk through an older section of your community or a trip to look at historical buildings can be valuable if well planned. You might also want to visit your local historical society or museums where artifacts show what the community was like years ago. Often it is best to visit such museums at the end of a unit so that students will have more understanding of tools or other objects they may see.

Students can also be encouraged to bring to the class artifacts that their families may have from the past. They may have written records, such as a relative's discharge from the army, or a penmanship book that is many years old. Be careful, however, if the artifacts are valuable since it is almost impossible to replace them if they are lost or damaged.

Children's Literature.   A fourth strategy to bring history or any of the social sciences to life is the use of children's literature or trade books. Literature can bring past events into the lives of students. Literature is usually more people-centered than text material and can give fresh insight into the ways of life in our culture—past and present—as well as cultures of other places and times.

Biographies and novels are especially powerful. Stories can combine historical incidents with emotion and conflict. Kieran Egan suggested that, for students up to the age of 7, stories with clear conflicts between good and evil and fear or security are best.[1] Students from ages 8 to 13 are in the romantic stage and prefer to read about people who struggle courageously with real problems. Children want to know how Sojourner Truth

---

[1] Kieran Egan, "What Children Know Best," *Social Education* 43 no. 2 (February 1979), pp. 130–139.

felt in the face of great odds, for instance, and will often be interested in books depicting human suffering.

In the following list of historical fiction that might be used in teaching "Immigration and the New American Experience," the order is broadly based on grade level:

Bunting, Eve. *The Happy Funeral.* Harper, 1982. A Chinese-American child experiences the traditional way her family observes her grandfather's death. Grades one through four.

Levinson, Riki. *Watch the Stars Come Out.* Dutton, 1986. Grades one through three.

Blain, Marge. *Dvora's Journey.* Holt, 1979. A lively account of Dvora, a twelve-year-old girl, vividly brings to mind the struggles that the Jews endured as they left their homeland, Russia, in 1904. After many hardships, Dvora reaches America and pursues her dream of becoming a teacher.

Clark, Ann Nolan. *To Stand against the Wind.* Viking, 1980. Younger readers empathize with a South Vietnamese family, consisting of three generations living together in mutual duty and affection, whose members' lives are disrupted by war. When those who survive are forced to flee, young Em must assume duties as head of the household and help others to learn how to cope as strangers in the United States. Grades four through eight.

Gilson, Jamie. *Hello, My Name Is Scrambled Eggs.* Lothrop, 1985. When Harvey's family sponsor a Vietnamese family, the boy's plans to Americanize 12-year-old Tuan become more complex than he expected. Grades four through six.

O'Dell, Scott. *The Captive.* Houghton Mifflin, 1979. Julian Escobar, a young Jesuit seminarian, joins a Spanish expedition and sails for the New World to be a man of God to the natives. Shipwreck, treachery, and greed change his life. He finally must choose between death for himself and the enslavement of others. Set in Mexico in the 1500s. Grades four through six.

Snyder, Carol. *Ike and Mama and the Block Wedding.* Coward, 1979. When Mr. Weinstein loses his job in 1919, everyone on East 136th Street turns out to provide his daughter Rosie with a fine block wedding. This book depicts the warm immigrant neighborhood that refuses to be ground down by poverty. Grades four through six.

Yep, Laurence. *Dragonwings.* Harper, 1975. A young Chinese boy adjusts to life in San Francisco during the time of the earthquake. Grades four through six.

Beatty, Patricia. *Lupita Manana.* Morrow, 1982. Lupita faces obstacles as an illegal immigrant from Mexico. The novel offers no easy, happy ending, even for a girl like Lupita, who has spunk and character. Grades six through nine.

Branson, Karen. *The Potato Eaters.* Putnam, 1979. The O'Connor family experiences many hardships in Ireland in 1846. Potatoes come up black and rent and taxes are high, but the family stays together despite increasing difficulties of illness and hunger. Finally, they emigrate to America. Grades six and over.

Madison, Winifred. *Call Me Danica.* Viking, 1977. A 12-year-old girl dreams of leaving Croatia and moving to Vancouver, where she has relatives, but expectations don't match reality. Grades six through eight.

Where can teachers of the social studies find additional good books? Each year the journal *Social Education* publishes a list of notable children's trade books in the social studies field. These books are selected because they (1) are written for readers from kindergarten through the eighth grade, (2) emphasize human relations, (3) present an original theme or a fresh slant on a traditional topic, (4) are highly readable, and (5) include maps and illustrations when appropriate. The number of good books is increasing. Who would not be excited by a book such as *The Inheritance* by Claudia Von Canon (Houghton Mifflin), set in Spain at the time of the Inquisition? The hero comes home to claim his father's estate; his father, suspected of helping the Jews, had committed suicide rather than submit to the Inquisition. The hero has to decide whether to stay in his hometown under suspicion of the Inquisition or flee for safety.

Biography and autobiography on the lives of people such as anthropologist Margaret Mead; Thomas Gallaudet, a pioneer in education of the deaf; American Indian Squanto, and others are always popular, as are folk tales and legends of various cultural groups. In addition, books on controversies such as acid rain or the nuclear arms race can provide different viewpoints for students.

Consult your librarian to see what is available in your school related to the social studies, and indicate your preferences for future orders. Some teachers read a little from an interesting book to entice students to read further on their own. Take care not to kill student enthusiasm by assigning only dull reading reports.

These four strategies will help children get a sense of the past and make history come alive when moving beyond the textbook. Other techniques include role playing or dramatic play. Have children research various occupations in a New England town at a particular time, and then set up shops (general store, blacksmith, print shop, church, jail, bakery, inn/tavern, furniture/cabinet, barber/doctor, and the like). Include in your debriefing discussion an analysis on how accurately the children played their roles. Try a *history day*, increasingly popular in some states, in which children portray life in colonial or other earlier times. All of these techniques require active participation from students and move well beyond traditional textbook teaching.

Geography

The academic discipline of geography is changing rapidly with new technologies such as remote sensing and electronic data processing. Using airborne and space-borne radar, new instruments can gather information on things such as forests and ocean currents. But although the academic discipline of geography is moving ahead, professional geographers are concerned that little of geography is being taught in the elementary schools. Survey after survey has found that both adults and children often have little notion of where the major nations of the world are located. In addition, tests show that often map-reading skills are not well developed, with some adults unable to read road maps or similar everyday tools.

To help the teaching of geography, the National Council for Geographic Education and the Association of American Geographers in 1984 prepared guidelines for what should be taught in geography education in kindergarten through grade 12.

1. Location—position on the earth's surface
2. Place—the physical, human, and observed characteristics that distinguish one place from another
3. Relationships within places—how people have modified or adapted to natural settings
4. Movement—movement of people, ideas, and materials
5. Regions—areas that display unity

The guidelines state that in grades 3 and 4 students should learn to locate and describe major geographical features and regions and recognize how they change through time. Then they should concentrate on American geography and the use of more complex maps. But map skills are not an end in themselves. Rather, maps should promote understanding of the major geographic concepts.

Chapter 9 provides more detail on teaching the interpretation and making of maps. But we should mention here that a critical concern about how geography is taught is that the stress is *only* on map skills, rather than on the major concepts of geography as outlined by the National Council for Geographic Education and the Association of American Geographers. Students may learn the topography of their state or a nation but pay little attention to how that topography has been modifed or how people have adapted to the natural settings. In studying Brazil, for instance, students often learn that Brazil has a large forest area and that its major cities are located on the coast but not that Brasilia, its capital, was carved from a high plateau once thought uninhabitable or how the migration of Japanese into Brazil has changed the character of the nation.

In teaching map-reading skills, you need to be aware of the differing levels of ability among your students. Map reading may be too difficult for some students in grades four and five, especially if the maps contain too much data. There is evidence that girls at the elementary level do not do as well as boys in map-reading skills and geography. You should be aware of your own teaching methods and make sure that you give girls as much time and attention in reading maps as you give boys.

A second criticism of how geography is taught is that thinking skills are underemphasized and low-level memorization is overemphasized. Rather than having students simply locate cities on a map, have them find common elements about the locations. They may be surprised to note that some 90 percent of all major cities are located near waterways. For those that are not, like Madrid or Phoenix, ask them to hypothesize why not. Do politics and technology influence the location of cities? Are newer cities more or less likely to be located near waterways? Why? Or rather than simply having students learn about the climate of their own region, have them compare it to other climates. How does climate influence the way we live our lives? The way we dress?

There is no best way to teach geography just as there is no one best way to teach history. As with history, however, you need to make geographical concepts concrete by designing learning experiences for your class that use their environment and fall within their range of readiness. Take your students on a walk around the school, and then have them make a map of the route they traveled. Walk the same route again, this time making maps as you go. How close do their remembered maps come to their actual maps? What problems do mapmakers face when confronting new territory? (Three-dimensional maps, with boxes or blocks representing buildings, can be particularly fun—but don't use up more time than the concept requires.)

Make students aware of how the place that they are studying relates to the place where they currently live and of where places that they are studying actually are on the map. Use the textbook maps to point out the major cities of your state in the fourth grade or the major sites of revolutionary battles in the fifth grade. Figure out how many hours it would take to get from your community to Philadelphia, where the Constitution was written, by horseback or carriage and by plane; measure it off. If you live four days by horseback, talk about it on Monday, and on Thursday remind your students that they would just now be arriving at their destination.

In addition, try to tap as many actual student experiences as possible. Ask your students where they have lived or traveled, and have them talk about those places. Talk about your own travel experiences as well.

Using controversial issues also helps to bring life to major geographical concepts. Some ecology or environmental issues lend themselves naturally to a consideration of major concepts of geography. Should a given piece of land in the community be developed? How should it be developed? Should it be made into a shopping center or housing for low-income groups? This can lead to a better understanding of the advantages and disadvantages of using a land site for different purposes as well as showing how people can modify their environment. All of these means, and especially using the local community as a concrete illustration, can help to improve geography education by moving beyond the textbook.

Exercise 5.2   *YOUR VIEWS ON GEOGRAPHY*

What do you remember about your own exposure to geography in elementary school? Jot down some things you remember about how geography was taught. How comfortable do you feel about teaching geography? Have you had a college-level course in geography?

Economics

Knowing about the economic world is important for every student. All students will eventually need to have skills and knowledge to be able to earn their own living. In addition, economic or financial considerations invade almost every decision we make—large or small. Students face the problem of whether or not they can afford to buy a certain piece of sports equipment or a bike. Governments as well as families face the problem of what to do with limited financial resources. Scarcity and limited resources are always a problem and the main focus of economics.

An important source of resources for teaching economics is the Joint Council on

Economic Education, 2 West 46th Street, New York, NY 10036. This organization will send you information on where your local or state centers are located. You can secure sample units and background information from them to help in planning the teaching of economics in the classroom.

Economics, like history and geography, often contains difficult concepts. Gross national product, scarcity, income distribution, depressions, comparative advantage, opportunity cost, and so on can be hard for students to understand. In addition, economics (a policy science) has ideological issues connected with it, and some groups become very upset if the schools appear to be advocating anything but our present economic system. Free materials, including films from business, labor, or other groups, should be viewed with a critical eye when presented to students. But the controversial nature of economics can be a plus by adding interest and relevance. How much money should be allocated for defense? Welfare? AIDS? Students often have opinions on these issues.

As with history and geography, abstract economic concepts can be made concrete more easily if you use the community and other resources in addition to the basic textbook. Students can see what jobs are performed in their own community and make comparisons with other historical periods. Field trips and resource people will help students understand local businesses. Students can participate in simulations like *Mini-Society* (Addison-Wesley) to get a feel for how economic concepts work in our society.

Some teachers follow up field trips and visits from resource people by having students make and sell some product of their own, such as school T-shirts, cookies, or holiday gifts. In this way, students can actually act out the various roles involved in producing and selling a product or service.

Two areas that are related to economics are consumer education and career education. Your district may have guidelines about teaching them; if not, you will want to decide how much to include in your own curriculum. For both, but particularly for consumer education, you will need to determine whether a specific unit should be included each year or whether the topic should be integrated into other units. Many experts feel that unless they are taught as separate units, these topics will get scant attention.

Consumer education lends itself well to correlation with other subject matters like math and language arts. Students can make price comparisons of similar products at the supermarket. They can become more aware of what advertising is trying to do by analysis of commercials on television and ads in newspapers and magazines. Consumer education can tie in with the study of nutrition and how we all can improve in what food we buy to eat. Consumer education helps students develop skills to live more intelligently in the real world.

In a similar manner, the rationale for career education is the fact that all adults need to be self-supporting, and this usually involves having a job. Some argue that girls and minority groups need specific career education to help them raise their sights and prepare to enter more responsible jobs and nontraditional careers. The recent rapid changes in the job structure, however, suggest that *everyone* has to be prepared to make work and career changes, and therefore a flexible attitude toward change as well as skills are necessary in the adult work market.

Career awareness and exploration can take many different formats. For the primary grades, parents representing different careers can bring what they wear to work and what they use as tools or equipment when they tell about their work. In grades four through eight, field trips to institutions such as hospitals may show the wide range of skills that a hospital needs to be able to offer its services. Students should move from the more familiar doctor and nurse to a consideration of people such as the X-ray technician, the dietitian, and the nurse's aide. Visits to hospitals, stores, offices, or factories can also illustrate the division of labor that is necessary in our modern society. But do not visit a factory or business that is too complex or abstract for your students. Generally, visiting an office or computer center is not as useful as visiting a place that makes a single product such as soft drinks. Services that are more difficult to "see" such as banking and finance also may be poor choices.

Along with increasing your students' focus on the wide range of occupations that exists in our society, be certain to include the affective domain. By the upper grades or junior high school, students can do a variety of value exercises on what they like to do and what their interests are. Then they can think of how their individual abilities and values may lead to possible career choices. At the elementary school level, however, no student should feel that something is wrong if he or she does not have a career choice. Students should be encouraged to be tentative about career goals and to be aware that each person has the potential for success and satisfaction in a number of occupations.

Exercise 5.3   *ROLE OF CONSUMER AND CAREER EDUCATION*

What role do you think consumer education and career education should have at the elementary level? Write down your ideas, and compare them with those of others in your class.

Political Science

Knowledge about the key concepts of government is essential for citizens to participate in our democratic society. Instruction in civics or government has been part of the elementary public school program for a long time. Yet in terms of producing active citizen participation even at the simplest level, voting, educators still have a long way to go.

What teachers and the schools do about citizenship skills is related to their ideas of what a good social studies program is. Those who follow the cultural transmission model described in Chapter 1 probably will not take as many steps to see that the social studies program is producing active and knowledgeable citizens.

In Chapter 6 we will focus in detail on citizenship education, both in the school and beyond the classroom, and address topics such as the teaching of the Bill of Rights. But here we will briefly discuss law-related education, a promising development to help improve the teaching of civics and government at the elementary level. Law-related education seeks to promote an understanding of society and its system of laws so that students learn how they may effectively function within the law. In addition, law-related education tries to teach critical thinking skills regarding laws and issues facing our nation.

Law-related education has made use of case studies that focus on fictional or more simplified versions of actual cases. Case studies have been constructed from incidents such as William Golding's *Lord of the Flies*, in which boys isolated on an island by a plane crash deal with the problem of trying to govern themselves, with some unfortunate consequences. Case studies appeal to human interest since they show individuals caught between conflicting demands or facing a real crisis such as a prison sentence. A good case study should illustrate some principle or concept; otherwise, students may miss the point of the exercise. In addition, students must accurately understand the facts in the case so that they can make a good decision about what action should be taken.

Again, as in the teaching of history, geography, and economics, the local community can be an important resource in law-related education. Law-related education can use field trips or guest speakers from one or all of the following agencies: the local, state, and national justice agencies such as the local police, the state police, and the Federal Bureau of Investigation; the local, state, and federal courts; the offices of the public defender and the public prosecutor; and the various people and facilities connected with corrections such as probation officers, work camps, and detention halls for juveniles. In addition, lawyers are always a good resource.

Use of field experiences and guest speakers can put meat on the dry bones of textbooks. Speakers reflect current views. As always, using these resources effectively requires planning and helping students both to observe and to ask good questions. Debriefing and summarizing the experience are always worthwhile in assessing what has been learned. To make the social sciences and history meaningful in the context of a student's own interests and experiences, teachers need to be careful planners and use a variety of methods.

CURRENT EVENTS PROGRAMS

What is the role of current events or current affairs programs in the elementary school? Part of the rationale for such programs is the assumption that all citizens must eventually be aware of current issues in order to vote and make intelligent decisions. One of the purposes of teaching current events, then, is to begin to get students interested in keeping up with what is going on in the outside world.

In your own classroom, current events can be the glue that binds all other social studies elements together. A newspaper article about an earthquake in Chile can bring together history (have there been earthquakes there before?), geography (where is Chile, and what region did the earthquake affect?), economics (what will be the long-term economic damage to the people who have lost their homes?), and political science (how are the relief efforts organized?). Frequently, current events can be related to whatever unit you are studying; to reverse the process, you might ask students to look for newspaper articles about the country or period you are studying. It makes sense, if you are studying China, to have your students be aware of what is happening now in China.

Because current events programs serve multiple purposes, it is little wonder that different teachers use different formats, as the following cases illustrate:

Case 1. Barbara Carpenter, a fourth-grade teacher, has current events every day after lunch. Students are encouraged to bring in newspaper clippings that are of interest to them to share with the class. There are no specific criteria about what should be brought in, so the items range from what is happening in South Africa to local crime reports. There is only accidental correlation between current events time and what is happening in the social studies program.

Case 2. Maria Gomez, a fifth-grade teacher, has current events every Friday. She has a set of classroom newspapers, *The Citizen Edition*, published by Scholastic for the fifth grade, that is passed out and read during the social studies period. Ms. Gomez likes to use the Scholastic Junior classroom newspapers because many of her students come from families in which not much attention is given to current events and few if any newspapers and magazines are delivered to their homes. In addition, the Scholastic series tries to coordinate some issues that are commonly taught at the fifth-grade level. Ms. Gomez thinks the students enjoy reading the junior newspapers and she finds the suggestions for the teacher helpful.

Case 3. Samuel Bronski, a sixth-grade teacher, has current events every Thursday. At that time he uses the day-old local newspapers that are delivered to the school free. Mr. Bronski never forgets to have current events day on Thursday, because otherwise, the stack of newspapers becomes a nuisance since they take so much space. His last social studies class of the day gets to keep the newspapers. Sometimes Mr. Bronski finds that certain sections like the sports section disappear before the last period of the day. Throughout the year Mr. Bronski has explained the different parts of the newspapers to the students. To make sure that they do not read only the comics, Mr. Bronski prepares a few questions for each student to answer during the current events class period. He thinks that the students enjoy having a copy of and reading the adult newspapers.

Case 4. Andrew Oleson, a seventh-grade teacher, focuses the current events program with the unit he is teaching. When they are studying the Soviet Union, only items from newspapers or magazines that relate to the Soviet Union can be brought to the class to be reported on. The items then are put on the designated bulletin board, which has the heading of that nation. Students get extra credit for the news items that they bring to report to the class. Current events teaching occurs only within the regular social studies period.

Case 5. Ann Bronstein, an eighth-grade teacher, has current events every Friday. At the beginning of the year, five categories are chosen: international news, national news, state news, local news, and sports. The category of sports is a concession to students' high interest. At the beginning of each week, five students are given one of the above topics to report back to the class on Friday. All students eventually have a turn, and every five weeks a new cycle is started. The students use the format of a television show with each specialist reporting on his or her category. Students are encouraged to make use of magazines such as *Time* or *Newsweek*. Students are also motivated to illustrate or use the chalkboard to help explain what is happening since they each receive a grade based both on content and delivery.

Exercise 5.4 *YOUR VIEWPOINT ON CURRENT EVENTS PROGRAMS*

Which of the above current events programs do you like the best? What appear to be the strengths or the weaknesses of each program?

You can see that some teachers use current events as a separate subject with little or accidental correlation with the social studies program, and other teachers use current events to supplement or reinforce what is going on in the regular program. Only in very rare cases would you see a teacher use current events as the basis for actual social studies units, since it is difficult to plan units around unpredictable events. However, a teacher could start a unit, especially on a given nation like Iran or Israel, by focusing on what is happening to that nation at present.

A second area of difference among teachers is what sources are used by both teacher and class to get data about current events. This decision can be affected by the teacher's knowledge of the background of the students' families. Students from families that have a wide range of printed material probably do not have to use the junior newspapers prepared specifically for the schools. However, there are several advantages of using commercially prepared classroom newspapers published by Scholastic and Bruce Seide Publisher (*Weekly Reader* for kindergarten through grade six and *Current Events* for grades seven and eight). If the newspapers are in the class, you are more likely to use them. In addition, they are objective and try to have articles that are within the range of interest and comprehension of children. But some teachers do not use the commercial junior newspapers as a learning experience. Instead, they pass them out when there are only ten minutes left in the day. Students then get the message that current events are just a fill-in for killing time. It is little wonder they move at once to the more enjoyable features of the commercial junior newspapers.

Ideally, as they grow older, students should move into using adult sources of information. For this reason the use of newspapers can provide an opportunity for learning skills that are valuable. Students can profit by exercises showing how an index called something like "Today's Contents" or "Inside" helps to locate specific features of the newspapers. Reading headlines is important, and it is especially helpful if your community has two local newspapers so that students can compare the headlines on a given day for the two newspapers. Occasionally, bringing in a well-regarded national newspaper such as the

New York Times or the *Los Angeles Times* is helpful as a comparison with local newspapers. Bringing in foreign newspapers as well as specialized newspapers such as the *Wall Street Journal* can also help students to see the wide variety of different newspapers that are available.

Distinguishing between an editorial and a news story is also an important skill. Give students a news item that is accurate, fair, and objective and, on the same topic, an editorial. Ask them which article wants action to be taken? Which article best describes what is happening? Which article tells the writer's feelings?

Current events may be related to the teaching of controversial issues since many items of current events at the local, state, national, and international levels are controversial. Here again, the teacher as a decision maker must decide what role she or he will take in the teaching of controversial events. Using a wide variety of sources of information such as newspapers and magazines is more likely to point out to students the emotional impact of a division of opinion on a given issue as well as the differences in viewpoints. Many teachers encourage students to bring news items for a bulletin board. If this is done, students should change the news items frequently. Nothing is more deadly than old torn news items whose usefulness has long passed.

TEACHING CONTROVERSIAL ISSUES

As students become older, they become better able to discuss controversial issues. There is no shortage of controversial issues in our society; economics and government policy, for example, have always provoked differences among citizens. What should be done to improve the economic well-being of our nation? There is certainly a wide divergence of opinion among citizens as well as between groups such as business and labor. What should be done to promote a better defense system for our nation? Again, a wide difference of opinion exists within the military as well as among civilians.

Among social studies educators, there is much debate over what role teachers should assume in the teaching of controversial issues. Teachers have been criticized in their communities on what they have or have not done. There have been court cases in which the question of academic freedom to discuss controversial issues for both teachers and students has been considered. In general, the courts have ruled that teachers can discuss controversial issues if they are appropriate to the academic subject area. This means that a math teacher would probably not be protected by the courts if he or she talked about abortion during a math class.

Here are four typical roles that teachers take in teaching controversial issues:

Case 1. Gloria Young does not discuss any topics in her fourth-grade class that she thinks are controversial. She believes that the classroom should be a neutral place and does not like it when students argue and bicker among themselves. Ms. Young thinks that it is best also to shield students from unpleasant topics that may only upset them. She believes that it gives children more of a sense of security to imagine that all is well in their community and that they should not be unduly worried about what is happening there or in the broader world. Ms. Young also thinks that her principal appreciates the fact that she causes no problems with parents who might be upset to learn that controversial issues are being discussed in the classroom.

Case 2. In the next room, teaching the fifth grade, is Carol Taylor. She is a civil rights advocate and a feminist and has a deep commitment to make students conscious of the injustices that both women and other minority groups such as blacks have suffered in the past. In her teaching of United States history she emphasizes how these minority groups were unfairly treated.

Ms. Taylor believes that she knows the right position on controversial issues that come up in the classroom and made clear to the parents who came to an October open house how she feels. She argues that all Americans should have equal rights. Unlike Ms. Young, Ms. Taylor does not ignore controversial issues. She welcomes the inclusion of controversial issues, especially as they relate to her teaching of United States History. Ms. Taylor is constantly bringing up questions on how the budgets of governmental units should be changed with more emphasis on job retraining and ending discrimination in all forms.

If a student with a different viewpoint suggests a different idea, Ms. Taylor calmly ignores it and goes on with presenting her point of view. Ms. Taylor thinks that students hear and learn more in the media about the status quo and not making changes to improve the position of women and blacks. She sees her job is to free them from these false ideas.

Case 3. In the seventh grade in the same school is Marianne Ash. She believes that controversial issues should be discussed in the classroom. However, she also believes that she should be neutral and downplay her own views on certain issues. Even when students ask her how she will vote on a certain issue or what she herself thinks about which policy should be favored, Ms. Ash does not think it is appropriate for students to know. She is afraid that some students might take her position without considering it carefully or that a few students who are not fond of her might immediately take the opposite position.

Ms. Ash encourages her students to present a variety of viewpoints on a given controversial issue. She tries to guide the discussion toward which people will benefit from a given issue such as rent control and which people will be the losers. Ms. Ash believes that with rational discussion students can clarify their own positions after hearing a variety of viewpoints.

Case 4. In the eighth grade, in the same school, is Shirley Baker. Like Ms. Taylor and Ms. Ash, Ms. Baker believes that controversial issues should be discussed in the classroom. But unlike Ms. Ash, Ms. Baker gives her own point of view on issues. She tells students how she will vote on certain issues, and on her car is a bumper sticker indicating her viewpoint on ecology. In her classroom, Ms. Baker thinks she should be a model of a politically active citizen. She tells the students about the organizations she belongs to that have a political focus. In the classroom, Ms. Baker brings in a variety of speakers of different points of view. She also uses a combination of other methods such as library research and group discussions to help students clarify how they feel on a given controversial issues.

Activity 5.5 *VIEWPOINTS ON CONTROVERSIAL ISSUES*

Which position do you think is the best of the four described above for the teaching of controversial issues? Which one would you like to model? Give your reasons for your position.

As you can see, there is a variety of opinions on the proper role of an elementary teacher in teaching about controversial issues. But in the above four cases there is another person that we may have overlooked. That person is the principal of the school, Dr. Jane Menshi. She keeps hoping that the school district will issue some guidelines on the teaching of controversial events and the role of academic freedom for teachers and the students. She knows that her teachers are doing a lot of different things in the teaching of controversial issues. She has received a few complaints from parents about Ms. Taylor's strong position but was able to tell the parents that at least Ms. Taylor is open about where she stands, and if the parents wish to bring up additional facts to teach to their own children on what they think is right, they should do so. Dr. Menshi always points out to parents that the research on political socialization shows that parents and the family are the most important factors in what children believe about political issues. So far her discussions with parents have worked out, and no one has pushed any further complaints onto higher administrators.

Dr. Menshi, however, is a little concerned about the social action that Ms. Baker wants to take. Ms. Baker believes that students need the experience of working in the community in areas that they favor. She wants students to help support local political candidates of their choice. The students would attend meetings of these political candidates and do tasks such as handing out political literature for the candidates for office. No student would be forced to do this community action, but in the back of their minds, students who want an A in the class probably realize that Ms. Baker is apt to look with favor on those who participate actively in community affairs. Baker even suggested to Dr. Menshi that students help in the political campaigns of school board members. What would the board members think of that? Dr. Menshi was very worried about this but did not know what she should do. What do you think would be the best position for the principal to take with regard to outside political action on the part of the eighth graders in her school? Can your class role play some of the alternatives?

In looking over the four teachers' positions on teaching controversial issues, you can see that each has some advantages and disadvantages. The four positions move along a continuum from the teacher who does nothing about controversial events to the teacher who would like her class to take social action in the community. Social studies experts themselves disagree on the proper position for teaching controversial events, but most of them would not support Ms. Young's total avoidance of controversial issues in the classroom. This is simply an unrealistic position in an age in which students are bombarded by the media with news of their community, nation, and the world. Children are aware of problems and controversial issues outside of the classroom, and sheltering them from these real problems, especially as they are growing older, does not make much sense. To become effective citizens, students need to be able to make judgments on issues. Furthermore, even if she does not realize it, Ms. Young is teaching values. Her stance as a person unconcerned about controversial issues is probably not a good model of what a teacher should be.

Ms. Taylor deliberately is trying to get students to accept certain positions. In effect, this is a form of indoctrination. Other viewpoints are not given much attention. Although in this case Ms. Taylor is supporting a liberal position, advocates of indoctrination can range from Marxists to conservatives, all of whom believe it is their duty to pass on their particular ideology. These true believers are really being authoritarian teachers with regard to the teaching of their own value systems. They are not giving students the opportunity to hear other points of view.

The advantages of Ms. Ash's position are that students are exposed to a wide variety of viewpoints on a given issue, and Ms. Ash also uses a variety of methods for the students to study the issue. Ms. Baker's position is similar to that of Ash, except that Ms. Baker gives her own position on issues. She makes clear to the class where she stands.

Is this good? At least teachers like Ms. Baker let students know what they believe. In many cases, students are perceptive enough to guess where teachers such as Ms. Ash stand by "reading" verbal and nonverbal clues. For example, without realizing it, teachers often do not write on the board the ideas suggested by students that they themselves do not like.

In effect, Ms. Ash and teachers like her want to play the role of a nonpartisan referee. This position probably receives the most support in the teaching of controversial issues. It is also a noncontroversial point of view with the community which normally does not object if the teacher plays this role. Advocates of social action like Ms. Baker, especially if they become involved in politics of the local community, are likely to find themselves being attacked for pushing young "impressionable" students into political action. In some cases, however, teachers have been rewarded with praise and publicity, especially if the social action takes the form of doing something popular like cleaning up the local beach or getting out the vote.

The proper role of teachers in the teaching of controversial events is not yet settled and is not likely to be in the near future since it is basically a value issue. The most controversial teaching area is probably war and peace and especially the danger of a nuclear war. But areas such as abortion are also highly sensitive in many communities. Court cases on the rights of teachers and students continue to define the limits of academic freedom and free speech. Policy statements by local districts on the teaching of controversial events are helpful, since generally these statements support academic freedom. But regardless of what position you take on the teaching of controversial issues, you need to recognize that ultimately all students as citizens will have to make decisions on where they stand on controversial issues.

SUGGESTED READINGS

Guidelines for Geographic Education, K-12. Published jointly by the Association of American Geographers, 1710 16th Street, N.W., Washington, D.C. 20009, and the National Council for Geographic Education, Western Illinois University, Macombs, IL 61455, 1984.

Levstik, Linda S. "Teaching History: A Definitional and Developmental Dilemma." *Elementary School Social Studies: Research as a Guide to Practice.* Bulletin 79. Washington, D.C.: National Council for the Social Studies, 1986, pp. 68–84. Discusses different approaches including Kieran Egan's ideas on the use of narrative as an aid to historical understanding.

Provenzo, Jr., Eugene, and Provenzo, Asterie Baker. *Pursuing the Past: Oral History, Photographs, Family History, Cemeteries.* Menlo Park, Calif.: Addison-Wesley, 1984. Good on past oral history.

Wronski, Stanley P., and Bragaw, Donald H., eds. *Social Studies and Social Sciences: A Fifty-Year Perspective.* Bulletin 78. Washington, D.C.: National Council for the Social Studies, 1986. Changes in both fields during the past fifty years.

CHAPTER

6

Elementary Citizenship Education

We view citizenship education from a broad perspective in this chapter. Not only is citizenship defined, but also the concept is related to the classroom, the school, and the community. These sections will assist you in gaining this broad perspective:

1. Defining Citizenship
2. Discipline and Decision Making: Classroom Citizenship
3. Linking Schoolwide Citizenship to the Community
4. Instruction in Citizenship
5. Global Citizenship
6. Putting Citizenship Education Together

What do you think of when you hear the term *citizenship education*? Doesn't it sound abstract and far away from the elementary classroom? It is true that children entering school have 12 years before they can exercise full citizenship rights. We need to remember, though, that in 1969 the U.S. Supreme Court recognized students as having First Amendment freedom of expression rights.[1] But what children experience in elementary school can directly influence the attitudes and ideas they gain about citizenship. One of public education's major mandates is to prepare children for the citizenship role. To do this, we need to explore two questions. First, we must consider what attributes or knowledge the citizenship role requires. Second, we must consider how children can best acquire these attributes.

---

[1] *Tinker v. Des Moines Independent Community School District*, 393 U.S. 503 (Iowa 1969).

DEFINING CITIZENSHIP

What does a citizen do? Often the answer we give depends on our frame of reference. "Good citizens" in elementary schools are children who obey and cooperate. "Good citizens" in our local communities are those who perform acts of conserving public property, coming to the aid of someone in distress, and so on.

As teachers, our orderly classroom frame of reference can cause us to focus entirely on good citizenship as obedience. We lose sight of the larger goal of preparing children for an active, participatory citizenship. Knowing about the system of government and how it works is basic to a broader definition of the citizenship role. Good citizens protest misuse of authority by the police. Good citizens urge new laws as a way of making desirable change. This concept of citizenship requires that citizens be active, that they stand up for their rights and those of others, and that they consider the common good when making choices and decisions. Citizenship in our society requires knowledge of how to make the system work positively for us. While we keep the orderly frame of reference, we must, somehow, also promote the active side of the citizenship role in elementary classrooms.

Some Basics of Democracy

> Each person has one vote.
> Citizens have equal protection under the law.
> Decisions are made by majority vote.
> Decisions and laws can be reviewed and amended by lawful process.
> Decisions and government acts are based on law.

Our next consideration is how children can acquire the attributes necessary for citizenship. We know that children learn from example and practice. They also learn from the written word. But they learn more meaningfully when they can interact with the written information in an active way. Educational theorists such as John Dewey have demonstrated that children learn from experience. The Lab School he directed at the University of Chicago in the early 1900s promoted children's learning by projects and group planning and research.[2] Recent longitudinal data from the High/Scope preschool curriculum suggests that when at-risk children have experience in the area of planning and evaluation of daily activities, they achieve greater sociopersonal success as young adults. It was found that the successful children internalized a greater ability to take charge of and initiate their own learning and become contributing members of society.[3]

What do these two illustrations have to do with citizenship in classrooms? We believe that the goal of citizenship development that includes democratic values should guide the way we organize our classrooms and learning experiences. Knowledge about the way children learn suggests that care must be taken in the way citizenship attributes are

---

[2] John Dewey, *How We Think* (Boston: Heath & Company, 1933).

[3] W. S. Barnett, *The Perry Preschool Program and Its Long-Term Effects: A Benefit–Cost Analysis*, High/Scope Early Childhood Policy Papers, no. 2 (Ypsilanti, Mich.: High/Scope Press, 1985).

developed. The old adage about the futility of "do what I say, not what I do," is pertinent to learning citizenship. Telling children about democratic citizenship is not the best learning mode. Nor will children learn to be active citizens by following a set of rules and behaviors prescribed by the teachers or the school that requires absolute, unquestioning obedience.

Currently, several discipline, or classroom-management, systems are popular in classrooms. Assertive Discipline and Jones' Classroom Mangement Training Program are two of the better-known systems. Each system has its own merits. Each can be helpful in making us think about and organize the way we handle our students so that they all can have an orderly and pleasant place in which to learn. However, when we consider adopting any classroom-management system we should ask ourselves these questions about it:

> Does it promote self-regulating behavior?
> Is it consistent with the way children learn?
> Does it promote critical thinking and decision making?
> Does it promote positive self-regard?

Affirmative responses to these questions are good indicators that the management system is consistent with the goal of developing democratic citizenship capabilities for children.

Most teachers find that no one classroom-management system meets all of their preferences and settings. Choosing from various sources still leaves several basics of management to be covered. Discipline and decision making both need to be taught consistently.

DISCIPLINE AND DECISION MAKING: CLASSROOM CITIZENSHIP

The major task we elementary teachers have every new school year is teaching our "system" to new students. Routines—for entering the classroom and leaving, for getting supplies, for getting information from the teacher, for keeping the classroom orderly—are modeled and practiced. Teachers necessarily are "lawgivers" in this phase of the school year. Children must learn to handle these routines for the business of the class to run smoothly.

Here are strategies you can use to help children perfect these routines:

1. Begin a day or period by discussing and planning a schedule.
2. Reinforce children who perform the desired routines.
3. Conduct evaluation at end of day or period that discusses "how we did with our routines," "what we need to finish tomorrow" and how we can improve our work.

By following these steps students are learning to play the procedural, or disciplinary, side

TABLE 6.1   STUDENT-ACTIVITY CHOICES

Kindergarten	Third Grade	Fifth Grade
Sand table	Computer	Typewriter/Computer
Painting easel	Listening post	Experiment table
Carpenter corner	Filmstrip viewer	Art project
Typewriter/computer	Library corner	Media/library
Dress-up corner	Math games, experiments	Listening post
Block corner	Art projects	
Book corner		

of citizenship in a classroom society. It is imperative, for everyone's benefit, that this "discipline" be taught and learned.

It is further imperative for developing active citizenship skills that decision making be added to the class system. Some teachers build student choice periods into their daily or weekly schedule (Table 6.1). During these times students sign up for their choices. These teachers usually have a poster or bulletin board with slots where students may place their names to assist with traffic control and the negotiation of "equal access" to the most popular activities.

Organizing students to assume responsibilities for classroom duties is another important way for children to practice citizenship. Typically, duties include clean-up and leadership roles. The variety included in this array depends on the student age and class-room design. Here is an outline of fourth-grade jobs developed by Joan Elston and Barbara Mumma.[4]

President

Take attendance.
Pass lunch tickets.
Lead flag salute.
Greet visitors.

Vice-President

Do daily checklist.
Take over when president absent.
Take attendance to office messenger.

Secretary

Write thank-you notes.
Keep field-trip checklist.
Fill paper drawers.

Treasurer

Record service points.
Collect field-trip money.
Distribute book orders/books.

Room Maintenance (4)

Wash boards.
Open, close, windows.

Audiovisual Engineers (2)

Set up and operate tape recorder,
   filmstrip, movie projectors.

[4]Outline of fourth-grade jobs developed by Joan Elston and Barbara Mumma, Collins School, Cupertino, California.

Empty pencil sharpener.
Empty wastebasket.
Scour sink.

Table Chairperson

Lead group tasks.
Distribute dittos, paper, supplies.
Collect papers.
Check desks for neatness points.

Elson rotates children through these roles. Her goal is to permit each student to have practice in both leadership and "followership," starring and support roles. All who visit this classroom sense the ownership and pride this system gives these students.

Classroom meetings are another essential strategy for modeling decision making. Decisions about real choices must be the agenda. Whatever the issue, the meeting should have the following criteria:

1. A signal for wanting to speak
2. A discussion leader (teacher for earlier grades)
3. A discussion of the choices that looks at good and bad possible results of each choice
4. The possibility of seeking more information before voting
5. A way of voting secretly so that each child votes his or her own feeling
6. A way of following through to see that vote is honored

Look for these criteria in the following transcript. As you read, think about what payoffs for citizenship skills children gain from classroom time spent this way.

SAMPLE CLASSROOM TRANSCRIPT 6.1
Classroom Decision Making

Mr. Cervantes wanted his first grade to thank the fifth-grade class that had brought their puppet show on important U.S. presidents to their classroom. Mr. Cervantes opened the meeting with this question: "Who remembers some of the things we learned about the presidents from the fifth graders yesterday?" (Various children volunteer information they remember.)

    Mr. Cervantes: What were some of the things you liked most about the show? (Various children describe what they liked.)

    Mr. Cervantes: How could we thank the fifth graders?

        Jesus: We could tell them on the playground.

Mr. Cervantes: Yes, that would be one way. Does anyone else have a suggestion?

Kerry: We could send them a letter.

Mr. Cervantes: Yes, are there any more suggestions about how we could thank them?

Erin: We could go to their class and tell them.

Mr. Cervantes: Those are all suggestions I want us to think more about. What would be good about telling them on the playground?

Jake: It's easy to do.

Jenny: Not for me.

Mr. Cervantes: What are some problems with telling them on the playground?

Jenny: I don't know who they are.

Mr. Cervantes: Well, let's think about the second suggestion. What are some good things about the idea of sending a letter? (Mr. Cervantes leads the discussion to cover all suggestions.)

Mr. Cervantes: You've given some good things for us to think about. Are you ready to decide? So that we each vote the way we think, I'm going to ask you to close your eyes and raise your hand when I ask for the choice you want. Are you ready? How do you show me?

Postscript:

The class voted to go to the fifth graders and tell them, not Mr. Cervantes' choice. He wanted to use the event to write letters. Now he's thinking about how to honor the vote while capitalizing on the language arts opportunity of going to the other class. What would you do?

Zooming our imaginary lens back into the classroom, we see that Mr. Cervantes is quickly taking them into preparing a choral reading "thank you" that will have all of the children saying "we learned a lot from you," interspersed with individual children telling one thing they learned such as, "George Washington had false teeth made of wood."

Exercise 6.1   *BOUNDARIES OF COOPERATIVE PLANNING*

How would you change the roles if instead of a first-grade class thanking a fifth-grade class the fifth graders were thanking the first graders. Did Mr. Cervantes manipulate the situation when the children did not prefer his choice? Or did he follow the spirit of the class? Would the same method work with a fifth grade?

There is a moral to this episode. Teachers should not embark on class decision making unless they are willing to abide by the decision the class makes. As the example showed, Mr. Cervantes structured the decision-making episode; he did not dictate the decision. He integrated language arts with the experience but not the element of language arts he had envisioned. As teachers, we choose issues that are appropriate to class decision making.

How do you feel about the class deciding whether to study math or social studies? We think that would be going too far. As teachers, our professional responsibility is to organize investigation in the different curricular areas and make decisions about how to present something or in which ways or about which choice from a list of choices is appropriate for elementary students.

Group Decision Cases

Classroom meetings are advocated by some authorities as appropriate strategies for helping individual children become better classroom citizens.[5] As with any group process, leading the class meeting requires that the teacher think on his or her feet about where the discussion is heading and, more importantly, the implications the discussion is having for the individual worth and dignity of the children. Consider the criteria for evaluating classroom management strategies as you read the following two examples for solving a problem:

Bernie the Bully. A fourth-grade class is just back from recess during which Bernie reportedly shoved Sharif to the ground when Sharif came up to take his turn kicking in the dodgeball game. The teacher, Ms. Stearns, convenes a meeting to discuss better ways of sharing on the playground. Ms. Stearns asks Sharif what happened during the dodgeball game. Sharif hangs his head and says nothing. Penny, the original reporter, raises her hand and repeats that Bernie wouldn't let Sharif take a turn and pushed him down.

Bernie glares at Penny and grunts a noncomittal "Yeah" to Ms. Stearns' query for confirmation. Ms. Stearns turns to the class and asks, "How can we be certain that this type of problem does not happen again?"

Several children make comments to the effect that they don't have the problem, that Bernie does. Ms. Stearns asks Bernie how he can change his behavior. Bernie scowls and spits out, "Let 'em play."

Dodgeball Dodgers. Several children request to stay inside during recess. After the rest of the class goes out, Ms. Stearns asks the group why they suddenly chose to stay inside. They make comments that recess is boring and that if you're not a superstar, it's better not to play in the dodgeball game. After recess Ms. Stearns convenes a class meeting with the question "What could we do to make sure everyone has a good time during recess?" Children suggest various ideas, some of which are about sportsmanship on the dodgeball field. Having listed their ideas, Ms. Stearns asks the children to vote for the two most important ideas to put into practice during recess. One of the most-voted items is to "stop calling bad names during dodgeball." The other is "don't keep the same team members every recess."

After negotiating how to put the team item into practice, Ms. Stearns closes the meeting by charging everyone to put their ideas into practice next recess time.

---

[5] William Glasser, *Schools Without Failure* (New York: Harper & Row, 1969).

Thinking about the Cases.   What did Ms. Stearns accomplish with these class meetings to address a problem? Are positive behaviors reinforced? Do students gain positive self-regard? Is critical thinking promoted? If you feel more comfortable with the second episode, your instincts are in tune with ours.

Ms. Stearns may be helping Sharif get a chance to play, in the first eipsode, but she's probably used a sledgehammer to kill a fly as far as Bernie is concerned. Frankly, we would not like to be in Penny's shoes either. In the second episode individual children are not singled out for "repair." Group suggestions are prioritized and put into action steps.

We must be cautious that in our zeal to promote class resolution of problems we are not creating more individual problems. In other words, individual problems are not the best topics for group decision making. It will always be true that individual students will require continuous and special attention beyond group strategies.

Earlier, we tied classroom management, or discipline, to decision making. Clearly, class meetings, rotating class duties, and frequent sessions for planning and evaluating with the class do not cover all of the management needs of a classroom. Even so, when we consider the typical management problems—students rowdy and aimless, students not taking initiative for learning, students refusing to do assignments—we are convinced that many could be worked on through the use of these three strategies. Experienced teachers find that careful and consistent work with these or similar strategies resolve most classroom-management issues.

LINKING SCHOOLWIDE CITIZENSHIP TO THE COMMUNITY

Providing children access to the community outside school is an important element in the development of citizenship. One way to guarantee these links is by curriculum integration of a community strand into each grade level (Table 6.2). School staffs taking the time to coordinate which public agencies they will link to in each grade level are ensuring that children have a broad foundation upon which to understand how community business gets done. The agencies and activities are interchangeable, especially within the primary grades. The crucial element for citizenship is that the activities are based on children's firsthand exposure to real institutions and situations.

A second means that schools traditionally have used for linking children to the world of citizenship happens at election time. Some schools import campaign paraphernalia and hold mock elections. Social scientists tell us that children replicate their parents' political orientations and choices. Even though results of school mock elections may be interesting to teachers, the child receives little concrete citizenship development from such an exercise. In fact, the contrary is true. In voting for candidates children typically get no buildup to make their decisions. They probably do not know what the candidate stands for or what the important issues in the campaign are. They are generally forced to rely on media images

TABLE 6.2 COMMUNITY CURRICULUM LINKS

Grade	Group	Activity
Kindergarden	Police	Visit police car and traffic crossing, practice emergency reporting.
First	Fire	Visit station, practice safety routines and emergency reporting, have fire-hazard inspection.
Second	Sanitation	Visit dump and recycling sites, organize clean-up campaign.
Third	Transport	Visit bus-maintenance yard, take traffic and road surveys.
Fourth	Health	Visit hospital and retirement home, adopt patients.
Fifth	Courts	Visit municipal and traffic courts, survey local statistics.
Sixth	Social Service	Visit children and homeless shelter, campaign for food and clothing.
Seventh	Environmental	Visit animal and wild life refuge, participate in clean-up.
Eighth	City, County Council	Visit council session, survey agendas for issues and media for facts, debate issues.

and home orientations. School elections then can take on the aspects of a horse race where winning is the only issue. We must ask ourselves if this is the substance about elections that we wish to have the school propagate. Elections need to be studied and given attention in the classroom, but we should keep voting in perspective. Voting is the last act in a long process of making choices. It is the process, not the vote itself, that must be emphasized.

Middle- and upper-grade children are capable of following political campaigns. They should be encouraged to do so. Keeping track of candidate statements over time and collecting facts about issues to display and analyze are essential current events activities. Analyzing the way candidates portray themselves and the issues on television, counting the number of times the name is mentioned, and noting the main and underlying messages alert children to how the media is used to shape our opinions and ideas.

Some teachers fear that students will become less patriotic as adults as a result of analyzing issues and questioning candidates. As teachers we need to examine what we mean when we say that our goal is creating future patriotic citizens. We have all been taught that patriotism is a good and necessary value for our nation to survive.

In most public schools, love of one's country is instilled in us. We learn to revere national symbols—the flag that flies in front of the school, the reproductions of historical scenes—George Washington, the Minutemen fife and drum corps, and the signing of the Constitution—and we continually repeat the rituals of loyalty in the Pledge of Allegiance and national anthem. Most of us believe that these symbols and rituals are appropriate, even essential, elements of school culture since the activities create a sense of national identity and pride essential for young children living in this country.

Exercise 6.2 *PERSPECTIVES OF COUNTRY AND IDENTIFICATION WITH PLACE*

Patriot	Chauvinist	Provincial	Ethnocentric
Cosmopolitan	Parochial	Zenophobe	Catholic
Expatriate	Nationalist		

Do you have positive and negative feelings about these terms? Try putting them on a continuum. What polarities did you use to define your continuum?

Indeed, children seem to depend on these rituals happening in school as a necessary part of daily routine. Our examination should take us back to our objectives. What are we after when we incorporate these rituals in our classroom routines? Do these rituals accomplish our purpose? What are young children learning as a result of participating in these rituals?

Jean Piaget demonstrated that young children have great difficulty with the concept of country as an entity that is also part of, yet different from, community, county, and state. In the late 1960s Wallace Lambert and Otto Klineberg found that by the age of seven, children were specific about their own national identification.[6] Furthermore, they had internalized an international pecking order that included derogatory national stereotypes about other nations. Children of other nationalities tended to see Americans as a high-status group, as did the Americans themselves. (More recent surveys find that American children see Japanese as the current high-status nationality.) Other studies found that by the age of 10 children had internalized an attitude about their own power within the political system. This sense of power was related to the children's own family socio-economic status. Teachers were found to modify their approach to citizenship-related activities according to the socioeconomic status of children in their schools. Teachers emphasized obeying laws and fulfilling responsibilities to children of poorer, blue-collar families. In contrast, teachers of middle- to upper-class children tended to emphasize problem-solving approaches to citizenship topics.

We have no evidence that the pledge to the flag and singing a patriotic song or voting in a mock election are harmful to children's positive regard for national identity and citizenship. If our purpose is to develop a love of our nation and feeling of belonging to it, these activities are just the first step. To be effective these rituals need to be accompanied by further activities that link all children to their school and local community. As we have seen, some of these activities are planning and evaluating the school day with children, involving children with the responsibilities and decision making of running the class and school, and organized exposure to the public institutions. In addition to these three strategies, children need direct instruction in the basics of citizenship under our system of government.

---

[6] Wallace E. Lambert and Otto Klineberg, *Children's Views of Foreign People: A Cross-National Study* (New York: Irving, 1967).

INSTRUCTION IN CITIZENSHIP

Functioning effectively in our modern, complex society requires sophistication. We must understand what our rights and responsibilities are. We must be able to locate and deal with a myriad of public institutions. We must be able to locate and deal with a myriad of public institutions. We must know how to seek and use information we need from the mountains of information that is available but not always easy to find. We must understand what the rules of the game are under our system of government. Beyond the classroom, school, and community activity arenas, children need instruction in three general topics—the rule of law, our system of justice, and the global nature of citizenship. This section suggests how to organize these three topics.

The Rule of Law

Typically, the "formal" aspects of learning what the law is and how it can be extended or changed are reserved for segments of the fourth, fifth, and eighth grades. The basis for understanding our formal system needs to be laid, as we examined earlier in this chapter, by a link to community functions at every grade level as well as citizenship activities that become part of the daily classroom life. Young children, as well as middle graders, can profit from formal consideration of the need for rules.

Young children are socialized rule followers by the time they reach kindergarten. They need to discuss what rules they have at home or in the classroom and why these rules are important as well as what the consequences are when the rules are not followed. Questions such as "why do we have to raise our hands in class?" or "why do we have to put garbage in the garbage cans?" are essential beginnings to discussions in later grades about the documents that define our society's rule of law.

Several commercially available videotapes and filmstrips give teachers an animated stimulus for the discussion of rule-observing behavior as a basic social skill:

> "Beginning Responsibility: Rules Are for Gorillas Too!" Animated gorilla escapes to street. Discovers rules keep us safe, make play easier. (Coronet Films, 1983. K–3. Video, $195.)
>
> "Good Citizenship with Winnie the Pooh" (five sections). Pooh makes mistakes. Children led to discuss by defining problem and solutions, evaluating choices, and selecting most appropriate. (Disney Educational Media, 1985. K–3. Filmstrip, $169.)
>
> "Understanding Right and Wrong" (four sections): Conscience: Why Do I Feel So Guilty? Rationalization: All the Kids Do It, Motivation: I Didn't Mean To, Point of View: How Would You Feel? Concrete situations leading to class discussion of topics. (Learning Tree Filmstrips, 1983. Grades 5–9. Filmstrips, $86 each.)

In each example, the concepts are tied in with a broad definition of *citizenship*. These media present stories involving characters in situations that test the need or usefulness of rules and cooperative social behavior.

The media presenting the general place of rules need to be followed by a specific study of American documents that support the rule of law in our society. Middle-grade children need to translate into everyday language the documents that establish the basics of citizenship in our society. Documents that should be discussed in this fashion are the *Declaration of Independence*, the *Constitution of the United States of America*, and the *International Declaration of Human Rights*. For example, asking fifth graders to read the Preamble and give six main reasons that the representatives of the Constitutional Convention stated they needed a constitution can help to define the historical context as well as make the content of the remainder of the document more meaningful.

> We the people of the United States, in order to establish a more perfect Union, establish justice, ensure domestic tranquility, provide for the common defense, promote the general welfare, and secure the blessings of liberty to ourselves and our posterity, do ordain and establish this Constitution for the United States of America. (*Preamble of the United States Constitution.*)

Unfortunately, not all of the Constitution is as easy to decipher as the Preamble. Middle-grade children need an overview of the structure that the Constitution creates for the way our society is governed. One way to outline the main ideas contained in the Constitution is through use of a visual outline or advance organizer such as that illustrated in Figure 6.1. Bulletin boards depicting main ideas about our system of government, such as the separation of powers and how a bill becomes a law, are keys to unlocking the lines of printed text for many students.

Making the Bill of Rights live for middle graders requires involving them in relating the document to hypothetical situations. Through lessons, such as the following fifth-grade example, students gain a knowledge-level awareness of their citizen rights.

SAMPLE LESSON PLAN 6.1
Bill of Rights: Can This Be Done?

Objective:

Students categorize hypothetical situations as being protected or not protected under the Bill of Rights.

Materials:

For a class of 30, one copy for each student of Bill of Rights, one transparency of "Am I Protected?" and chalkboard or butcher paper chart for recording answers.

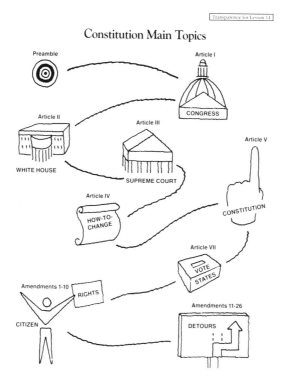

Constitution Main Topics

Figure 6.1 Advance organizers visually assist student comprehension of abstract, complex topics.

Source: You and the Constitution, by June R. Chapin and Rosemary G. Messick. Addison-Wesley, 1987. Reprinted with permission of Addison-Wesley.

Procedure:

1. Explain that Constitution gives each citizen certain protections, or guarantees that the government may not take away. "Our task in this lesson will be to discover what our citizen rights are and decide whether certain situations interfere with these rights."
2. Divide class into groups of three and assign amendment to each group.
3. Distribute amendment list giving groups a minute to read their amendment and skim the others.
4. Explain that you will show a situation on the transparency, and each group must decide if (1) their amendment related to that event and (2) whether the event interferes with their rights according to the amendment.
5. Show events one by one, recording student decision in category columns by event number (see recording chart).

6. Conclude by asking students to list what they learned about the Bill of Rights through this exercise. Ask how these events relate to real life.
7. Assign "I Learned" statement to be written and handed in in five minutes.

Evaluation:

Did students relate acts to amendments? Could they generalize from amendments and acts to make statements about their citizen rights?

Transparency:

"Am I Protected?"

1. You own a hotel. The president calls and asks you to keep 10 soldiers there as they are on duty in the neighborhood and have no place to stay.
2. You are against a Supreme Court decision. You write a letter to the editor of your paper stating your opinion.
3. You were freed by a jury decision from charges of robbery. Now, five years later, the bank that was robbed brings charges against you.
4. A policewoman knocks on your door. She shows you a search warrant and wants to come in to search your apartment.
5. You own a hunting rifle. Your neighbor says you have no right to have it at home.
6. You are asked to give evidence about a traffic accident you were involved in while under the influence of alcohol.
7. Arrested for driving while drunk, you are put in the county jail for a year and fined $10,000.
8. You are 14 and want to get married.
9. The public school now begins each day with Bible reading.

Sample Recording Chart *"Am I Protected?"*

Permits	**Does Not Permit**
1.	
2.	
3.	
etc.	

This lesson requires critical thinking and discussion. By presenting situations familiar to students, the relevance of the Bill of Rights to their daily lives becomes apparent. They may not be, and should not be, required to remember every detail of the First ten amendments to the Constitution. They will, however, gain a sense of the importance this document has. Pedagogically, note that small groups read and discuss *before* the whole class discusses the lesson. Without the small-group step, most children will miss the "opportunity" personally to read and discuss, thereby circumventing real contact with the material. The extra class time small-group work takes is crucial to this lesson.

The Justice System

Formal instruction is necessary to supplement the real and vicarious contact children have with our system of justice. Their real contact may have come when a highway patrol person pulled their parent over to issue a traffic ticket. Or they may have testified in a divorce hearing concerning child custody. Television provides them with a vicarious contact. The view that a show such as "Miami Vice" gives of the system of justice is counterbalanced somewhat by "Peoples' Court" and "Superior Court."

As citizens living under the system of justice, as well as consumers of televised criminal justice shows, children need an overview of what the steps and requirements of law are when involved in incidents that could lead to court involvement. Reviewing a televised episode with a copy of Figure 6.2 would permit middle graders to become more critical of what they see.

Upper-grade students need specific instruction in the justice system. This instruction should include textbook study and classroom discussion. Possibilities for bringing textbooks to life include visiting courts in session, interviewing officials of the justice system, reading and dramatizing case studies, and participating in mock trials. Local bar associations are another resource for bringing the justice system to life. Associations are usually eager to send representatives to classes. Without getting into the finer points of contracts and torts, attorneys are able to illustrate how civil issues and criminal charges are resolved.

Thus we see that intruction about the justice system is a necessary complement to direct experiences that schools can provide future citizens. To round out further their instruction toward becoming future citizens, children need to consider their roles as citizens of the world.

GLOBAL CITIZENSHIP

As our world community contracts to become a global village with nearly instantaneous communication and certainly eventual interconnections between all spheres of endeavor, our definition of citizenship must also change to fit this new reality. Children in our classes are, in fact, citizens of the world as well as our nation. As such, they need to develop a loyalty to and identity with earth's fellow creatures.

Three Themes of a Universal Curriculum

1. We are all global citizens who share a responsibility for solving the world's problems and for the creation of the world we desire.

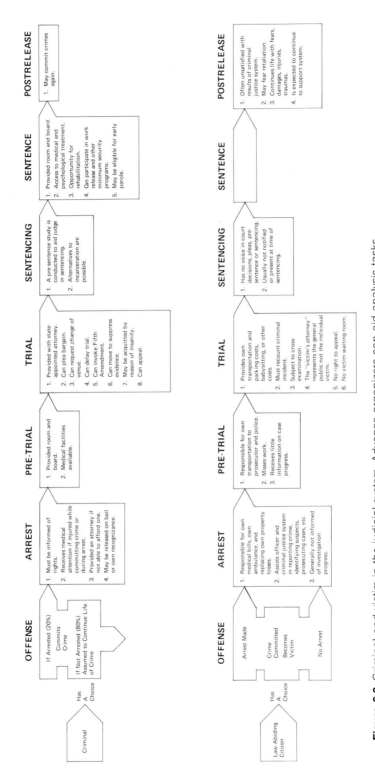

Figure 6.2 Criminal and victim in the judicial system. Advance organizers can aid analysis tasks.

Source: Reprinted by permission from *Excel in Civics: Lessons in Citizenship* by Steve Jenkins and Susan Spiegel; Copyright © 1985 by West Publishing Company, Pg. 57. All rights reserved.

2. We are all members of the family of humankind. We are responsible for understanding and caring for people of cultures different from our own.
3. We are stewards of the earth, which is our home and life-support system.

Instruction that incorporates a global perspective on ecology, resources, cultural variety, and human choices is a challenge. A favorite topic easily adapted to a global dimension is the study of endangered species. Rather than limiting the species in the sample to local or national examples, animals from the whole world can be included. From research about which animals are endangered and where their habitats are located, children should be led to deliberate about what strategy they can take to help save their favorite animals. To do this they will need to do further research into what is causing the animals to disappear. They need to search for connections between human and environmental change. The next step is to decide what kind of action to take based on this further information. Children can become effective lobbyists by letter even in the international arena. The last process that evolves from this global approach is valuing. Children should be prompted to state what they have learned from this process about their relationship to the planet.

SAMPLE LESSON PLAN 6.2
Feeding the World

Objectives:

Students gain relative perspective of global population groups and food supplies.
Students suggest ways to respond to problem situation.
Students see global situation from simulated, foreign perspective.

Materials:

World map, colored chalk, baguette of French bread and regional identification cards with following data:

Asia—54 percent population, 5 percent food supply
Africa—10 percent population, 1 percent food supply
Latin America—8 percent population, 15 percent food supply
Middle East—2 percent population, 5 percent food supply
West (U.S., Canada, Western Europe)—26 percent population, 74 percent food supply

Procedure:

1. Tell class that for today they are going to represent all the people in the world.
2. Divide them into 5 groups proportionately. For example, for a class of 30, Asia would have 16, Africa 3, Latin America 2, Middle East 1, West 8.

3. Show or have member of each group come forward and identify its space on the world map. Have each group move to its own seating area, which should be roughly proportionate to its geographical occupation of the planet.
4. Bring out a baguette explaining that it represents the food of the world and that you are going to divide it according to how much each region actually has.
5. Tell class that their groups are to discuss three questions once they get their part of the world food supply.
6. Show questions previously written on chalkboard:
   How does your group feel about its food supply?
   What could your group do about this situation?
   Are your responses like those of people in the real world?
7. After groups have discussed their answers to the questions, call on each group to share their information with the whole class.

Evaluation:

1. Ask large group what they learned in this short experience. Ask what questions they now have about world hunger and write them on butcher paper for future reference.
2. Ask individuals to write a paragraph or draw their feelings about the session.

Providing children with information about global problems is not enough. Avenues to personal efficacy in relation to these problems must be part of the instructional sequence. In the case of world hunger, children should be led to decide how they can help alleviate the problem. (Note that the lesson "Feeding the World" can be used as an opener to a unit but is unsatisfactory as an isolated experience.) Students may wish to work on a local food-distribution effort or raise funds to support a child through one of the international charitable organizations. Or they may wish to compose letters to appropriate authorities expressing their concerns and points of view about how to address the problem. They should learn the story of Samantha Smith, the young girl from Maine tragically killed in an air disaster, who wrote a letter to the premier of the Soviet Union that sparked a new round of communication about peace between the peoples of the United States and the USSR.

Some groups working on the global sphere for international improvements are entirely voluntary. That is, they are not supported by any government or international governmental organization. Green Peace and Amnesty International are some of the more newsworthy contemporary examples. Many of these organizations are willing to send representatives to schools in an effort to gain support for their causes. Before inviting guest speakers into our classrooms, however, we need to review our responsibilities in citizenship education. Are we providing the children with an opportunity to experience data from a variety of opinions about the issue we are studying? Do we ask them to question the opinions and data they gather? We need to explain these responsibilities to representatives invited to present their group's perspective.

Exercise 6.3 *BEGINNING A UNIT*

How would you begin a unit on endangered species? Your unit objectives are to make children aware of the global nature of the problem, to develop their ability to use library research sources and put together a short presentation using their research data, to value the importance of saving species enough to take some action in favor of the value. What should you do first? (1) Invite a representative of a local environmentalist group to tell what the group is doing to help save a species. (2) Use the National Institute for Urban Wildlife's "Habitat Pac" on Endangered Species. (3) Show a film about Canadian seal hunts. (4) Ask children to write letters about saving the whales to the Japanese prime minister. Rank your choices. Then check with another student or discuss the pros and cons of each in class.

Learning about human rights programs and goals is another vital part of global citizenship education. Many states have required genocide and holocaust study. California has developed the following guidelines for instruction about human rights and genocide:[7]

1. To help students understand that prejudice, intolerance, and hatred of other people are the seedbed for violations of human rights.
2. To make students aware that acts of genocide do not happen randomly; they are purposefully planned and occur with government sponsorship.
3. To help students understand that attitudes that permit seemingly small violations of human rights could pave the way for the acceptance of genocidal actions.
4. To demonstrate through historical and contemporary examples the variety of ways in which human rights can be violated.
5. To help students understand the calamitous effect of human rights violations, including the loss of rich cultural traditions through the crime of genocide.
6. To make students aware of the Declaration of Independence as a statement of the natural law philosophy of human rights.
7. To make students aware that human rights are best protected in a democracy where there are limits on the power of the state and all people have full civil rights and political liberties.
8. To make students aware of the human rights guarantees contained in the Bill of Rights and subsequent amendments to the Constitution of the United States.
9. To help students understand the responsibility of governments, including the United States government, for protecting human rights.
10. To acquaint students with organizations outside of government that are devoted to the protection of human rights.
11. To help students understand that there is a pattern and a clear story about how rights have been lost and how they are protected.

---

[7] *Model Curriculum for Human Rights and Genocide* (Sacramento: California State Department of Education, 1986).

Knowledge of past atrocities can help children see that they, as world citizens, have a relationship to these events.

Although it may be politically popular at present to criticize the United Nations, the fact remains that it continues to be the structure that facilitates communication and programs that attempt to address global needs. Older children should compare the similarities between the United States Constitution Bill of Rights and the Universal Declaration of Human Rights. Younger children should have exposure to both lists and discuss what, for example, freedom of opinion and expression means. One way to make the rights vivid for children is to relate current events to them. What human right, or rights, are refugees from Central America or the Caribbean area seeking by coming to the United States?

Universal Declaration of Human Rights (1948)

> Equality before the law
> Protection against abritrary arrest
> Right to a fair trial and freedom from ex post facto criminal laws
> Right to own property
> Right to political asylum
> Freedom of thought, conscience, and religion
> Freedom of opinion and expression
> Freedom of peaceful assembly and association

International Covenant on Economic, Social, and Cultural Rights (1966)

> Right to work and choose one's work freely
> Right to earn equal pay for equal work
> Right to education
> Right of all peoples to self-determination
> Right of ethnic, religious, and linguistic minorities to enjoy their culture

Discussions about how current actions of governments fall short of the ideals of human rights can provoke feelings of impotency in children. Unless you are prepared to take citizen action steps such as letter writing, discussing current events using a human rights context is not recommended. To ignore, however, this important avenue to awakening the moral concerns of children is to deny our responsibility for world citizenship education.

Global citizenship is a complex and contradictory and often, controversial notion. Many Americans argue that global education activities undermine our national interests. Indeed, this may be the case. Nations, ours included, tend to see resource issues according to their own perspectives. As we attempt to address instruction about citizenship, we need to consider what instruction best serves the children.

PUTTING CITIZENSHIP EDUCATION TOGETHER

To summarize our exploration of citizenship education, we need to recall that it is one of the major historical goals of public education in our country. Traditionally, young children have been civically prepared by ritual inculcation of loyalty and formal instruction in our system of government with the addition, in some schools, of action programs in citizenship. We agree with Morris Janowitz, University of Chicago sociologist, in his assessment that we must reform our citizenship education. He said that old-fashioned, simple-minded patriotism is not effective in our current interdependent world. He believes that civic consciousness is a more relevant approach to creating a persistence of love or attachment to a country—a territorially based political system.

Janowitz argued further that the vitality of democratic citizenship cannot be maintained by the existing range of political forms such as voting and political participation. He believes that some form of national service is necessary to give the idea of civic obligation concrete meaning.[8] We agree with Janowitz's critique. Although the idea of national service is beyond our topic here, we believe that citizenship education in school should include service and decision making.

In this chapter we have tried to suggest that concrete, direct experiencing of decision making as well as learning about our system are both necessary to prepare responsible citizens. To guarantee that children have opportunities for civic observation and participation and decision making, we suggest specific planning across the grade and schoolwide curricula. As an element of culture learning, citizenship development needs to be integrated into the processes we use to organize our classroom communities. Beginning instruction about the rights and responsibilities and procedures of the various governmental levels is an essential building block, as well, for citizenship development. The key to internalizing the citizen role, for most elementary students, is active, personalized involvement.

SUGGESTED READINGS

Gibbons, M., and Neuman, M. "Creating a Curriculum for a Global Future." *Educational Leadership* 43 (December 1985–January 1986): 72–5. Suggests reasons for globalizing the curriculum.

Janowitz, M. "Toward a New Patriotism." *Curriculum Review* 24 (March–April 1985): 14–18. Argues need for youth service and involvement to create civic responsibility.

Kaplan, Dan; Taylor, Jr., W. Frank; and Soldy, Ann. "We the People." *The Instructor* 96 (October 1986): 94–96. Teaching ideas about the Constitution for younger children.

Kniep, W. M. "Global Education in the 80's." *Curriculum Review* 25: (November–December 1985) 16–18. Urges need for more global view in curriculum.

[8] Morris Janowitz, *The Reconstruction of Patriotism: Education for Civic Consciousness* (Chicago: University of Chicago Press, 1983).

7

Culture Learning

As a result of reading this chapter, you should have a broad view of the ways that schools influence children's learning of culture and how we can pursue social studies goals as we organize culture learning. Specific objectives for the chapter are that you can describe how culture is learned in three spheres of schooling and can suggest various strategies for exploring cultures and resolving intercultural conflicts in a classroom. To help you toward these objectives, the chapter is organized in four sections:

1. Getting Started
2. Classroom Organization and Culture Learning
3. Classroom Instruction about Cultures
4. Intergroup and Multicultural Problem Exploration

GETTING STARTED

Culture learning as part of the social studies can be seen from a variety of perspectives. To get a sense of these perspectives and which ones you share, respond to these multiple-choice items.

Exercise 7.1 *SELF-ASSESSMENT*

1. What is the most significant goal children can gain from learning about their own and other cultures?
   a. Knowledge about how peoples of various cultures live and what they value

    b. Appreciation for the diversity of ways of life

    c. Ability to accept people from different ways of life or different appearance

    d. Ability to communicate and work together with others toward common goals

2. What is the *best* strategy for improving the ability of children from diverse groups to live together in a positive way?

    a. Present lessons about different ethnic groups.

    b. Celebrate holidays of significant ethnic and racial groups.

    c. Structure classroom tasks so that children must learn by working together.

    d. Involve children in direct contact with members and activities of ethnic and racial groups of the community.

3. What is the best strategy for resolving differences between racial or cultural groups in the classroom?

    a. Prohibit discussion about this kind of thing in the classroom.

    b. Read stories about conflicts that have "happy endings."

    c. Discuss racism, stereotyping, and scapegoating with the class.

    d. Invite adult members of the groups to the class to present their points of view.

    e. Role play conflict situations that lead children to practice conflict resolution.

Did you have difficulty choosing one best answer? Clearly, each item has more than one possible choice. Part of the difficulty you experienced in this forced-choice exercise probably is due to uncertainty about the term *culture learning*. You may not be accustomed to the broad definition we give the term. In our broad sense culture learning occurs at every grade level in two ways. First is instruction. Traditionally, we have concerned ourselves with culture and culture learning as the content of our curriculum. We teach facts and generalizations about peoples of various times and places. For example, children learn that family loyalty is a high value for the Chinese. We teach about our esteemed literary and artistic accomplishments, which some call "high brow" or capital "C" Culture. Thus Aaron Copland's "Billy the Kid" or Mark Twain's *Huckleberry Finn* may be taught as much for their cultural recognition as for the content they portray.

Immersion is the second way that children learn culture. Children absorb unconsciously what will become their culture by the close contacts of their daily living. They may learn that their school values quiet behavior. They may learn that they feel good about associating with some groups and uncomfortable about associating with others. This kind of culture learning is a process. This kind of culture learning, both positive and negative, goes on in schools as naturally as breathing.

Culture learning is assimilating the official curriculum and the ways and rules of daily living. To improve children's opportunities for becoming culturally knowledgeable with positive self-esteem and ability to get along with "different" others, we need to plan for both of these ways of culture learning, to keep the virtues of our tradition of transmitting knowledge about culture and cultures, and to add a consideration of the way we live together in classrooms as one of the most powerful culture learning experiences in a child's education.

CLASSROOM ORGANIZATION AND CULTURE LEARNING

You can plan for culture learning by examining the following three aspects of classroom life: *motivation*—the way you introduce, organize, and reward academic performance in your classrooms: *instruction*—the content you offer about the ways of life of groups of people; and *problem solving*—the ways in which interpersonal and intergroup problems are observed, discussed, and resolved.

Motivation and Classroom Organization

Classroom interaction teaches children more than the contents of your lesson plans. Children learn from the way you organize how work gets done, from the way you call on students, and from the way students are seated and prompted to move about the classroom. Unfortunately, what they learn from these aspects of classroom life may not be what you would wish. They may learn that being quiet and compliant earns them more teacher approval than when they ask uncalled for questions or want to discuss fairness issues. This kind of learning is known as the *hidden curriculum*. The hidden curriculum is the culture of the classroom. It teaches children how to get along in the system. But the rules of the hidden curriculum may contradict those of the formal, projustice curriculum. To use the power of the hidden curriculum, you must examine some of our assumptions about how to help all children learn in positive ways; take the power of interaction in classroom cultures from its hiding place.

Comparing our beliefs and what happens in our classrooms is one way to uncover the hidden curriculum. We teachers and future teachers all agree that our basic goals are to guide children to realize their potentialities and to learn to live and work with others in a rewarding way. Yet our classroom organization and management often denies the second goal. We use individual rewards for learning and group rewards for behaving. For example, we give stars to individuals who complete work successfully and top grades only to those who do better than others. Groups that behave as we would wish are permitted to leave first for recess. Peer pressure is used for social control and rarely to promote learning.

The message children take from this situation is that learning and working together are not related, that children who are not academic learning stars have less value. School appears to grant almost exclusive recognition and value to children who excel at individual, academic achievement. In classroom settings with various culture and racial groups represented, the children of "less value" are often members of social or economic minority groups that have less status in the outside community. Thus our reward system often has the effect of reinforcing the divisions and inequities of the adult society. We do not attain our basic goals of realizing individual potential while learning to work together for all children.

There is new research on what the classroom can accomplish toward our goal of educating children to relate positively to all people and groups and to improve their own academic performance in the process. Researchers concerned with intergroup relations and minority-group achievement have begun to verify that the way we structure expectations in our classrooms can have a positive effect on intergroup relations and achievement. Basing their procedures on Gordon Allport's earlier theory that "prejudice may be reduced by equal status contacts between majority and minority groups in pursuit of common goals," researchers organized nonsuperficial, noncompetitive, equal-status contact in classrooms.[1] These structures are known as cooperative learning.[2] In cooperative learning students in small groups learn from one another and are rewarded as a group. Learning becomes an active, cooperative, social effort.

Below is a glossary of terms that indicate the crucial, yet illusive nature of preparing for culture learning in the classroom. There is societal disagreement about the relationship of instruction in schools to these terms. You will develop your own unique perspective about how to work with children concerning these concepts. Our purpose here is simply to alert you to the pervasiveness and complexity of the issue of culture learning.

Exercise 7.2   *TERMS FOR REVIEW*

Review these terms. Do they have specialized meanings to you? Do you disagree with these definitions? Can you give examples of each term? Note any related terms that you believe should be included in a glossary about culture learning.

assimilation: person of one culture merging his or her ways of living, or culture, to another, usually dominant culture.

bias: acts or attitudes that favor an individual or group over others.

bigotry: acts of intolerance due to individual's belief in a particular creed or practice or opinion.

culture: way of life and belief of a group passed from one generation to next.

Culture: examples of art and literature esteemed by "educated" individuals of a shared culture.

discrimination: favoring or rejecting an individual because of his or her group identification.

ethnic group: group that shares a distinctive culture for racial, religious, or historical reasons.

ethnic studies: units or courses that study the history, culture, and contemporary issues of an ethnic group.

ethnocentrism: belief that one's group or culture is inherently superior, leading to contempt for other groups or cultures.

multicultural education: process of positive interaction between individuals of

---

[1] Gordon Allport, *The Nature of Prejudice* (Reading, Mass.: Addison-Wesley, 1954).

[2] Robert E. Slavin, "Cooperative Learning: Applying Contact Theory in Desegregation Schools," *Journal of Social Issues* 41, no. 3 (1985): 45–62.

different groups that leads them to value their similarities and differences; note that there is no general agreement about the definition of this term.

pluralistic society: society composed of multiple ethnic, and cultural groups.

prejudice: unfavorable feeling about members of a group formed without knowing individuals of the group.

scapegoat: a person who is blamed and made to suffer for a group.

stereotype: unchanging idea about group that defines individuals of that group without regard to their uniqueness as individuals.

Guidelines for Structuring Cooperative Learning

Various structures for organizing cooperative group work have evolved. Several guidelines are appropriate for all versions of cooperative learning:

1. Each student must have a role with defined tasks.
2. Materials must be readily available for student use.
3. You must keep in view all the time limits and group-procedure reminders.
4. You must lead students to evaluate cooperative procedures and goals for improvement after each session.
5. Group size may vary from three to six with group composition aimed toward including a variety of abilities rather than similar abilities.
6. You will act as a facilitator for group process but will not answer content questions.

When the learning task involves reading for new information that all must acquire, the subdivision of each group into "experts" on a section of the reading has been useful. After independent reading, the experts from all of the groups that read the same section meet and share their findings. Then they return to their original groups and "teach" about their section. In this manner each child brings something of value to contribute to his or her original groups.[3] When the learning task involves review, construction or experimenting, or performing, the roles should be distributed so that each student has something distinct to perform. Regrouping for expert sharing is not necessary for this kind of task.

SAMPLE LESSON PLAN 7.1
Landforms on Earth[4]—Cooperative Lesson Example

Cooperative lessons can take a variety of forms. This lesson plan illustrates one possibility. It is typical of a cooperative lesson based on review of textbook reading or research in

---

[3] R. E. Slavin, *Cooperative Learning: Student Teams* (Washington, D.C.: National Education Association, 1982).
[4] Lesson developed by Erika Gilbert, San Jose, California, 1987.

various sources. Since it is review, the groups do not break up into separate expert groups. They stay together and assume group roles pertinent to this lesson. Note that every child in each group has a specific role and task. Also, the group must come up with a product by working together. This type of lesson is appropriate for children who have been introduced, but are not yet accustomed, to cooperative learning. The process of this lesson is as important as the content.

Group Size: 4
Grade: 4–6   *Length*: 30–40 minutes

Objectives:

> Student identifies and defines 16 landforms.
> Student works cooperatively to teach and learn.

Materials:

Two pieces of large square (1/2 inch) graph paper for each group, one piece lined paper, pencils for each group, textbooks for groups.

Motivation:

How many people know what a word search is? Who can explain what a word search is for those who don't know? Demonstrate by writing one vertical and one horizontal word that intersect and fill in spaces with random letters. Create two questions for which the words will be answers. Locate and circle with the class.

Example:

rca i s
coa s t
ccr l a
ood a b
lav n l
ada d e

Where do water and land meet? What is Manhattan?

Procedure:

1. Show graph paper. Explain that each group will have two pieces. On one they are to make a word search. On the other they are to copy the word search and circle the answers; this is the correction key. Then they must write a question for each word in the search on the lined paper. When group completes search, they may trade with another group and find the words in the search created by the other group.

2. Explain roles for each group: "ones" will write questions group makes for each word in search; "twos" will lead discussion; "threes" will draw original word search on graph paper; "fours" will make answer key by copying completed search and circle answers.

3. Show list previously written on board:

canyon	coast	continent	delta	gulf	harbor
island	lake	mountain	ocean	peninsula	
plain	plateau	river	sea	valley	

Explain steps in making word search:
   a. "1" leads group in choosing terms and creating one question for each term on search.
   b. Recorder writes down question on lined paper.
   c. "3" writes answer on graph paper either vertically or horizontally.
   d. "4" copies answer on second graph paper.
   e. When 10 questions and answers are completed, group should fill in both graph spaces with random letters.

4. Count off students in groups of four. Move students into working arrangements. Call up "1's" to pick up materials.

5. Circulate, assisting groups in organizing their work.
   Answer procedural questions only.

6. Allow groups to trade questions and word searches as they finish; trade keys when group completes search.

Evaluation:

   1. Discuss what they liked about this way of practicing terms they need to learn.
   2. Discuss what helped them to work together and how they can improve the process next time they work together.

Cooperative learning apparently improves intergroup relations when used in racially and culturally mixed classroom groups. Furthermore, there is evidence that the average academic achievement improves when cooperative learning is used. What does cooperative learning have to do with the social studies? It is true that the structure of this strategy can be employed for any school subject. Given, however, that a major purpose of the social studies is to help children become active, critically thinking citizens capable of working together toward their common welfare, cooperative learning offers a positive approach to constructing a cultural milieu crucial to the process.

Cooperative-learning strategies create a classroom culture based on mutual assistance, equality between group members, and role diversity in learning tasks. In other words, this process itself teaches one of the social studies' major goals—learning to live positively with each other. But the content of culture is important and requires our careful thought. How shall we organize what we want children to learn about a culture?

CLASSROOM INSTRUCTION ABOUT CULTURES

When we prepare to study about a culture, we have sensitive decisions to make. Shall the traditional aspects of the culture be highlighted? Shall the aspects of a culture that are presented to tourists by representatives of that culture be questioned? When we focus on American immigrant cultures, shall the Americanized version or the old country version of the culture be presented? Shall the culture study be coordinated with the culture's celebration of holidays as we know them? Does the historical background of the group in the United States matter? Should groups be studied separately?

To answer these questions, put yourself in the shoes of a parent in a culture being studied. Would a Mexican-American parent, for example, want her children and other children to know about Cinco de Mayo? Hanukkah? St. Valentine's Day? Would that same parent prefer that children experience some of the food, music, and folk arts and crafts of his or her culture? What would that parent want us to know? For what purpose would that parent want to have his or her culture studied in the classroom?

Possibly a Mexican-American parent would want us to include study of her culture in the curriculum so that her children might feel their group is valued by the school and society. Whether the culture was included throughout the year in various activities related to the study of other cultures or was presented as a special topic during a concentrated period would probably not matter.

We drew these conclusions about our hypothetical parent by using her ethnic identity as the primary factor in predicting her curricular emphasis preferences. We may be right; a Mexican-American parent probably would be concerned, on the one hand, that her culture be included in classroom studies. But she may also define that culture in terms we have not considered. We have defined her as Mexican-American, one-dimensional, when, in fact, she may also be divorced, a medical doctor, and a fifth-generation American. Any one of these facets of her identity might be far more significant to her than her ethnic identity. (See Figure 7.1.)

Each of us is culturally multifaceted. To prove this, look at yourself. Identify who you are in each of the concentric rings of the cultural identity diagram (Figure 7.1). Which of these rings most defines the way you live your life? We have elements of culture related to whom we are sexually, how old we are, and what is our religious background. The interaction of these various facets, or microcultures, continually redefines and reshapes our

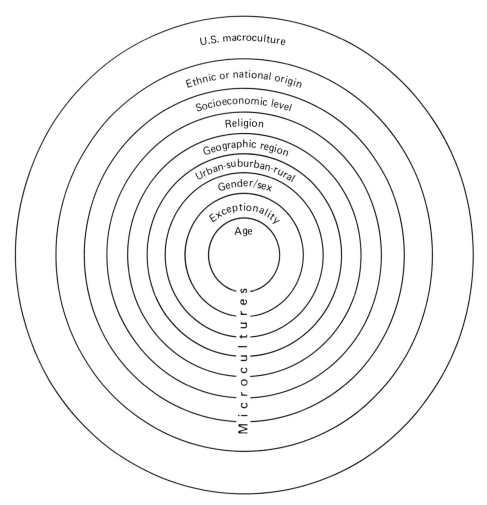

Figure 7.1 Cultural identity of an American. A widening circles arrangement with circles denominated from center ("Age") to outer ring ("U.S. macroculture").
Source: Multicultural Education in a Pluralistic Society by Donna M. Gollnick and Philip C. Chinn. Merrill Publishing Company, 1986. Reprinted with permission.

cultural identities. We also, to one degree or another, are shaped by and share in the national culture. Keeping this reality in mind should guide us away from presenting material that prompts children to draw stereotypic conclusions about people and groups they study. Children need to learn about themselves and others as complex, changing cultural beings.

SAMPLE LESSON PLAN 7.2
How Do We Know a Culture? Images of Japan

Our Stereotypes	Their Traditions	Japan Today
Kimono	Kimono times	Kimono times
Cherry blossoms	Spring festival	Spring festival
Hard work	Duty, loyalty	Work and play
Tea, rice	Tea ceremony	Coffee, tea, etc.
Manufactured goods	Calligraphy	Revere art, technology
Look alike	Geisha, coman	Dress varied

Using pictures cut from magazines focusing on a single culture or national group or a combination of them, have students categorize them according to these three divisions. They should find some pictures that fit all three categories and discuss where we get our images of groups or nationalities. Do we get our ideas about groups within our society in the same ways?

Learning from Each Other

Each new school year brings a new cultural configuration to our classrooms. Informal culture learning can be promoted by taking advantage of the cultures of children in our classrooms throughout the school year. Finding out who we are and where we come from serves to instruct us about others as well as make us feel valued for who we are. Promoting the children's exploration of who they are does not directly address the "learning-about-culture" issue. But by valuing individual children for whom they are, we hope the messages children translate are: "I am worthy and welcome," "My classmates are like me in many ways," "My classmates like me," "My classmates are different from me and that's interesting," "I have something from home that is worth teaching my friends about."

SAMPLE LESSON PLAN 7.3
"Learning about Us"—Activities for Classrooms

Primary

"Profile of the week": Paper silhouette or photo of child posted with "things I like about . . ." comments from classmates about spotlighted child. You can collect and write statements during sharing period.

   "The Way We Were": Baby pictures of class posted with birth information and favorite toy and first words.

"Our Gang": current, Polaroid photos of children posted with name and favorite things such as color, food, activity.

Our Gang Follow-Up: Number photos and have children draw number. They write "What I like about . . ." sentences to display under picture they wrote about. Can be repeated periodically.

Culture Cooking: Collect simple culture-related recipes and schedule parent to assist classroom-cooking session on monthly basis. Have parent describe ingredients and where to get them. Compile class cookbook.

Body Prints: Children trace each other on butcher paper. Outlines are colored by each child, cut out, and displayed in classroom. Discuss how we are alike and different.

Self-Portraits: Crayon drawings or tempera paintings of self that are named and displayed as body prints.

Intermediate

"We're Here": World map connecting student names or pictures to place of birth.

"What's in a Name?": Research bulletin board with each student telling what she or he found out about first name—why parent chose, meaning, origin.

"Book of Origins": Individual research on family that can include story starting with grandparents detailing where they lived and what they did illustrated with timeline and map of origins.

"Our Resumes": Self-assessment of favorite things, abilities and talents, and future goals collected into class book.

The majority of many classes will come from single-parent or blended families. Assignments requiring children to research their family connections need to be presented to parents in a nonthreatening, flexible manner. The last thing we want from a school assignment is to have it create dissension at home, insecurity, or even shame for the child. We need to inform parents about upcoming assignments that might involve family sensitivities and ask that they alert us if there are activities that might be uncomfortable for their child.

Learning from Our Community

Parents and grandparents are a source of learning about cultures that we often hesitate to tap. We may feel that because of language or social inhibitions some parents would not come to our classrooms to share their cultures. Breaking down these inhibitions might be easier if we gave choices of times and tasks for parents and other relatives to come to the class to share. The sharing can be simple and brief. It can be a picture, religious object, game, song, story, newspaper; accept anything and offer suggestions if a parent does not know what he or she has to share. The payoff of parent presentations is multiple. Parent and child feel valued and included. Other children begin to see similarities between their ways and those of their classmates. Having parents in the classroom provides face-to-face contact between parents and children from different groups. We know that this kind of contact reduces fear of the unknown for all.

Basic Ideas for Primary Grades Instruction in Cultural Diversity

1. There are many kinds of families.
2. All kinds of people live in our community.
3. There are some ways in which we are all alike.
4. There are some ways in which we are different.
5. We work together in our community.

Excursions into the community as field trips and walking tours can also be used to highlight learning about local cultural or ethnic groups. As they study their community, attention should be given to the stores, resturants, theaters, churches, cemetaries, and clubs that are ethnically or culturally identified.

Often local ethnic organizations are willing to send a representative to classes to tell children about their group and share some of its local history. Children can get more from these visits if they discuss why the visitor is coming before the day of the visit. They should list the questions they would like to ask and decide how they will make the visitor feel at home in the classroom. Following the visit is a fine occasion for the practice of thank-you note writing and the further study of group issues that the visitor initiated.

Exercise 7.3 *MATCHING ACTIVITIES TO BASIC IDEAS*

Categorize the activities in the list below according to the basic idea they best fit. Then develop two more activities for each category and share with a colleague or your class. When you have finished, you will have a good beginning for integrating the affirmation of cultural diversity in your social studies program.

——Make a class book of individual pictures and stories of people of different cultural heritages working.

——Celebrate holidays honored by various cultures.

——Gather pictures of all kinds of families from different cultural groups. Ask children to find a family with a grandmother, two brothers, etc.

——Talk about what children do when they are with their families. Make a language-experience chart about the discussion.

——Take walks or trips to see community workers on the job including a variety of ethnic and racial groups in your selection.

——Have children categorize pictures of people according to basic activities of eating, working, wearing clothes, playing, and living in their homes.

——Share a book with children that shows a child cooking, making music, celebrating a holiday, carrying out a daily routine or communicating in a culturally identifiable way.

Teachers who take their classes to a culturally related community celebration such as Chinese New Year, Greek Festival Days, Japanese Obon, or a Native American Powwow need to secure the assistance of a member of the group whose celebration is being visited. This person should serve as a cultural interpreter. Children should find our what the costumes and foods and music and dances represent. They should find out how that group came to the community and something of the local history of the group. They should find out how children of the group being visited are involved in the celebration. They should find out what activities the group organizes to teach the children their traditions. Furthermore, children should discuss why the group chooses to keep these traditions and whether the traditions are the same here as they are in the country or region of origin.

The excursion should be followed by a review and discussion of the event visited. Further interviews with the cultural interpreter may be needed to answer the questions children have about what they saw and experienced. Individual pictures or stories or newspaper-like accounts of the experience are appropriate ways for children to integrate the event in their experience.

Learning about Cultures from Secondary Sources

Learning about a culture from books and films or other materials is like learning another language from a textbook and tapes. Being where the language is spoken makes all the difference, just as a firsthand contact is the best way to learn culture and learn about culture. Since, unfortunately, we are not usually able to take our students to live with other peoples, we are forced to rely on books and mediated images as sources for learning about cultures.

Selection of authentic and contemporary materials about cultures is a sensitive task. In recent years major textbook series have made substantial efforts to include a greater variety of cultural and racial group representation as well as to make that inclusion an authentic, nonstereotypic portrayal in their material. We must go beyond textbooks, however, if we want to gain depth of understanding about a particular group. Most texts are organized as factual surveys. Children need more material than a text provides to investigate a given culture.

Teachers' editions may give us some leads as to enrichment materials such as trade books and films about cultures they touch upon in their texts. Other sources of materials about various cultures and ethnic groups are listed in the bibliography of this chapter. Whatever your source of trade books and other media, you should preview them before using them with children.

Using Holidays as Critical Thinking Times

The activities you organize to celebrate holidays in school may have the effect of reinforcing stereotypes and racism. One example is Thanksgiving. In many schools Thanksgiving is the time for the "Indians" in fringed brown paper bags decorated with painted tempera symbols to sit down with the Pilgrims in tall-brimmed black construction paper hats and white Kleenex caps at the same table. The motivation for this activity is to lend a sense of history to the holiday. No matter that this sense of history is a distorted version of the real events; the fact that such a ceremony portrays a historical myth and offends Native American groups never crosses our minds. Have we been doing this routine too many years to break the mold of tradition? How could this holiday be made more meaningful and truthful for children? Activities that lead children to consider what they have to be thankful for and how to help people in need are more within the spirit of the holiday.

Examine the possible motivation behind holiday art activities. For our national culture, why was it important for Americans to remember President Washington as a young boy who always told the truth? Once children have explored the cherry tree chopping as a morality tale, making cherry-festooned hatchets of construction paper can have more meaning. Making connections between the holiday and children's lives is another way to explore holiday motivations. For example, children might discuss how they get ready to give up a favorite food or toy as a lead to understanding Catholic cultures' pre-Lenten celebrations variously called Mardi Gras or Carnival. Do they indulge one last time before they begin the abstinence? In bringing this critical thinking element to holidays we help children understand the importance of ritual and celebration in all of our lives.

CLASSROOM INTERGROUP AND MULTICULTURAL PROBLEM EXPLORATION

Are we preparing children to live in our culturally and racially pluralistic society when we structure more equitable learning settings in our classrooms and celebrate ethnic holidays and heroes and incorporate ethnic history in our presentation of the American experience? All of these attempts are important; they open vistas to the reality of our society. In and of themselves, however, they are not sufficient. They do not instruct children in ways to live and positively interact with situations where power, prejudice, stereotyping, and status create conflict in personal interactions. Bringing problematic and conflictual situations into the classroom for controlled exploration adds a practical dimension to preparing children to live in our multicultural society. Learning to deal with new situations and people takes practice. Looking at alternatives is a learnable critical thinking skill, and looking at a situation from another point of view is an attitude we need to model.

To many of us, the idea of intentionally including conflict in our classrooms is threatening. We may be highly trained in conflict avoidance; we may prefer not to recognize conflict when we see it. By controlling the situation, we hope the reasons for the conflict will disappear. Sometimes they will. Or we hope that we can prevent conflict by instructing children to treat one another with respect. Surely, we need to communicate this message in the hope that conflicts will be averted.

Figure 7.2 Decision making about unplanned conflict situations.

Still, conflicts will always arise. Our task is to decide what to do about the conflict we see that arises out of individual interactions among our children and to incorporate lessons in conflict resolution into our curriculum on working and living with others.

Handling Intergroup-Based Conflict

What about dealing with conflict that rears its unwanted head as a result of interaction among students, or between students and teachers? Figure 7.2 relates four basic options you can consider when intergroup conflict occurs. This continuum is based on how much attention a teacher decides to give a conflict incident. You can ignore the incident, perhaps believing that it will go away. You can stop the conflict, declaring that "we don't do this here," while hoping this declaration will erase the motivation that provoked the conflict. Or you can opt to discuss the issue with the parties directly involved, deciding that the conflict should be treated as interpersonal. You also can involve the whole class in a discussion: "How would we feel if ...," aiming to clear the air by having children consider reversing roles.

Exercise 7.4   *SELF-CHECK ON INTERGROUP CONFLICT IN SCHOOLS*

Examine your feelings about conflictual classroom situations by choosing the one response that best matches what you would prefer. These sample conflict situations are designed to prompt your thinking about where you stand intellectually and emotionally on these issues.

Situation 1

Anton, a black child, comes to you after recess and tells you that Chad, a white child, called him a "Nigger" while they were standing in the third-grade line.

1. You tell Anton not to pay attention to Chad.
2. You get the children to work and call Chad to the hall to have him explain why he would "name call," asking him never to do it again.
3. You seat the class and give them a "lecture" on words we do not use in polite society.
4. Later that day you use the event as a situation for the class to explore through two puppets, one black and one white.

Situation 2

Your fifth graders are buzzing about the new second-grade teacher, Mr. Todd, who is a dwarf.

1. You discuss the term *stereotype* with the class.
2. You tell the class that they should treat others as they would like to be treated.
3. You invite Mr. Todd to your class to tell them how he feels about being a "little-person" teacher.
4. You ask the children to write about how they would feel if they were suddenly transformed into dwarfs.

Situation 3

A newly arrived, adopted Korean child enters your kindergarten. Chungsoon can speak no English. This is a novelty to all the other English-speaking children. They are laughing and pointing.

1. You ask children to think of ways they can make Chungsoon feel at home in the class.
2. You appoint Angeline to be Chungsoon's special friend.
3. You read the book *I Am Here: Yo Estoy Aqui* about Luz, a kindergarten Spanish-speaking child who learns to communicate with the other children through a Spanish-speaking classroom aide.
4. You make a special place separate from the other children for Chungsoon to work and give her special, individual attention with gestures.

Examine Your Choices

If you selected number 1 in the first situation, number 2 in the second situation, or number 4 in the third situation, you need to examine why you are more comfortable ignoring the conflicts in these situations. Conflict can be turned into a learning experience for you and the children. If it is swept under the rug it will not go away; it will become part of the hidden curriculum, the nonpositive classroom culture. If you choose number 2 in the first situation, you should consider the effect of this method. It may keep Chad from name calling in your presence, but it also may inspire Chad to call Anton "tattletale Nigger." If you choose to lecture the class, you are, in effect, telling them what not to do. Yet they need to know why. They need to explore how it would feel to be called a similar name. The choices that involve presenting the conflict as an exploration using different characters requires fantastic readiness to "seize the moment of teachability" on your part. Can you be that alert? Ready? Adroit? What if you do not observe situations that are auspicious lead-ins to these vital issues?

There is no course that can totally prepare you for the decisions you will have to make about how to handle intergroup conflict. What you can do is discuss the situations in this self-check and others in which you have been. Be assured that as a teacher you will be involved in working with children on issues of stereotyping and name calling and prejudice. Only experience informed by your attentive eyes and ears of social justice can bolster your self-confidence and courage in handling this kind of culture learning.

Teaching about Interpersonal and Intergroup Conflict

Techniques and materials for the exploration of conflict usually fall into the bibliographic categories of role playing, problem solving, and critical thinking. Typically, more than a verbal prompt is used to initiate this kind of classroom episode. Prompts vary from staged incidents to photographs portraying children in dilemmas to puppets that get into conflict situations to filmstrips that lead into a crisis point to trade books that portray social, racial, or cultural dissonance.

Using dolls dressed as people who have come to the classroom is another effective way to involve children in a longer-range "living with" people who are different from them or people who have difficulties to resolve. "Persona Dolls" are introduced to the class by the teacher as people who have come to join the class as portrayed in this dialogue.

Mrs. Lever introduces Brian, an orthopedically handicapped third grader, to the class one morning during opening exercises. She brings in a doll dressed as a third grader seated in a wheelchair.

> *Mrs. Lever:* Class, we have someone who will be joining us. His name is Brian. He comes to us from Children's Hospital where he has just learned to use his new wheelchair. His mother tells me that Brian is eager to be in our class. Brian was hurt in an auto accident. He cannot use the lower half of his body. He will need our help to do certain things. Do you have questions about our new classmate?
>
> *Melissa:* Can he talk?
>
> *Mrs. Lever:* For now, Brian will talk through me. Later, some of you may learn enough about Brian to talk for him.
>
> *Vito:* How come he's coming to our class?
>
> *Mrs. Lever:* He lives in our neighborhood and finished second grade last year.

This line of questioning continues until children have discovered that Brian will need help for bathroom visits, drinks, and getting in and out the doors. Mrs. Lever then sets up a buddy schedule for Brian for the rest of the week.

A few days later, Mrs. Lever asks the children to share what they have learned now that Brian is in the class. Brian's buddies tell about their troubles in bathrooms and with doors. Mrs. Lever leads them to explore how they would feel if they were Brian. Finally, Mrs. Lever asks that they be thinking about what they could do to make their classroom and school an easier place for Brian to be. She fully expects that the group will begin a campaign to prepare the school for children such as Brian. She expects that they will speak with the principal and write to the school board about their concerns.

Under the guise of fantasy you can introduce explorations of real-life problems and conflicts. Classrooms can accommodate more than one Persona Doll. In settings where children would not have contact with certain "different others," the dolls can provide opportunities for empathy-building experiences that lead children to think critically about human variety that is outside their life spheres.

Lesson Ideas for Understanding Prejudice and Name Calling

Staging classroom incidents is one of the most effective avenues into open discussion and more personally perceived insights about the effect of prejudice. Here are three classic ideas that have proven adaptable to a variety of ages and settings.

Blue Eyes and Brown Eyes.   This is a teacher-instigated experiment in social control and prejudice. Separate children according to some observable trait. Do not use skin color since this experience is intended to be analogous to the real experiences that happen as a result of prejudice based on skin color. Treat representatives of one trait, such as brown eyes, with great favor. Allow them to sit in the front of the class, have more privileges, be first in line, have all of the recess equipment, and so on. Treat the blue-eyed children with disdain. When they make any error call attention to it and say, "Well, that's what I would expect from a blue-eyed person." After a day, or less for younger children, of this kind of teacher treatment, hold a class discussion on how each group felt. Extend the discussion to whether this kind of thing happens in the real world. Discuss what children have learned from this experience that they can use the rest of their lives.[5]

The Museum.   This experience is to help children recognize the stereotypes they have and consider where they got them. It is appropriate for middle graders. Ask children to discuss what a museum is for. Ask them to tell what would be in a museum about people. Ask children to close their eyes and imagine that they are in an ethnic museum. Their purpose is to imagine a display in the Black Room of the museum. Allow some silent time before proceeding. Then suggest that children move to another room. Use a group that has significance for the class for the next mental display organization process.

After silent imagining time, ask children to describe what they put into the Black Room. Record their contributions. Then, going down the written list, ask where each idea came from. Categorize responses into "firsthand" and "secondhand" information.

Discuss whether members of the group being discussed would decorate their room the same way.

Finally, discuss what happens when we think about individuals only in terms of the group with which we identify them.

---

[5] Jane Elliott and William Peters, *A Class Divided: Then and Now* (New Haven: Yale University Press, 1987). PBS video also available.

What Did You See?   This is a dramatic way into the topic of how selective memory distorts the way we remember events and individuals or groups. With no warning, stage a classroom interruption that will be witnessed by the children. You could have two children from another class, preferably from differing racial or cultural groups, chase each other into your room shouting at each other, using derogatory names, over a playground argument that you end by sending them to the principal's office.

Once calm is restored, ask the children to write about who they saw, what they said, what happened first, and what the scene was about. Then have them compare their stories. Are they the same? What kinds of differences are there? Are there differences related to mixing facts with conclusions or inferences? Are there differences of interpretation that stem from the racial or cultural identity of the players?

This experiment is much broader than intergroup relations. It should inspire more critical thinking about what children see and read in the news.

Apartheid.   This lesson is an adaptation of one done in greater detail by Carolyn Pereira "Elementary Teaching Strategies" in *Social Education*.[6] By giving racial identifications and physically rearranging children within the classroom, they can begin to grasp the meaning of South Africa's current situation. Give enough paper squares of four different colors to represent South Africa's four official racial categories: for a class of 30–71 percent black, or 21; 16 percent white, or 5; 10 percent colored, or 3; 3 percent Asian, or 1. Pass out papers arbitrarily telling children that the papers will help them learn the meaning of a new word. Write "apartheid" on the chalkboard.

Write the color of paper and the racial group it represents on the chalkboard. Move half of the blacks to the back of the room. Send one white to join the blacks in the back. Place the rest of the blacks in the front of the room. Squeeze them into one corner of the front. Scatter Asians and coloreds close to the two groups of blacks. Allow whites to sit scattered in the middle of the space.

Explain that this arrangement represents how space is organized in South Africa. Ask children to think about the facts you present as though they were members of the South African racial group represented by the paper they hold. Write the facts on chart paper or strips and unveil them as you proceed for dramatic effect and to help the children recall them.

Facts

Apartheid means apartness. Laws forbid any mixing of races in neighborhoods, schools, and jobs.

Blacks cannot vote or hold government positions.

The color of a person's skin determines how free he or she will be in South Africa.

Coloreds are mixed-race people. The government does not treat them as white,

---

[6] Carolyn Pereira, "Elementary Teaching Strategies," *Social Education* 51 (2 February 1987, pp. 128–29). Reprinted from *Social Education* with permission of the National Council for the Social Studies.

although some speak Afrikaans, a white language, and are members of the
Dutch Reformed Church.

Asians are originally from India. They are segregated from whites and not accepted
by blacks.

Whites in farm areas own land. Blacks are allowed only poor places to live.

Ask the children in each group how they feel about these facts. How do they feel
about each other? Have children predict what may happen in this situation. How does this
situation affect us in the United States? Do we have any situation that is or was similar?

SUMMARY

In this chapter we have reviewed three ways that culture learning can occur in the
elementary classroom. The way we organize learning is potentially a culture-forming
process. Cooperative-learning modes appear to offer us a powerful tool for building
positive interactions between children who may perceive themselves as different in cultural
ways from others. We may learn about cultures in ways that take advantage of the cultures
that children bring with them to school. Recognizing that each individual identifies with a
variety of microcultures can guide us in the way we orient children's study of groups of
people. We may learn about dealing with differences in our own and others' cultures by
practicing the skill of seeing a situation from another perspective and exploring alternative
resolutions of conflicts. Finally, we clear a path for creating new ways to behave in our
culture by seeking solutions to real problems related to group identities.

SUGGESTED READINGS

Cangelosi, James S. *Cooperation in the Classroom: Students and Teachers Together.*
Washington, D.C.: National Education Association, 1986. Review of cooperative
learning strategies.

Gollnick, Donna M., and Chinn, Philip C. *Multicultural Education in a Pluralistic Society.*
Columbus: Merrill, 1986. Textbook on foundations of education with multicultural
perspective.

Thomas, Marlo and Friends. *Free to Be . . . A Family: A Book About All Kinds of Belonging.*
New York: Bantam Books, 1987. Songs, stories, comics for classroom sharing, a
sequel to earlier *Free to Be.*

Johnson, David W.; Johnson, Roger T.; and Holubec, Edye J. *Circles of Learning:
Cooperation in the Classroom.* Alexandria, Va.: Association for Supervision and
Curriculum Development, 1984. Practical suggestions for implementing cooperative
learning.

Kendall, Frances E. *Diversity in the Classroom.* New York: Teachers College Press, 1983. Text suggesting techniques for recognition and honoring student diversity.

Ogubu, J. U. "Research Currents: Cultural-Ecological Influences on Minority School Learning." *Language Arts* 62 (December 1985): 860–69. Insightful analysis of minority status based on religious, social, and immigration identities.

Slavin, Robert E. *Student Team Learning: An Overview and Practical Guide.* Washington, D.C.: National Education Association, 1986. Research-based manual for implementing jigsaw versions of cooperative learning.

Tiedt, Pamela L., and Tiedt, Iris M. *Multicultural Teaching.* Boston: Allyn and Bacon, 1986. Text of extensive resource ideas for every curricular area.

8

Communication Skills in the Social Studies

In this chapter we discuss how to help children develop their communication skills, with a special focus on writing skills in the social studies. These topics are examined:

1. Relating the Social Studies and the Language Arts
2. Developing Oral and Written Expression in the Social Studies
3. Organizing Research Projects
4. Finding and Organizing Information
5. Developing and Presenting Writing Skills

Teachers and writers often make similar kinds of statements when they discuss the personal effect of teaching and writing: "I gained a real understanding of the concept only after trying to teach it." "I write to work out a problem." Both teaching and writing force us to organize our listening, reading, and thinking in a way that others can understand. When we communicate, we also internalize knowledge. Writing and other expressive modes help both children and adults structure their learning.

Guiding children to communicate effectively is a major challenge. Consider the communication requirements of living in our country. We must listen and read with understanding just to keep up with what is happening. Being clear on the telephone, giving directions, and explaining are oral skills we need to order our lives. Equally important are the writing demands of adult living. Our lives are filled with ordering goods and services, making consumer complaints, filling in all kinds of forms from income tax to accidents to college admission, performing the writing chores of businesses and organizations such as keeping minutes, formulating agendas, submitting proposals, writing reports and letters or memoranda, writing contracts, and issuing work orders. Effective communication is vital to our lives. Writing regulates our way of life. We may complain about the paperwork we must wade through, but without it our lives would become even more frustrating. The old American custom of "putting it in writing" is here to stay. This custom demands that children become critical readers, logical thinkers, and concise, persuasive speakers and writers.

RELATING THE SOCIAL STUDIES AND THE LANGUAGE ARTS

The social studies should be a major vehicle for transporting children to expressive skills. Reading, speaking, and writing opportunities can result naturally from social studies topics. Indeed, language-arts skills are best taught when integrated with topics from content areas such as the social studies or science. Good writing skills develop from a well-developed oral language.

Apparently, many teachers and schools do not take full advantage of the possibilities for using the social studies as a vehicle for developing communication skills, especially writing. Results of recent nationwide assessment testing demonstrate that writing is one of the skills areas in which students perform least well. Students were able to write simple descriptions or give information. They were much weaker in writing tasks that required analysis when explaining, supporting, comparing, and contrasting were required. Nor did they perform well at writing tasks that demanded pursuasion.[1]

To explore how we can develop communication skills in the social studies, this chapter focuses on the necessary integration of language-arts skills and social studies projects. The first section examines a classroom incident to illustrate the use of a social studies theme to develop communication skills. The second section presents an overview of teacher decisions concerning communication skills development in project-oriented instruction. The third and fourth sections suggest strategies for the phases of project work that require children to gather and organize information and, finally, to present or write their findings.

DEVELOPING ORAL AND WRITTEN EXPRESSION IN THE SOCIAL STUDIES

Read this vignette and look for these aspects: what communication skills were being developed? What sequence did the teacher use to develop them?

Veteran kindergarten teacher Barbara Schubert, tired of the inanity of most sharing times, decided to introduce a global aspect to the routine. She added a globe and a package of red stick-on dots to sharing. Children continued to bring in toys and other significant objects to share. Ms. Schubert directed them to look for where the toy, or object, had been

---

[1] National Assessment of Educational Progress, *WritingReport Card* (Princeton, N.J., 1986).

made.[2] Quickly, children learned the words Korea, Taiwan, Japan, and Hong Kong by sight and by location on the globe. After they shared, they placed a stick-on dot on the globe marking the place where what they shared had been manufactured.

Thus each child's oral patterning was prompted to include the usual information of what I brought (naming and describing) and how I got it (sequencing), in addition to the extension of where it came from and where that place is on the globe (identifying origin).

Then serendipity entered! One morning a child asked, "What are we going to do about all the volcanoes?" Uncertain of the child's meaning, Ms. Schubert responded, "What volcanoes?" The child brought the globe to the circle and pointed to the mounds of red stick-on dots on Japan, Hong Kong, Taiwan, and Korea, which reminded him of red mountains about to explode. Astutely, Ms. Schubert moved into questions about what the dots meant. They were off and running, at their level of comprehension, on the implications of the balance of trade.

After some discussion, the children dictated the beginning of a chart story with Ms. Schubert asking the children to tell what described most of the toys they shared. After listing several ideas—"mine has batteries," "it transforms," "from Japan," "orange and black"—they decided that none was true for all of their toys.

> *Ms. Schubert:* Then what is true? Think about where the volcanoes are.
> *Children:* Asia!
> *Ms. Schubert:* Can we begin our story with a sentence about toys and Asia?

The children directed Ms. Schubert to write: "Most of our toys come from Asia." Then Ms. Schubert asked them to tell her more details about the first sentence. They added: "Our toys are made in Korea, Hong Kong, Taiwan, and Japan. They are imported."

Schubert asked the children to talk about these facts with their parents and to come to school the next day ready to tell more facts and feelings about what the red dots meant. Again she led them to compose a paragraph starting with one general statement followed by two more sentences that added detail to the topic sentence.

As they wrote more about their investigation, Ms. Schubert had them find statements of fact and feeling in their writing. Many children brought their parents in to see the "volcanoes." The topic extended into looking at labels on their clothes to see where they had been made and reaching the conclusion that we buy things from many other nations. Then Ms. Schubert asked the children to investigate if their parents could tell them of things other countries bought from the United States. The informal theme of global trade and interdependence produced several pages of chart stories that year. Children continued to bring parents into the classroom to read the results of the children's investigation into world trade. Parents were astounded that kindergartners could become articulate about a topic that is usually part of a college-level economics course.

This vignette illustrates our contention that young children can investigate apparently sophisticated social studies topics with great interest and profit. The teacher also taught

---

[2] Barbara Schubert, Blackford School, Campbell, CA.

them an expository paragraph composition form. Development of communication skills—orally describing, categorizing, and drawing conclusions and then putting them into a group-written story, "reading" the story, and performing further oral activity followed by further writing and reading—was an integrated part of a social studies theme. This kindergarten episode also shows that through writing the results of their study, children are led to think more consciously about what they are learning. Ms. Schubert did this by approaching the topic using concrete and emotionally meaningful objects and experiences. She built upon the children's contributions and gave them a purpose for further investigation by involving their parents as an audience for its process and its results.

Her strategy facilitated the children's development of expressive skills. She gradually helped them make the transition from telling to writing, from idiosyncratic recall to recall based on facts, from stream-of-consciousness recall to more logically considered relation of observations. All of these things are facets of thinking. Writing the charts was, in essence, a thinking exercise flowing from a lot of oral exchange.

Expressive Skills

We know that children who read and write with facility usually have a greater oral-language facility. So our first concern in developing expressive abilities is to provide a rich oral-language environment. Children must be exposed to oral language from a variety of sources ranging from the teacher's own inventiveness to hearing stories read to them or watching and listening to media. Immersion in a content-rich environment supplies children with expressive ammunition from which they draw upon when they have opportunities to recreate their knowledge. Every time they recite rhymes, sing songs, assume roles in dramatic enactments, tell experiences, retell stories, discuss how to resolve problems, or make decisions, they are enlarging their language and thinking potential.

Experts list three purposes for writing most related to the social studies. One is informative or investigative, a second is interpretive, and the third is persuasive. Can primary children pursue these three purposes? They can if we think in broader terms. Instead of just writing, we need to consider all forms of expression. In their speaking, drawing, and group compositions, as well as their writing, children can develop their thoughts according to these purposes.

> The typical expressive objectives for primary grades include:
> Recalling facts about . . .
> Listing characteristics or properties about . . .
> Creating categories based on properties
> Relating events in sequence
> Stating opinions and supporting them with facts

These are narrower and more behavioralistic statements than the major purposes of social studies writing. However, these statements can be applied to the three purposes for social studies writing or expression. Recalling facts and relating events is done to inform. Listing properties and making categories serves an interpretive purpose. Supporting opinions with facts is persuasive.

Perhaps the real issue, then, is not so much that primary objectives are incompatible with the purposes we should strive for in social studies expression. The real issue is that what we typically require at this level, and other levels, too, does little to help children develop these writing, or expressive, purposes. Observation in classrooms shows us that the typical expressive tasks are limited to answering questions from the textbook or other book read to the class, doing fill-in-the-blank items, or matching items in workbooks. Book reports or other reports are usually left to the children to structure. Furthermore, observational studies of elementary classroom activity find that little or no instruction in how to perform expressive assignments is given. (See the Chapter 3 section "Direct Teaching.")

Strategies for Developing Expressive Objectives

Developing young children's expressive abilities is an ongoing, multifaceted, overarching goal. (see Figure 8.1). A good classroom will have various and simultaneous expressive activities related to all curricular areas. The strategy, or methods, used to develop these abilities effectively are applicable to the social studies as well as to other areas.

Children's less-than-adequate performance in expressive tasks can usually be traced to a faulty instructional strategy. Children who are enthusiastic about a task usually have an audience in mind. Children who make a speech to tell why they favor or oppose letting pets roam free usually have been instructed about the form a persuasive talk should take. A class in which most children complete expressive tasks successfully has probably been through most of the steps listed in Figure 8.1.

Exercise 8.1 *ANALYZING A CLASSROOM EPISODE*

You may find it useful to read the kindergarten vignette again to identify the strategy elements Schubert employed. What do you think was important in keeping the children's interest, enthusiasm, and expressive productivity going?

Expressive Activity Ideas

Expressive activities vary in length. They can take one session or extend over a longer period. Try to vary the purpose and form you build into expressive activities.

Expressive Activities

1. Imaginary dialogues between historical figures (recognized and nonfamous): George Washington and soldiers at Valley Forge.
2. News reports about events: gold discovered in California.

Step 1:
Concrete experience:
Exposure to picture, story, other information
Experiment, visit, event

↓

Step 2:
Discussion:
Making terms clear
Outlining sequence, findings, questions

↓

Step 3:
Motivation:
Considering purpose for using information
Establishing need to organize our information

↓

Step 4:
Definition of expression:
Deciding form of expression
Making structure of expression explicit
Developing samples of structured expression

↓

Step 5:
Expression:
Providing time to develop expression
Assisting expression development
Providing time to stare expression

Figure 8.1 Developing expressive abilities.

3. Letters from people settled in new place: Oklahoma settler to family in Ohio.
4. Promotional brochures: on attractions of county.
5. Editorials for or against any topic contemporary or historical: Lincoln's decision to hold federal property in seceded states; writing a new U.S. Constitution.
6. Scroll movie: westward movement accompanied with audiotaped narrative.
7. Photo essay: community services.
8. Directions: tell how to do something such as make candles or to go somewhere such as to the capital of our state.
9. Explain pictures and maps: describe important features of historical painting such as John Trumbull's signing of the Constitution or describe dangers faced by explorers on the Oregon Trail.

10. Interviews: retell information about school in grandmother's time.
11. Diary: personal record about my activities at home or imaginative response as person in historical event such as being a child on the Mayflower.

Children delight in attempting to use different genres. In varying the purpose and form, teachers guarantee children a better chance to develop broader expressive competency.

ORGANIZING RESEARCH PROJECTS

Children like projects. Topics explored using the project mode appeal to children because they have a beginning and an end, whereas textbook-dominated work seems to go on forever. Projects that involve children in gaining information and presenting it in their own way can be called research.

A project is more satisfying when children have some choice about the topic and how they present it and when the project is assigned with an outline or sequence of steps to follow in developing it. Handling a project is like doing a mosaic. Unless we know what we are striving for, working on the separate areas of the mosaic is not meaningful.

From the teacher's point of view, projects offer several advantages.

Projects

> Promote group work
> Allow individualization according to preference and skill needs
> Prompt active learning
> Integrate and apply communication skills
> Provide a vehicle for summarization of various experiences and data from various
> > sources

Planning for project work requires that you organize groups and topics that are age appropriate and sequence experiences so that communication skills are taught as they are needed. Units and projects may be synonymous. Projects may, on the other hand, be part of a larger unit or stand alone. Projects of all types offer opportunities for the development of communication skills.

Developing Project Options

Increasing communication opportunities through projects requires that you plan in two areas: how to subdivide a topic and what to suggest as ways that children can choose to present their project. Several factors need to be considered when deciding on group-project topics: Does the library have sufficient materials for each group to use? Does the topic have enough facets for group work? Often social studies textbooks suggest topic

TABLE 8.1 PROJECT PRESENTATION OPTIONS

Oral	*Written*	*Graphic*
Report	Report	Poster
Script	Newspaper	Collage
Panel	Brochure	Bulletin board
Role play	Letter	Mural
Quiz show	Editorial	Scroll movie
Debate	Journal	Timeline, map

subdivisions that are appropriate for group work. The primary topic called "types of communities" is a good example. Group work can be done according to the kind of community—urban, suburban, rural—or according to the way different life activities—transportation, getting food, working, housing—are organized in each community type. Thus in a project or unit on Africa, different groups might select different countries. Within each group individual children would be responsible for subtopics such as geography and climate, people and customs, products and trade and history. Or in a shorter project where the topic was making a poster about school clean-up, one child would contribute ideas for each of the subtopics—restrooms, playground, halls, cafeteria, classroom—to the group effort.

The choices you give students in preparing their topics can promote or inhibit communication. Combinations of these topics flow naturally from work within each group that is presented to the whole class or another audience. Children's interest levels will be kept higher if you vary the kinds of expressive choices from one project to another. Again, to promote oral communication, children must have individual subtopic responsibilities to present to their groups. (See Table 8.1.)

Grouping for Projects

Group projects foster oral language. They can be structured to promote social cooperation and group decision making. Children in primary grades need projects they can accomplish in one or two sessions. They work best individually, perhaps communicating about how to share materials. They can also work with a partner when the roles are defined and the task is to construct a product such as drawing a story sequence.

Rebus-writing instructions that outline work steps help keep younger children focused. (See Figure 8.2.) Center time may be a choice controlled by putting name tags on a sign-up chart until the number of positions available at the center is filled. After completing the task, the child removes his or her name tag from the sign-up chart, indicating that another child may come to the center.

Children in intermediate grades can work together on a project over several sessions. They work well in cooperative groups in which role responsibilities are taught and posted for reference. These roles typically include a group leader who will organize the group and get tasks distributed and set meeting times; a recorder who will keep track of which

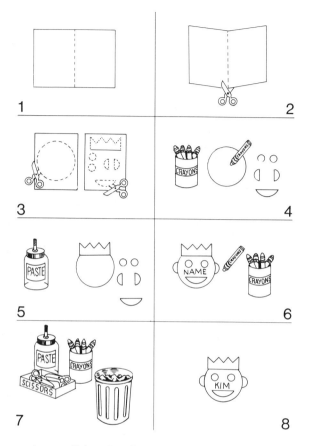

Figure 8.2 Rebus-project; outlining visualizes verbal instructions.

members agree to do what and fill out any group forms that are part of the project; and other roles that vary according to the project and may include chairperson, artists, presenters, word processers, and so on necessary to the group's final product. (See Chapters 3 and 6 for more on cooperative learning.) Rotating the group roles from one session to another and allowing children to choose a different group when projects change helps give all children a variety of role experience and opportunity to learn to work with different classmates.

FINDING AND ORGANIZING INFORMATION

The process of gathering and organizing information requires communication skills. These skills range from defining a purpose for collecting information from reading or interviewing to devising schemes for recall and telling others about it. These skills need to be taught. Notice how a skill necessary for children to do productive reading is introduced in the following classroom transcript.

Structuring Reading Purpose

Ms. Ishikawa's fourth-grade class is studying cultural diversity in their state.

Ms. Ishikawa: We've been studying about diversity in our state. In addition to doing our general reading and study, we are going to do some personal investigation. One part of the investigation will be to inverview people in our families. The part we want to begin work on today is our library research about our immigrant roots.

Before we begin, we need to decide what kinds of information we all need to look for even though we will be learning about different places. I will keep track of your ideas on the chalkboard. Who can get us started?

Cathy: My family came from Ireland and England. What do I do?

Ms. Ishikawa: I suggest you make one choice, but if you have time, you may want to research both. If Cathy chooses Ireland, what should she try to find out?

Lloyd: Maybe where it is?

Ms. Ishikawa: Good start. What else?

Cathy: What they wear.

Ms. Ishikawa: [Writes and uses body language to call on others; different children add items such as language, kind of work they do, climate, the way it looks, etc.] This is a good list. Now we need to look at it and see if there are certain things that could go together. Let's do some clustering. If I write land [she moves to another chalkboard segment], what would go with it? [supplies population as a second category; asks students to supply others; they come up with land, population, resources, famous places, way of life, and why people left]. Tomorrow when you find your country in the encyclopedia, how can you use these categories?

Students tell how they can write down information they need to recall under each one as they read. Then Ms. Ishikawa instructs each student to fold a blank sheet of construction paper into six parts and write one of the topical headings at the top of each part.

By exploring together what they need to look for before they read, these children defined a purpose for reading that will give them a structure for recalling what they read. Giving students a teacher-made list of questions to answer as they read is another way to establish a reading purpose.

Practicing Reading for Detail and Main Ideas

Let us return to the example of Ms. Ishikawa's fourth-grade class to see how she further prepared the students to gather information. This time we follow her lesson plan. Ms. Ishikawa wants the students to practice looking for details and main ideas before she asks them to work independently. She knows her students can find encyclopedia entries, but she wants students to learn to paraphrase and summarize the information they find. Here is the lesson she used to follow the first project session.

SAMPLE LESSON PLAN 8.1
Using Encyclopedias for Main Ideas and Details

Objectives:

Students will skim encyclopedia article for specific details. Students will read encyclopedia paragraphs and state main ideas.

Materials:

Tape next to screen, sheet of butcher paper folded into six sections with categories labeled, magic marker, set of encyclopedias, transparency of Iceland entry, highlighter transparency pens, overhead projector.

Procedure:

1. Move students to carpet facing screen.
2. Tell students: "We are going to practice using an encyclopedia to gather information for our roots reports. There are two kinds of information we will need. One is specific numbers and facts. The other is more general ideas. Who knows how we go about looking for specific facts? [Children review skimming.] Who knows how we go about looking for general ideas? [Children review process for getting main ideas.]
3. "Let's look at our category sheet. Which of these call for specific facts? Which seem to call for main ideas?
4. "Now, let's pretend that my grandparents came from Iceland. What volume do I go to? [Have child find Iceland entry.]
5. "So we all can work together, I have a copy of the Iceland entry on this transparency. [Lead group to entry overview by asking questions about subtitles.]
6. "We should read the whole entry for our report. After the first reading we should look at our papers and see which of the sections to return to for information we want to write down."
7. Take turns orally reading entry, pointing out along the way when paragraphs contain information pertinent to categories on sheet.
8. Have volunteers highlight detail sections of transparency while you record in appropriate category on sheet in front of class their rephrasing of facts and information. For "way of life," review entry for ideas and have children highlight and come up with main idea phrases. Discuss how reading for general ideas is slower than skimming for facts.

9. Use thumbs up or down to check for understanding: "First thing I do is look for details" (down). "As I do the first reading I make mental note about what parts to come back to" (up). "Main ideas must be copied word for word" (down). "For the second reading I skim subtitles looking for places that should give me details" (up).
10. "Tomorrow we will begin our own encyclopedia reading. Who can review for us the steps for finding information from the article on our country?"
11. Continue independent practice using encyclopedias next session.

This direct-teaching lesson assumes that students will not take extensive notes and will work individually on this phase of the project. If the children had earlier practice in this kind of task, the teacher might have incorporated the use of individual note cards. There is no one correct way to take notes that works for everyone on every kind of topic. What does work is exploring the categories of information that need to be collected before beginning the information gathering process.

Gathering information independently may not be the best way to approach this kind of task. Some children are more successful when reading of this nature is presented as a team task. A technique that increases oral and listening skills while helping children focus on reading expository writing for main ideas is to adapt the SQ3R for use with two children.[3]

SQ3R: A Study Technique

S (Survey)   Read headings; look at illustrations, italics, questions.
Q (Question)   Make question(s) from heading(s) and write down.
R (Read)   Read orally to find answers.
R (Recite)   Discuss answers to questions.
R (Reread)   Read to check answers and write them.

Children take turns being reader and recorder. The recorder asks the questions and listens for the answers as the reader reads a section or paragraph. Both discuss what to write down. Then the recorder writes the agreed-upon main idea. The students reverse roles and proceed to the next section or paragraph. The result is an outline that can be used for team readers to explain their reading to the rest of their study group.

Textbook reading can be facilitated by the same techniques. Additional ideas that help children get meaning from texts or other kinds of reading materials are:

Reading buddies of more and less fluent readers
Teacher-taped passages that children "read" at listening posts
Vocabulary posters listing significant terms related to the topic being studied
Teacher reading aloud key passages

[3] Francis P. Robinson, *Effective Study* (New York: Harper & Row, 1970).

No one technique works with every student for every kind of reading task. In general, when children are involved and able to talk about the content they read, they will comprehend more.

Classifying and Organizing Information

Children need practice to gain confidence in developing their own categories and organizing information. They are assisted toward these skills when they have a structured purpose for reading and some method for getting the main ideas from what they read or see or hear. They need to work with writing and presenting structures that match their purposes.

SAMPLE OUTLINES FOR DIFFERENT PRESENTATION PURPOSES

Descriptive Outline

Introduction tells what will be described.
Major quality or event.
>   Two or more sentences that tell more details about topic
>   Additional major quality or event (as many paragraphs as needed)
>   Two or more sentences that tell more details about topic
>   Summary tells how major qualities fit together.

Persuasive Outline

Introduction tells what issue is.
State position.
>   Two or more sentences supporting position
State argument against position.
>   Two or more sentences telling why argument is not good (as many paragraphs
>   as needed to cover reasons for position)
Summary restates position and major reasons and why others should agree.

Comparison Outline

Introduction tells what is to be compared.
>   Two or more sentences describing what is to be compared
Describe major point of comparison.
>   Two or more sentences describing how comparison topics compare on this point
Describe another point of comparison.
>   Two or more sentences describing how comparison topics compare on this point
>   (as many paragraphs as needed to cover major points)
Summary states conclusion about how two topics are same or different.
>   Two or more sentences supporting conclusion

These basic outlines will be modified as children gain more facility of expression. There is nothing sacred about them. However, using such an outline will help you organize your ideas.

You will get better results when you work through a familiar topic with the whole class before asking individuals or small groups to put together a presentation. Initially, you will need to supply the main points of the report or presentation. If, for example, the general topic were to describe life in the American colonies, you could pick a colony such as Georgia and lead the class in the development of it by supplying the major points and leading the group in the elaboration of these points. After several projects have been developed in this manner, children can be asked to come up with the major points as part of the prewriting or preparation for an oral presentation.

Sample Writing Outline

> *Introduction:* Georgia was one of the most British colonies.
> *Major point:* Landowners lived like aristocrats.
> *Major point:* Plantation owners were interested in cash crops.
> *Major point:* Plantation owners organized society to suit themselves.
> *Conclusion:* Georgia was a unique American colony.

Exercise 8.2 *DEVELOPING A WRITING OUTLINE AS A TEACHING TOOL*

Choose a social studies writing topic appropriate for the middle grades and decide which presentation purpose—descriptive, persuasive, or comparative—it best suits. Develop a sample outline you could use for teaching this writing or speaking purpose to a class. Share your outline with your colleagues. What did you learn using these structures? What do you think about these propositions? (1) Teachers must master a skill they expect to teach. (2) Teachers who write have more success in getting children to write. (3) Teachers who share their writing with students encourage students to write. These statements paraphrase research questions currently being studied on the teaching of writing.

Another way in which children gain confidence in their ability to gather and organize information is by knowing where to look for the kind of information they need. A whole variety of locational skills is implied when we mention using library reference skills. Everything from using tables of contents to indexes to card files to computer access is involved. Typically, most schools have library programs that provide sequential development in these important subskills. You can support these efforts in several ways. You can coordinate their assignments with the library program so that children have a classroom purpose to apply skills the librarian teaches. You can develop classroom games and contests that involve children in using reference books. You can provide children with repeated overview possibilities previous to a library assignment as in this example:

Exercise 8.3 *SAMPLE LIBRARY REFERENCE PURPOSE: WHERE WOULD YOU LOOK TO FIND ...*

1. When the first Olympic Games were held
2. What the zip code is for Indianapolis, Indiana
3. How far it is to Anchorage, Alaska, from here
4. Who the richest people in the world are
5. Where the Mason-Dixon line is
6. What people thought of the Constitution in 1787

Which reference book(s) would be the best place to find answers to these questions: encyclopedia, *Guinness Book of World Records*, world almanac, telephone book, world atlas, historical atlas, card catalogue, dictionary, textbook, *The Book of Lists*?

Children may learn to use specific reference books through trivia contests. Once a reference book has been introduced, the children can be invited to submit questions on index cards based on using that reference. The cards are signed and deposited in one box, and answers are deposited in another. The children can earn trivia points in their free time by correctly finding the answer or adding questions to the discover box. Children earning an agreed-upon number of points over, perhaps, a two-week period are rewarded with ribbons or privileges.

Skill building in structuring their reading, knowing where to look for information, finding main ideas, putting information into categories, and organizing information according to a presentation purpose is a lifelong process. To grow in these skills, children need constant contact with projects and lessons that require them to practice. We need to provide children with models of how to perform these skills and organize a variety of projects that enable them to apply our models.

DEVELOPING AND PRESENTING WRITING SKILLS

As we have seen, preparing children for presenting what they have learned orally and in writing is a complex process involving many skills. To ensure success in these areas, there are still more steps to follow once children get to the point of putting together their information. Before investigating suggestions for the composition process, review the four general steps of the whole process:

Steps in the Presenting and Writing Process

Step 1: Prewriting—topic selection, consideration of audience and purpose, data gathering, and organization.

Step 2: Drafting—write out ideas using notes.

Step 3: Revising—make changes in ideas.

Step 4: Editing—look for errors in mechanics, grammar, spelling, punctuation.

In essence, the first two-thirds of this chapter focused on the step that is called prewriting. Without engaging in at least some of the prewriting activities, preparing an oral or written presentation becomes, for most children, an excruciating and even impossible task.

Using Checklists to Guide Presentation and Writing

Children need guidelines about the form a presentation should take. They want to know how their presentation will be evaluated. Over the years some traditional elements of effective presentations have been identified. The two presented below are typical for the intermediate grades:

Oral Report Checklist

1. Practice at home in front of mirror and time yourself.
2. Get attention with riddle, picture, gimmick.
3. Announce your topic.
4. Use notes to keep on topic.
5. Use at least one illustration.
6. Speak in loud voice.
7. Look at your audience.
8. Use good posture.
9. Make summary.
10. Watch time and stay in time limit.

Written Report Checklist

1. Submit your outline.
2. Your report must follow the outline.
3. Outline must have:
      Introduction—you tell what it's about.
      Body—you make a point in each paragraph.
      Conclusion—you tell what report means.
4. Report must show it has been edited for mechanics, punctuation, spelling and grammar.
5. Report must be in your language, so tell what you think is important.
6. List your sources of information.
7. Label any pictures, tables or graphs.

Such checklists are most meaningful when the teacher and students develop them cooperatively. Primary grades profit from checklists with items appropriate for that level. For example, younger children could attend to items 3, 6, 7, 8, and 9 from the oral checklist. Rather than the more extended writing checklists, a checklist that reminds them of a specific structure for a paragraph is appropriate. Many teachers use the expository-writing competencies from J. E. Sparks for paragraphs. The program develops the skills of relating main ideas to supporting details. A beginning level would have a checklist outlining a paragraph, using the jargon of the program: first power sentence; two second power sentences using power transitions; form, spelling, and handwriting.[4]

Step One: Gathering Information and Reorganizing.   Once the reading is completed, children need to be instructed in ways they can go about rethinking the initial outline. One additional suggestion that may be helpful in getting them to plan before they write or order their presentation is to ask them to answer these questions:

> Why is this *topic* important?
> What are the points that tell why the *topic* is important?
> What illustrations will help readers understand the *topic*?
> What is my conclusion about the *topic*?[5]

Children can substitute their topic names in place of the underlined word to help them personalize their thinking. These questions put children in the position of imagining how they can best present their topics to people who do not know about their topic. The answers they get sometimes yield a trail to follow in their writing that is different from their original outline.

Another time-tested method for rethinking the original outline is to try different arrangements of the cards they put their notes on or to cut up the folded paper on which they put notes about different categories. They can rearrange these pieces until they find a workable order. Some children order according to simple, linear progression such as beginning, middle, and end; others invent their own arrangements. The important point is that the initial outline that guided their information gathering be reviewed and perhaps revised before they begin to write or prepare the presentation.

Step Two: Get Your Ideas Down.   This phase of the process probably represents a reversal from the way most of us learned how to approach writing. Instead of spending time reviewing the mechanics of writing, the emphasis is on the content. Children are directed to get their ideas down on paper. They should record them in cases of oral presentations.

The microcomputer is an excellent tool. Many children have skill with word pro-

---

[4]J. E. Sparks, *Write for Power* (Los Angeles: Communications Associates, 1985).
[5]Ann Humes, "Putting Writing Research into Practice," *Elementary School Journal* 84, no. 1 (September 1983): 3–15.

cessing. Composing on it is not burdened with writing that is illegible even to the author or paper that rips or pencils that break or erasures that smudge. Whatever the writing tool, encourage children to get down their thoughts before they do anything else. When children seek advice about where to put a comma or how to spell, they should be redirected to what they want to say. The motto is: "write thoughts first; worry about details later." Their outlines are an enormous help in keeping them going. Getting a version of their thoughts on paper or a floppy disk is the goal of this step.

Step Three: Revise.   Children learn more from this process if they are placed in groups that assist each other. Roger Applebee, an authority on helping young people write, has found that writing response groups of five students encourage examination of ideas. Under his method, each student reads his or her report or report segment to the group. The group then follows a three-step sequence in discussing what was read. First, they *praise* what they think is good. Second, they *question* what they do not understand. Third, they suggest places where *polishing* or improvement needs to be made. The same procedure can be followed with an oral-presentation tape.

Most teachers find that having the response group share the writer's outline helps them tune in on the ideas presented. Under Applebee's method, individual authors can accept or reject their response group's suggestions. Usually, they incorporate them in some manner in their draft or tape revisions. Children should be encouraged to share their revised product with the response group.

All children learn through this process. Listening to the process other children go through helps the listener learn to look for logical sequence and make suggestions about style. This is the last step of the process for oral presentations.

Step Four: Edit.   It is time to look for the mechanics of writing after the content is organized to the writer's satisfaction. Typically, both response groups and the teacher contribute to this part of the process. The final version is completed after editing.

To be sure, the writing process requires more in-class time to undertake. But the additional time this process entails is well worth the investment. Through it children are acquiring a procedural structure through which their confidence and independence in written expression grow. Other advantages of the process are that your role in correcting initial drafts is lessened and the writing produced is more likely to be of a better quality. Perhaps the highest recommendation for the process is that it teaches children that they can help each other learn.

SUMMARY

Communication skills are intimately tied to the social studies. Without content to give writing real purpose, skills practice in letter writing, narrative, or explanation is not a meaningful task for most children. Without instruction and guidance related to the process of gathering and communicating information, the learning potential in social studies remains largely unexplored for children. The suggestions in this chapter should serve to make your instruction in both areas more powerful.

SUGGESTED READINGS

Hoge, John D. "Improving the Use of Elementary Social Studies Textbooks." In *ERIC Digest*, no. 33. Bloomington, Ind.: Clearinghouse for Social Studies/Social Science Education at Indiana University, 1986, pp. 2–3. Lists ways to get more meaning from text reading.

Humes, Ann. "Putting Writing Research into Practice." *Elementary School Journal* 84 (September 1983): 3–15. Suggests steps from research for classroom.

Langer, Judith A. "Learning through Writing: Study Skills in the Content Areas." *Journal of Reading* 29 (February 1986): 400–406.

Pradl, Gordon M., and Mayher, John S. "Reinvigorating Learning through Writing." *Educational Leadership* 42 (February 1985): 4–8.

9

Teaching Special Social Studies Skills: Time, Space, Microcomputers

In this chapter we talk specifically about teaching skills intimately associated with the social studies:

1. Learning about Chronological Time
2. Map and Globe Skills
3. Technologies for the Social Studies

LEARNING ABOUT CHRONOLOGICAL TIME

You already know that one of the important goals in teaching history is to have children develop a sense of time and chronology. We all operate in a time-space dimension and constantly view social phenomena in a time-space orientation. We describe events by stating, for example: "Throughout the whole fifty states, the United States celebrated the bicentennial of the Constitution on September 17, 1987"; Or: "Yesterday I attended the meeting of the local teacher's organization at Washington School." Time and space are interrelated. For our purposes, however, we will consider them separately, first time (history) and then space (geography).

You know that when you are enjoying yourself, time seems to pass by quickly. On the other hand, when you are waiting in the post office line or for a medical appointment, time seems to go slowly. We as adults know that these are *subjective* conceptions of time. However, children do not necessarily know that the differences they experience in time are an illusion. They do not comprehend the uniform motion or velocity of a clock. They believe that the clock works more quickly or slowly depending upon how they experience the time. Some children have reported that school time really seems to drag.

To make time more *objective*, humans use mathematics and astronomy. In our modern technological society we measure time not only in years, months, and days but in smaller periods of specified length such as minutes and seconds. Computer-calculated time is measured in milliseconds and microseconds. The trend toward even smaller units of objective time will probably continue.

This section on time and chronology is organized in the order that material is usually taught in the primary grades and then in the upper grades. However, there are no firm rules on when to introduce time and chronology. In addition, it is often necessary to reteach to maintain some of these skills.

1.	Learn to tell time by the clock.	Primary grades
2.	Use calendar to find dates.	Primary grades
3.	Understand timelines.	Fourth–sixth grades
4.	Learn to translate dates into centuries.	Junior High
5.	Comprehend the Christian system of chronology— A.D. and B.C.	Junior High

Most children learn to tell time at home and in school, although the increased use of digital watches and clocks means that they are less familiar with the so-called face of the clock. Almost all children eventually learn to tell objective time through the use of clocks, calendars, and time-zone maps in their mathematics and science work. What is unique about the social studies is the addition of the *cultural* aspect of time. Students learn the distinction between B.C. and A.D. and the meaning of the terms *decade, century, millennium,* and the like. Teachers frequently use terms like *ancient times,* the *Dark Ages,* the *colonial period, prehistoric time, several centuries ago,* and the *beginnings of modern times.* We need to make sure that our students know what these terms mean.

Like all abstract concepts, time must be personalized and related to a child's experience if it is to be understood. One way to organize and understand time is through a *timeline.* A timeline is one of the simplest ways to organize historical information. Draw a line. It should be drawn to consistent scale; each inch might equal ten years, one year, or a hundred years, depending on what information you wish to include. Then write in significant events at the appropriate places. A timeline reads from left to right, with earlier events on the left and more recent ones on the right, so children are using a reading convention like that of English with which they are already familiar. (See Figure 9.1.)

Students can begin to understand a timeline by looking at the simple timeline of a single person—not necessarily a famous person. Look at the example of the timeline in Figure 9.1. Ask your students when Dolores started first grade or what happened to Dolores in 1980. Students can also make timelines of their own lives or those of their families, noting important dates such as marriages, births of children, and graduations.

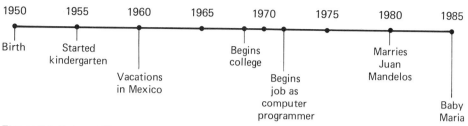

Figure 9.1 Dolores' life.

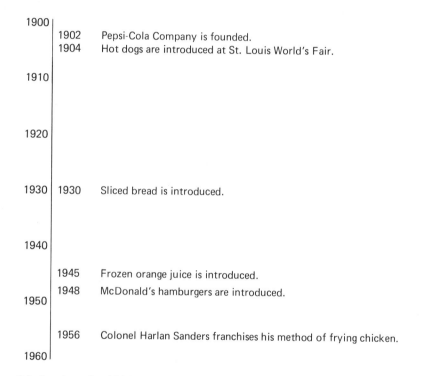

Figure 9.2 American food history.

Many teachers post several timelines around their classrooms and ask their students to add new dates as they study them. Symbols (such as a train for the completion of the transcontinental railroad) make the meaning of the dates clearer.

Continue to introduce more and more complex timelines to students throughout the year. Vary the format by moving the earlier events to the top of the page and the more recent ones to the bottom, as shown in Figure 9.2.

Ask your students in what year frozen orange juice was introduced. Then ask them how many years ago that was. But make sure that they are not simply calculating dates from the timeline; use timeline exercises to introduce critical thinking about the data shown. For example, can students hypothesize from looking at the American foods timeline what kinds of new foods might be introduced in the coming years? Or you might ask them to talk about the impact that nationally available frozen orange juice has had on our society in terms of family roles or its impact on the orange industry or on our relationship with Brazil, the world's largest exporter of oranges.

Timelines can be used to teach about historical themes (a timeline showing revolution throughout the centuries) or about specific regions or nations. Children's encyclopedias such as *The World Book* often provide timelines about important countries under headings like "Important Dates in Mexico." Consider, for example, the dates in the list below.

Important Dates in Mexico

1325	The Aztecs founded Tenochtitlan (Mexico City).
1519–21	Hernando Cortes conquered the Aztec empire for Spain.
1821	Mexico won independence from Spain.
1846–48	The United States defeated Mexico, winning much territory.
1910–11	Revolution.

The events above are simply listed in chronological order and are not scaled as they are on a timeline. What difference does this make in our reading of them? How does consistent scale teach historical lessons? You might provide students with a list like this and then ask them to make a timeline. How long did the Aztec Empire exist compared to the Spanish occupation? Timelines can provide *visual* reinforcement of historical concepts.

Timelines are excellent aids in teaching American history, or the history of specific states, since the periods involved in American history lend themselves to detailed timelines. A timeline covering 200 or 300 years—or even beginning in 1620, with the landing of the Pilgrims—enables you to include specifics about transportation, communication, and the development of industry as well as important dates in political history. Try having students find or draw pictures of citizens in typical dress for each century or half-century, and paste them to the appropriate parts of the timeline. Many students can calculate how many years ago the Pilgrims landed but have no real understanding of what life was like then or how long ago it was relative to the Civil War or the invention of the airplane. Why, they may ask, was setting out for the New World so frightening? After all, we now travel back and forth to Europe all the time. A timeline can help them understand.

After using simple timelines, students may be more ready to tackle concepts like *century*, a period of a hundred years. Explain that, in our culture, centuries are measured from the birth of Christ. A new century begins every hundred years. In the year 2001, a new century will begin. Provide your students with a Western history chronology by centuries, such as that below.

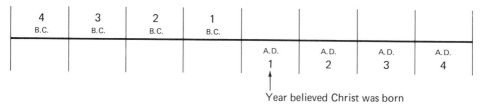

Figure 9.3 B.C. and A.D. centuries.

Historical Events Classified by Century

1700

      American Revolution

      French Revolution

1800

      Industrial revolution spreads

1900

      World Wars I and II

      Computers

      Space exploration

2000

Ask students to place specific events within the centuries. You can do this by giving students a random list of dates, including things such as 1776 (Thomas Jefferson writes the Declaration of Independence) or 1861 (American Civil War begins) or 1911 (Mexican Revolution). Don't use the dates of an individual's life, since they often overlap century boundaries. Now ask students what events happened in each century. In upper grades, you might ask if two historical figures might have talked to each other. Students should get a sense that James Madison could (and did) talk to Thomas Jefferson but could not have spoken to Woodrow Wilson or Franklin Roosevelt.

When they understand centuries, students may be ready to tackle the difficult concept of A.D. and B.C. The distinction between A.D. and B.C. is often a stumbling block even for junior high school students. Children need to be told that, in our culture, we use as a starting date the year in which people thought that Jesus Christ was born—*Anno Domini*, or A.D. 1. (*Anno Domini* is Latin for the year of our Lord.) A.D. precedes the year (A.D. 1988) whereas B.C. follows the year (673 B.C.). We are now living in A.D. 19__ (See Figure 9.3.) Give students a list of A.D. dates such as 1492 (Columbus discovers America) and 1812 (the War of 1812 begins); ask them to calculate how long ago these events occurred.

When students are comfortable with figuring out A.D. dates, explain that people lived before Jesus was born as well—before A.D. 1, that is. In fact, much of what elementary

A.D. 1 to A.D. 100	A.D. 101 to A.D. 200	A.D. 201 to A.D. 300
1st Century A.D.	2nd Century A.D.	3rd Century A.D.

Figure 9.4 Measuring centuries A.D.

students consider "history"—cave people, dinosaurs, the Ice Age—occurred before A.D. 1. (See Figure 9.4.) The year immediately before A.D. 1 is B.C. 1; there is no zero year. (B.C. means simply before Christ.) B.C. dates are like negative numbers, a concept your students may not be familiar with. To calculate how many years ago something happened, students must add the A.D. and B.C. figures together. Ask them to calculate, for instance, how long ago Rome was founded (753 B.C.) or Sparta defeated Athens (404 B.C.).

Students should also begin to learn how to use reference terms like the *second* century or the *twenty-first* century. Why, they may ask, do we call the century we now live in, 1901–2000, the twentieth century and not the nineteenth century? All years, after all, begin with nineteen. This confusion occurs because there was no *zero* century. A.D. 1 through A.D. 100 was the *first* century; therefore, A.D. 201 through A.D. 300 was the *second* century. Soon we will live in the *twenty-first* century, although the years will all begin with twenty.

Using simply A.D. dates, have students calculate both how many years ago an event took place and what century it was in.

A.D. 1451   First African slaves to Europe.
              Years ago _____   Century _____

A.D. 1534   Cartier claims the St. Lawrence.
              Years ago _____   Century _____

A.D. 1664   English capture New Amsterdam.
              Years ago _____   Century _____

To personalize this activity, ask students in which century they would have preferred to live.

Finally, the most difficult concept for most students is calculating centuries B.C. (See Figure 9.5.) Explain that centuries can also be counted in the period before Christ. Just as the 200s A.D. are called the third century, the 200s B.C. are the *third century* B.C. The complication is, once again, that there is no zero century B.C. You can repeat the same kind

300 B.C. to 201 B.C.	200 B.C. to 101 B.C.	100 B.C. to 1 B.C.
3rd Century B.C.	2nd Century B.C.	1st Century B.C.

Figure 9.5 Measuring centuries B.C.

of exercise for B.C. that you did for A.D. Ask students to calculate both how many years ago an event took place and what century it was in.

4000 B.C.   Agricultural communities in ancient China.
              Years ago _____   Century _____

1122 B.C.   Feudal states in China increased.
              Years ago _____   Century _____

221 B.C.   China achieves unity.
              Years ago _____   Century _____

202 B.C.   Han dynasty begins.
              Year ago _____   Century _____

As you can see, students often need explicit exercises to understand time concepts. In addition, you need to proceed slowly, one step at a time, making sure they understand dates first in A.D. and then in B.C. You typically cannot assume that everyone understands how to read timelines and can interpret the meaning of A.D. and B.C. or determine the century an event took place. At all times, examine the timelines in textbooks carefully and explain them to the class.

In this discussion, we have used the time frame or calendar of Western European civilization. Jewish and Muslim calendars are different since they use different starting points than the birth of Christ when counting the years. More advanced students can try to figure out dates using different calendars.

Exercise 9.1   *TIME CONFUSION*

Do you recall any confusion you had when you were young about time concepts? Do you think that elementary teachers should use terms such as the *nineteenth century* or the *twentieth century* while teaching? Or do you think it is better to say that in the 1800s the railroad was invented or in the 1900s the airplane was invented?

MAP AND GLOBE SKILLS

Too frequently, maps remain a mystery to adults. They simply have not gained much from their experiences in the elementary schools learning map skills. Map and globe skills are often taught for a few weeks at the beginning of the year, isolated from the rest of the social studies program. This practice has been encouraged by the fact that many publishers have traditionally started textbooks with a concentration of map skills in the first unit. That situation is changing. More publishers now provide a well-thought-out sequence of map skills in their elementary social studies series. In fact, of all the skills of the social studies—listening, small-group work, problem solving, and so on—map skills are probably receiving the most attention from textbook authors. In addition, of all the areas of elementary social studies, more computer software programs have been designed for teaching geography and map skills than for any other. Much of the computer software in the past, however, has focused on learning the state capitals and other similar low-level factual information.

Exercise 9.2   *MAP SKILLS IN TEXTBOOKS*

Check an elementary textbook series with regard to the map-skills program. If attention is being given in textbooks to map skills, why do you think so many children and adults have trouble using maps?

Although geography and map skills have been taught for generations, the research in this area is still inconclusive, especially with regard to when to introduce students to specific skills. In other words, although fancy charts on scope and sequence may state that children in grades four to six should use scale and compute distances or compare maps and make inferences, we are not really certain that all children are cognitively ready at these grade levels to learn map skills. Research has shown, however, that when teachers are well prepared and materials are carefully sequenced, most elementary students can indeed learn the basics of map "literacy."

If there is one "magic" guideline in teaching map skills it is to make the concept concrete. Relate what you are teaching to student experiences. Students in the primary grades, especially after exposure to globes, should be provided with the widest possible acquaintance with landscape features. Every school has a landscape that includes some of the geographic, geologic, and cultural features that students find symbolized on maps. But simply taking students outside for a walk is not necessarily productive. To make effective use of outdoor time, you need to plan activities before and after the trip, as well as planning the trip itself. If you do not plan carefully, you run the risk that students will think your walk is simply free time outside the classroom.

First, know what you want to achieve. This means visiting the sites your class will see ahead of time and identifying the major features; it also means communicating the purpose of your trip to your students.

There are administrative considerations to any field trip, even a short walk to local sites. Make sure you inform your principal, so that issues of legal liability and safety can be checked. Ask property owners for permission to make sure you're not trespassing, even in the case of an apparently abandoned cemetery. For longer trips, your school will no doubt have a policy about permission slips and number of chaperons.

During the trip, try to focus students' attention on what to observe. Students must understand concepts like *swamp* or *treeline* to understand the meaning of these symbols on a map. Symbols for cultural features (buildings, ruins, canals, dams, or even events like battles) must be explained; show students how the buildings they are seeing show up on maps. Finally, water and weather features are sometimes observable: dry salt lakes, tide pools, channels, coral reefs, ponds, warm and cold currents, prevailing winds. You may want to have students take pictures or fill out worksheets. Anything students can touch—rubbing their hands against rock formations, dipping fingers into ponds—will make the trip more memorable.

Finally, plan post-trip activities and use the experience in future classroom activities. Ask students their impressions and observations, and review your major objectives. Continue to bring the field trip up as a reference in future lessons. Students can make three-dimensional maps of the area they visited; tabletop maps, clay or sandbox constructions, or paper maps on the floor can also help students demonstrate graphically what they have seen. You might want to have them use blocks or boxes to show miniature buildings, schools, or neighborhoods. The more effectively children can use their experiences, the better they are able to understand the basic ideas and concepts of any field.

In learning map and globe skills, primary grade students, begin with a realization that their local area is only a tiny part of the whole world and move to a broader conception of the world. Your role in teaching children to become more careful observers as emphasized in the tips on having successful field trips is important. It is easy just to pass through an environment without noticing much about it. Skills in observing cultural and physical features can be gained through short walks, field trips, and students' trips with their families. This is especially important in the primary grades.

Because of the limitations of the local area, media—films, television programs, and so on—are usually needed to supplement students' understanding. But the importance of the local environment should never be forgotten at the elementary grade level. Frequently, teachers concentrate on a national commercial textbook and ignore what is right outside the windows of their classrooms. Given a map worksheet with directions on it, students can usually determine location of key items. But many of these same students do not know the directions in their own community. Ideally, children should learn the cardinal directions (north, south, east, and west) by the position of the sun (or shadow). Out-of-door exercises can be most helpful when introduced around the third grade.

We also recommend classroom signs or maps indicating north, south, east, and west. But what if you aren't sure where north is? This is not at all unusual. Many people drive freeways without any sense of direction; highway signs indicating east or west exit points mean little to them. Children who get perfect scores on map exercises in the classroom cannot walk or ride their bikes to a specific location using local maps because they cannot orient themselves to where they are. If you're not sure, ask or use a compass. Whenever you take students outside on walks or on field trips in a bus, indicate what general direction you are all going. Using a compass can often be fun; let students pass it around. Just as students now often know more about computers than their teachers, students sometimes have better senses of direction than their teachers. Identify these potentially helpful students as soon as possible. Often they are children who score extremely high on nonverbal and spatial areas of intelligence tests.

Along with labeling and identification of the local environment, map teaching involves a systematic, step-by-step presentation of a series of questions to help a student learn specific skills.

1. Students will identify continents by shape.
2. Students will identify hemispheres.
3. Students will find direction: compass points.
4. Students will understand and use scale.
5. Students will use a map key or legend to interpret symbols.
6. Students will identify common land and water forms.
7. Students will determine latitude and longitude.
8. Students will compare maps and draw inferences.

Each one of these skills may have to be explicitly taught. Although brighter students will absorb these concepts without much direct teaching, many other students will need as much assistance as you are able to give. Working in pairs may be helpful for many students when doing activity or worksheets on map skills; it also makes these activities more fun. Because there is often a sense of accomplishment in completing a map exercise, students have often reported liking geography and map work at the elementary level; unfortunately, this affection seems to fade in later grades.

What can be done specifically to teach these map skills? Look at the silhouettes of the continents in Figure 9.6. Ask students to label the continents. Once you are confident that students really know the shapes of the continents, move on to the identification of hemispheres and locating continents within them. Typically, students see maps only of the Western and Eastern Hemispheres. Occasionally, they are shown maps of the Northern Hemisphere (see Figure 9.7) but very rarely the Southern Hemisphere.

Yet it is important to be able to recognize continents from different perspectives. In effect, this is what happens to the astronauts. Try to show your students maps that were produced in other nations. Maps printed in Germany or Great Britain, for example, have the prime meridian in the absolute center of the map. World maps made in China or Japan show those nations in the center with the American continents squeezed into the right-hand edge. (Good sources for these maps are consuls' offices of different nations.) At first, students may say that something is wrong with these maps. This is a good lesson to show that people have different perspectives on what the world looks like.

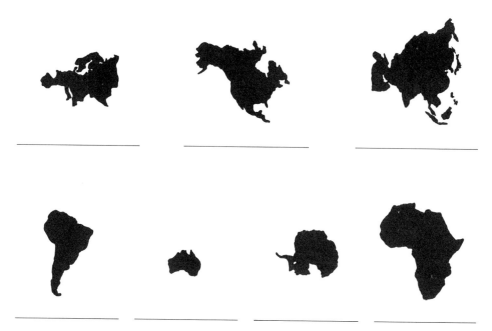

Figure 9.6 Outlines of continents.

As with chronology, specific map skills have to be taught and retaught, both as separate lessons or exercises and as integrated parts of other subjects. You cannot assume that students will transfer the learning of one map skill to another type of map skill or the use of map skills to "real life" without your help.

Almost every expert in the field has stressed the importance of introducing the globe to primary students and of explaining that globes are small models of the world. Some primary teachers bring in a model car to illustrate what they mean by a model so that students will not get confused and think that the world is the size of the globe shown in the classroom. Globes, and especially those with only water and continental land masses indicated, can help students visualize continents, a sphere, a hemisphere, and the equator. Furthermore, correlation with the science and math programs can help provide students with a general understanding of the rotation of the earth and seasonal changes. Photographs of the earth taken from outer space are also helpful in giving a new perspective on how the earth looks.

Flat maps are usually introduced in the intermediate grades, when students learn about scale, geographic grids, and the use of color and symbols in maps. Each skill must be taught and retaught separately. Students should become aware of the following ideas: (1) a map is flat and cannot show real roundness; (2) all flat maps have some distortion (although the technical reasons for different map distortions need not be explained); (3) the legend or key explains what each symbol means; and (4) the scale of the map controls the degree to which we can generalize.

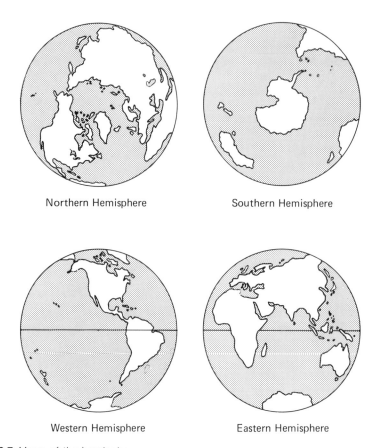

Figure 9.7 Maps of the hemispheres.
Source: "Teacher's Resource Binder—Level 3," *Communities Large and Small.* D.C. Heath 1985.

    Emphasize the information that a particular map provides. Intermediate-level students can be exposed to different kinds of maps: Students need to learn to interpret a temperature map, a time-zone map, a telephone-area-code map, a historical map (of the Roman Empire, for example, where the boundaries of Europe are different from what they are today), and a political map (of the United States, for instance, showing the number of members each state has in the House of Representatives).

    Intermediate students must also learn how to find places on a map. Most maps use a letter–number index to give the location of smaller cities or streets. Each student should have his or her own map to practice finding different places by using such indexes. Some teachers like to start this activity with small groups, but you must take care that each student learns the appropriate skill and that one student does not do all the work for the whole group.

No. 5. Center of Population: 1790 to 1980

["Center of population" is that point at which an imaginary flat, weightless, and rigid map of the United States would balance if weights of identical value were placed on it so that each weight represented the location of one person on the date of the census]

YEAR [1]	North latitude			West longitude			Approximate location
	°	′	″	°	′	″	
1790 (Aug. 2)	39	16	30	76	11	12	23 miles east of Baltimore, MD
1850 (June 1)	38	59	0	81	19	0	23 miles southeast of Parkersburg, WV
1900 (June 1)	39	9	36	85	48	54	6 miles southeast of Columbus, IN
1950 (Apr. 1)	38	50	21	88	9	33	8 miles north-northwest of Olney, Richland County, IL
1960 (Apr. 1)	38	35	58	89	12	35	In Clinton Co. about 6½ miles northwest of Centralia, IL
1970 (Apr. 1)	38	27	47	89	42	22	5.3 miles east-southeast of the Mascoutah City Hall in St. Clair County, IL
1980 (Apr. 1)	38	8	13	90	34	26	¼ mile west of De Soto in Jefferson County, MO

Figure 9.8 Center of population 1790–1980. U.S. Department of Commerce.
Source: Statistical Abstract of the United States 1981 (Washington, D.C.: U.S. Government Printing Office).

In the upper-grade levels, teachers should continually emphasize the interpretation and critical thinking aspects of reading a map. How will a map help answer certain questions? As seen in Figure 9.8, students can use a map and a table to recognize a trend such as the shifting center of population in the United States. Ask both specific questions (where was the center of population in 1860) and broader ones (what does this map tell us about our country?)

An activity that is both fun and instructive is that of comparing maps of Pangaea. Have students look carefully at a world map (top, Figure 9.9), especially the western Atlantic coast of Africa. Tell students to think of the continents as pieces in a jigsaw puzzle. Where would Africa fit? This relationship among the continents was first noticed in 1912 by Alfred Wegener, a German scientist. He proposed the continental drift theory, that continents had moved and drifted from one large land mass, called Pangaea (center, Figure 9.9). Research has upheld Wegener's basic idea, although scientists have made some changes in his theory. The bottom map (Figure 9.9) shows how present-day scientists think the earth looked more than 200 million years ago. Ask students what differences they see among the three maps. Then ask them to explain a bumper sticker on a car reading "Reunite Pangaea!" and why the bumper sticker is really a joke. Students who want to learn more about this can be advised to read about plate tectonics in encyclopedias and other sources.

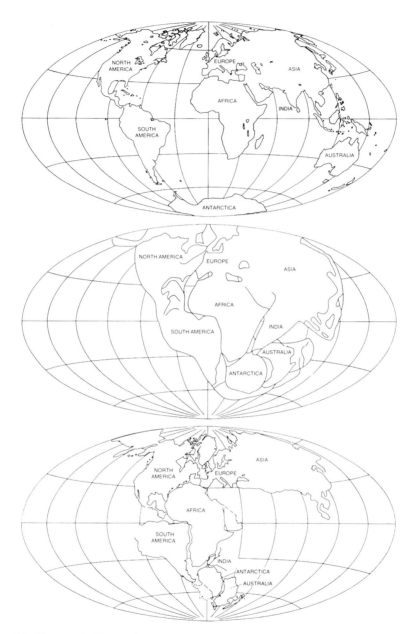

Figure 9.9 Changes in the continents.

Source: Adapted from "Alfred Wegener and the Hypothesis of Continental Drift" by A. Hallam. Copyright
© 1975 by Scientific American, Inc. All rights reserved.

Notice that we have thus far emphasized map-*reading* skills. Map*making* (or making one's own charts, cartoon drawings, etc.) is more difficult than simply reading or interpreting a map or table. Making maps requires visualization abilities. Mapmaking is the supreme test of map understanding; it may be an appropriate activity only for selected students. With proper instruction, however, most students enjoy map production.

The steps in making a map are somewhat similar to steps taken in making charts and graphs. They usually include (1) collecting or observing data, (2) organizing or simplifying the data, (3) planning the map (chart) in terms of scale, and (4) drafting or drawing the map or chart. Usually, students must be taught each separate stage before they can draw the map. One of the advantages of mapmaking is that students can present what they have learned, especially local data, in a simplified format.

Because of the time involved and the visual skills needed to make maps, many teachers ask students to place data on already assembled globes and maps. Unbreakable globes and wall maps that can be marked with crayons and washed off are especially useful. Even inexpensive outline maps (frequently found in teachers' guides for map exercises for students) that have a minimum amount of information on them can be used to real advantage.

We hope that teaching of map skills will move beyond the rote memory format that in the past has been typical of many map skills programs. Do you yourself recall the many hours you probably spent on longitude and latitude? How often in real life have you been asked to practice longitude and latitude? We should not forget that most adults commonly use road, newspaper, and magazine maps and do not have to compute longitude and latitude. But more importantly, we should try to teach students that map and globes are designed to help us to think. Maps in textbooks and globes should be used throughout the year and not just during a September unit. In this way, the teaching of map skills will enhance critical thinking, an area that needs as much attention as possible in the elementary school.

TECHNOLOGIES FOR THE SOCIAL STUDIES

How can we use technology effectively in teaching knowledge, skills, and values in the social studies? Technology in the social studies classroom can be divided into two major classes: (1) audiovisual media such as film, filmstrips, television, and videocassettes; and (2) computers and telecommunication. The first category can be considered *noninteractive* media, since the viewer cannot easily change the presentation. The wide range of materials in this category is often very useful in teaching social studies. These media can introduce new material, present information by visual means, increase motivation, or reinforce major ideas in a unit. Films, television, and the like can contribute an emotional dimension to your objectives. Much of our understanding about the Holocaust, for example, or about the recent famine in Africa has come through films and pictures.

The video revolution is a technological trend with great potential for classroom use. More and more teachers have videocassette recorders (VCRs) and frequently record programs at home to show to their classes. This offers an increasingly popular way to expand students' horizons; tapes of different nations or current events can be shown at timely moments in the classroom. You may have to do some editing, however, for best results. Copyright laws may eventually restrict the teacher's right to record from television; presently, teachers mays record anything. *Permanent* retention of videotaped programs, however, is a violation of copyright law.

The use of videocassette or videodisc technology should continue to make it possible for classroom teachers to tap the wide range of information that is available. Costs are expected to decline, and more will no doubt be done in these areas in the future. These techniques offer you the ability to show images from a wide variety of sources to make more concrete the material you are teaching. Videocassette technology can be especially useful in studying a culture such as the Balinese, about which teachers do not normally have a lot of material.

By using noninteractive media in the classroom, you can also help students become critical viewers both inside and outside the classroom walls (see Chapter 5 on the teaching of controversial issues and Chapter 8 on communication skills). Encourage students to listen to certain television programs that may be worthwhile and then discuss them in class. Always encourage students to keep up with current events through newspapers, magazines, and television.

The second important area of technology is *interactive* media: computers and telecommunication. The number of computers in schools will continue to grow. Parents and state legislatures put considerable pressure on schools in the belief that their children are being cheated if computers are not immediately available for educational purposes in the classrooms. Especially as costs go down, more computers will be placed in schools. Therefore, efforts are continuing to train both preservice and experienced teachers to use computers in their classrooms.

However, the physical placement of computers influences how computers are used in the schools. Is there a separate room with many computers that students are rotated into for specific purposes? Or is there one computer in the classroom to be used only by that teacher? Each of these arrangements has an impact on the use of computers in the social studies. In general, lab periods focus more on teaching and reinforcement of math and reading skills. If the computer is in the classroom, it is more likely to be used in other subject areas like social studies. Teachers who are flexible and persistent can work around almost any physical arrangement in using computers effectively.

First, computers function as word processors. Students are more likely to revise and edit what they have written if they use a computer. This means that written assignments in the social studies, especially longer ones, are promising projects for student word processing. Students can also learn to use software that checks spelling, a boon to all.

There are mechanical problems, however, that need to be addressed in using word processing. Children need to learn to type. Usually, students don't acquire this skill until about the sixth grade, although many schools have begun to introduce it as early as third grade. Students are often frustrated at "hunting and pecking." Unless they know how to type with some degree of accuracy, they spend more time correcting spelling errors than thinking about what they have written. In addition, students need to become familiar with the word processing program (*Bank Street Writer* is probably the most popular) that is to be used on the computer.

With these limitations in mind, teachers in the upper-grade levels should be open to word processing possibilities. More and more students at the middle school and junior high school levels now hand in assignments written with the use of a computer. Many students *do* have the skills necessary to use the word processing capabilities of a computer both at home and in the classroom. This, however, raises the issue of who has access to computers. Some argue that schools will eventually need to provide a computer at home for each student, so that no single student will be penalized for not having access to a computer at home. The costs of such an arrangement are beyond implementation at present.

In addition to doing word processing, computers can retrieve data. More and more social science data banks will be available to help students find information. At present, however, most of the software for social studies programs using data banks is designed for the high school level. *Scholastic* has been a leader in the use of data banks in geography and United States history. The geography program provides information about more than 100 nations in its data bank. Students can access general information about a given nation or answer specific questions such as what its major resources are. Most of these programs enable students to collect local data and add it to the program. Unfortunately, using data banks requires more computer skills on the part of the teacher as well as the students. This remains a stumbling block for implementation of data bases in general, although individual teachers have successfully "banked" information on, for example, Indian tribes in their states or particular nations.

As more people become more skilled, the trend will continue for them to use computers for data banks. More and more libraries at the university level as well as the Educational Resources Information Center (ERIC) are using computers to retrieve information. The card catalogue will probably become a thing of the past even in public libraries. Students will be able to tap into the larger data bases maintained by libraries to find information about what is happening in the stock market or current data about a single nation. In part, this is what we mean when we refer to telecommunication, the growing technology that links students and teachers with resources from every part of the globe. A number of corporations are presently trying to recruit educators to use their services, but many of their products are designed primarily for business use. Telecommunications are for the most part too expensive and inflexible for use in the average elementary classroom.

The question is how long it will take these technologies to make their way into the classroom, especially at the elementary level. When data retrieval does become feasible at the elementary school level, it should offer a much wider potential of finding and obtaining recent information about the global community than is now available. Some traditional library skills will no longer be necessary, but students *will* need the substantially more sophisticated computer skills than we now teach.

The third possible use of computers is in the presentation of data. As we have mentioned previously, it takes a higher level of skill for students to make their own map or chart than to interpret one. However, if computer programs are available to students, this job can be made easier for them. Simple statistical packages to help students find the mean (average) and significance of their own local data already exist. Present programs in this area still require some degree of computer sophistication, but in the future, simplified graphics and statistics will no doubt make them easier for both teachers and students to use.

The fourth and most common use of computers in the social studies at present is with commercially prepared software. How do computers fit into the picture of teaching skills and concepts in the social studies? Computer software has great promise for teaching skills and concepts. Software can set up activities for students to investigate such as the workings of a complex economic system. Students can make choices and decisions, and the results of their actions are immediately available to them. Such manipulation of data is not easily accomplished in traditional formats such as textbook teaching or a simulation not using a computer.

Software can also provide the opportunity for reinforcing basic skills, such as acquiring information from maps, graphs, charts, and tables. It can be designed to increase social participation skills, as when a small group works through a problem on a computer and must achieve some consensus on how to go about problem solving. The computer experience need not isolate students from each other. Potentially, computers can allow students to practice a wide variety of essential social studies skills.

But what is the reality? The prospect of teaching and using software for the social studies is discouraging to many teachers. First, the amount of commercial social studies software is limited compared to that available in other areas such as mathematics. Some publishers' software catalogues do not even have a subject area for the social studies. Second, the software that does exist concentrates mainly on drill and practice in which students review facts—names of continents, oceans, presidents. Unfortunately, this kind of software holds little interest and provides little motivation. As a result, many teachers look on the available social studies software without enthusiasm or recommend the purchase of poor software simply because nothing better is available.

The most promising area for computer use is simulations. Most social studies simulations are presently designed for secondary-level usage. You need to look carefully at publisher's statements on grade level, since publishers may give a wider range than is usable in order to sell the product. Simulations can tap high-level skills, and they can motivate student users.

The number of software programs available will probably increase. As for all materials used in the classroom, there is a need for teacher evaluation. Professional organizations now review software, as the National Council for the Social Studies does in its journal *Social Education*. Computer journals that cover all subject areas such as *Electronic Learning* also contain reviews of new products and software. In addition, many state and local organizations now devote an increasing number of conference sessions to the use of computers for instructional purposes. Exhibit areas at conferences are filled with computers. All of these efforts will probably make it easier for teachers to find good programs to use in the future. But the single factor restricting the use of computers now is the limitations of teachers. Although society is pressing for technologically competent students, many teachers are holding back students because of their own inability to use computers in a classroom.

The future of technologies for use in the social studies looks promising. Teachers soon will be able to tap wide resources that can help to expand the environment of students. Teachers will need to keep up with what is happening in these areas, however, and school districts will need to devote more in-service time to making their staffs familiar with the uses of new technologies.

Exercise 9.3   *EVALUATION OF SOFTWARE*

Run through three pieces of computer software on a given grade level at the elementary school. What are the strengths of each program? Disadvantages? Would you use this software in the classroom if available to you?

SUGGESTED READINGS

Buggey, JoAnne, and Kracht, James. "Geographic Learning." In *Elementary School Social Studies: Research as a Guide to Practice*. Bulletin 79. Washington, D.C.: National Council for the Social Studies, 1986, pp. 55–67. Good in showing that the research base on teaching geography is limited.

Diem, Richard A. *Computers in the Classroom*. How-to-Do-It Series 2, no. 14. Washington, D.C.: National Council for the Social Studies, 1981. Helpful for beginners.

Heinich, Robert; Molenda, Michael; and Russell, James D. *Instructional Media*. 2d ed. New York: Macmillan, 1985. Standard text on media.

CHAPTER

10

Evaluating Children's Progress in the Social Studies

In this chapter we describe the purposes and functions of evaluation in the social studies from various perspectives. We also discuss techniques of gathering data for evaluation of learning and explore ideas for matching data collection with instructional activities and communicating the data to parents and children. Finally, we present themes for evaluating our instruction. The following topics are covered:

1. Perceptions of Evaluation
2. Evaluation Techniques and Tools
3. Organizing Evaluation
4. Using Evaluation Data

PERCEPTIONS OF EVALUATION

Evaluation is something like beauty: Its meaning depends, in great part, on who views it. As teachers we play the pivotal role. We can manipulate the outcome of the scene. By examining the motivation of the other actors—the child, the parent, the school system— we can begin to get a better sense of the potential that our own role offers.

The Child

Remembering your own experience or that of your children is a good place to start when examining the impact that evaluation can have on a child. How many of us remember report-card day as a positive experience in our lives? Did we have a clue about why we got

197

the reports we did? Was the report itself important, or was the response our parents and friends had about our report what we remember?

From the perspective of a child, evaluation is synonymous with grades and report cards. Unfortunately, the connotation is most often pejorative. Children understand very early that grades represent a mysterious power over their lives. They know when they are grouped for instruction by ability. They are tuned in to any indication that a teacher may, or may not, like them and, seeking confirmation of their suspicions, they connect that indication to the grade they receive.

When questioned, children often do not establish a connection between work habits and grades. They usually do not link final results to a series of smaller steps in preparing for a test or project or presentation. They see evaluation as something outside their control. For many children, grades have little to do with learning or pride of accomplishment.

The Parent

Parents want their children to succeed. They want you as a teacher and the school to recognize their child for the special person he or she is. They want assurance that you know their son or daughter. Parents are often amazed to learn about aspects of their child's behavior that they have not seen at home.

Grades and reports worry parents because they represent judgments about their children—the first indications about how the children will do in life outside the home. They want to know if their children measure up to others of the same age. Most parents see reports and grades as stepping-stones or barriers to "the good life."

Parents want to know what their child is supposed to be learning. Many will want your suggestions about how they can help their daughter or son achieve what is required. Some may use reports as ways to either punish or reward their child at home.

The Teacher

Typically, we see evaluation as a necessary evil. It is a function we are forced to perform as a way of communicating how children are doing to them, their families, and the school system. Often, we do not agree with the way we are required to evaluate children: standardized tests and testing in general often intrude on the spontaneity of instructional time.

We intend to treat each child fairly as we collect impressions of her or his progress. We are channeled by our school system to work toward instructional objectives according to our grade level and subjects. We realize that these objectives may not be the most appropriate for every student. We are frustrated at our lack of time and energy and our inability to attend to every child's needs more adequately.

We are held accountable by parents to perform miracles with their children and by the school to produce the best possible test-score results. Sometimes it seems as though no one, not even the children, is accountable to us. We do not like being held responsible by both parents and the school for producing the results they both desire when not given enough support from either group.

The School System

Evaluation is the principal means of quantifying how students are doing in school. Keeping records of individual student progress is an essential way to communicate with parents and other schools about that student. Reducing the data to grade-level equivalents and numbers or letters is a more efficient way to communicate about individual student progress.

The more evaluative data you collect on students, the better analysis you can make of your programs. Decisions about new curricula cannot be made without data on student progress. Without standardized test data you cannot easily compare your district with other districts.

Student test data are also helpful in the evaluation of teachers. Other factors are important, but you should not throw out the insight that test scores offer to your performance over a long period.

The Experts

Broad views about the value of evaluation suggest that it should serve all actors—the child, the parent, the teacher, and the school system—of the school-achievement scene. Elliot Eisner listed five functions of evaluation:[1]

1. To diagnose what a child knows and thereby point toward appropriate instruction;
2. To provide data for the revision of curriculum both for the classroom teacher and the system;
3. To compare what children can be before and after instruction and with and without instruction;
4. To anticipate educational needs of children as they progress through a curriculum;
5. To determine if instructional objectives are being met.

Even though we may empathize with the wariness we see in the perspective of each of these groups, it is also important to be informed about the potential benefits all the people involved—students, teachers, parents, and school systems—stand to gain from an effective evaluation process. All these perspectives can be seen as interrelated. Notice that each perspective sees evaluation as a decision-making tool, not an end in itself. No one would object to a process where evaluation is an integral part of instruction, providing the momentum to move instructional effort toward some direction.

---

[1] Elliot Eisner, *The Educational Imagination*, 2d ed. (New York: Macmillan, 1985), p. 192.

Experts would want to change aspects of each perception described. They would want children to participate more in decisions about their learning. They would want parents to understand that evaluation is part of a process, not a final judgment about their child or a weight to be held over a child's head. They would want teachers to make greater use of evaluation results to guide their instructional planning. They would want school systems to collect evaluation data in the most unobtrusive, least time-consuming way possible.

These diverse perspectives are useful to recall when you examine your thoughts about the purposes of evaluation in children's learning. By focusing on the possible motivations for these various views of evaluation, you can more adequately communicate about a child's, or a group's, learning. To organize evaluation, however, you need more than empathy. You need to explore a repertoire of evaluation techniques and tools in order to decide which purposes and techniques best match.

EVALUATION TECHNIQUES AND TOOLS

The social studies aim at a variety of goals. Knowledge is important, but skills, values, and citizenship are equally important. Achieving sound evaluation results in such a wide-ranging subject requires multiple measures and methods. In this section we explore some of the data-gathering possibilities for evaluating children's progress in social studies. In the following section we reflect on the most appropriate times for using these techniques. Finally, we discuss using these data to communicate progress.

Observation

Teachers continually make judgments based on observations. They move a child so that he or she can do quiet work. They give more practice examples of how to calculate map distances when they see that several children need it. They compliment a child for picking up the project-work-area mess without being reminded. Rarely, however, do they keep records of these observations for purposes of communicating social studies progress.

It would be impossible, and not always germane, to record every incident of a child's behavior for evaluation purposes. But there is a useful middle point between recording nothing and recording everything. Observational data are especially useful for the social studies goal of citizenship. Objectives for this goal may be general and year-long such as "being responsible for myself and my things," or they may be related to a specific unit that involves small-group work with an objective of "sharing information for the benefit of the group."

You can, in the first type of objective, keep note cards handy to write the child's name and the date and a sentence reporting the behavior related to the objective (Figure 10.1). Some teachers like to send these "Super Citizen" cards home with children as they happen. Others prefer to accumulate the notes in a folder so that they can be used with parents at

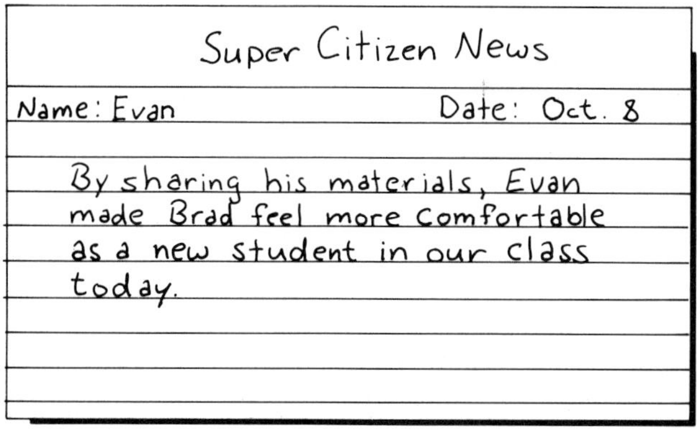

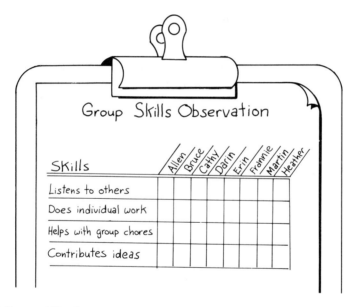

Figure 10.1 Super citizen news.

Figure 10.2 Group skills observation.

conference time. To benefit from this evaluation tool, keep a few specific objectives in mind to focus upon.

Observation by tallies is a convenient technique when data on particular behaviors are needed (Figure 10.2). Once the form is prepared, carrying it about on a clipboard during the monitoring of group work and recording what individual children do becomes a manageable task.

Observation as an evaluation technique is best suited, then, to situations of social interaction and independent work habits and group responsibility. Everyone agrees that these skill areas are crucial and must be developed. But student behaviors in these skill areas are not restricted to a part of the school day designated as social studies time. To use this observational technique, you must periodically schedule time to focus on these behaviors during a variety of classroom activities.

Sampling Work

Collecting samples of a child's expressive products over time is an important way to amass evaluative data. Drawing and writing efforts are particularily suited to this technique. Dating the samples and accumulating them in individual folders for each child is a management task for which children can be taught to become responsible. Teachers often have children choose their "best" story or drawing of the week or of the unit to file in their work folders. (See Figure 10.3.) Other teachers believe that sending all of the child's work home in a weekly folder for the parent to examine and return is a more consistent way to maintain communication about progress between the school and the home. But sending all of the work home erases a data base that is useful to accumulate for comparative purposes. With such a collection, the differences in what a child wrote or drew in September and December become striking. All members of the learning triad—child, teacher, and parent—can find edification and satisfaction in reviewing work portfolios.

Group products such as murals, roll movies, and skits do not fit into a single portfolio. You can informally record individual contributions to these products as they are presented and have the notes placed in the work folders. For intermediate-grade classes, you can ask that individual children write their own file notes about what they contributed to a group product.

Paper and Pencil Tests

Paper and pencil testing is most suited for assessing social studies goals in the knowledge and thinking skills areas. In our test-dominated age the use of paper and pencil testing in the social studies is often taken for granted, almost as a cultural imperative. Furthermore, tests provide a relatively easy means to gather data on what children know and can do. The data from objective-type test items are easily counted for ranking and averaging. Tests included in textbook-series materials make the chore of preparing tests easier. In addition, tests accompanying texts often have better coverage of textbook content and are written more clearly, especially multiple-choice questions.

Tests are here to stay. Most teachers use the commercially prepared tests that accompany textbook series. Feeling compelled to provide numerical evidence of student progress has pushed many teachers to reliance on textbook-related tests. Thus the content of their teaching tends to be tied to the textbook. You may think this technique of content selection is too narrow and limiting. Or you may believe that the content of texts you use

Last year my family and I went on a to Ohio. It took six hours to get to New Jersey where we stopped for the night. We stayed at the Holiday Inn. When we woke up we could see the Statue of Liberty.

At twelve that afternoon we left to go to Ohio it took one hour to get there.

We stayed there for three weeks.

My greatgrandpa ownstwenty acres of land and fifteen acres of water. When we were going to go into the lake we saw a dead cat fish on the shore.

I took my raft out and jumped into the lake.

There were big cat tailes sticking out of the water. There were at least one thousand sticking out of the water. Me and my dad went through the cat tails. The water was green and it seemed like we were in the jungle.

While we were there me my brother and my sister got to see my dad's cousins uncle and aunt.

I got to shoot a bow and arrow.

My dad borrowed a motor boat from a friend I got to drive the boat at full speed. My mom was scared when I let go of the stearing wheel and went in circles.

When we came back my grandpa was mowing the lawn with his tractor I got to drive the tractor.

THE END

written by: Greg Lanker, September

THE SUB HUNT

It was the day after Christmas and Mr. Smith got a call from the president saying, "Theres a U.S.S.R. sub in the Persian Gulf and Iwant you to find it and destroy it".

Mr. Smith was supprised that the president would give him such a order.

The next day Mr. Smith got twenty-five men and they all got in a p3.c orion. They turned on the engiens, taxied down the run way, and took off.

It took three hours to get to the Persian Gulf.

They turned on the radar and started looking for the sub.

One hour went by, two hours went by, three hours went by. Then finaly after three hours and 30 menutes went by they finaly found it.

Then they got a torpedo and droped it from 9 thousand feet in the air.

It was a direct hit the sub was destroyed.

THE END

Writen by: Greg Lanker, January

Figure 10.3 These writing samples show a student's progress from September to January. The earlier sample (a) recounts a recent experience. The January sample (b) uses fictional elements to elaborate on current events discussed in class and contains plot structure and dialogue. Spelling and usage problems can be worked on through the writing-editing process discussed in Chapter 8. (Samples written by Greg Lanker, Toyon School, fifth grade, Berryessa School District, San Jose, CA; Dick Pope, teacher.)

is appropriate as a basis for instruction. Either way, you need to be a critical consumer of prepared tests.

There are several criteria for selecting tests or test items. The principle criterion is to verify that the items are expressive of your instructional objectives. They should be expressive both in content covered and the level of thinking about the content you have led the children to experience. Choosing the kinds of test items that children have experienced, or that you teach them to work with, is another criterion. Providing sufficient items to check individual objectives is still another criterion. That is, we know more about a student's mastery of a concept if the student answers several questions about it.

Beyond the general criteria for test and item selection, each type of test item brings special considerations.

1. Short Answer.   This type of item is typically a statement with a key word or phrase missing. Which of the following pairs are the better items?

    a. The three large nations of North America _____.
    b. The three large nations of North America _____.
       1. Use the same language
       2. Have similar governments
       3. Have the same amount of land
       4. Have the same number of people

    a. Earth is a _____, and the sun is a _____.
    b. Earth is a _____, and the sun is a _____.
       1. moon   2. star   3. planet   4. pole

Both "a" items are inferior. They depend on answer invention. Some semantically appropriate answers, such as "fun" or "big" or "all-purple on the map," may not have any relation to the content covered. How many reasonable possibilities can you think of for the three large nations of North America? What we have done here to improve the items is transform the short answer into a multiple-choice item.

Short-answer items, and all pencil–paper items, can be criticized as testing reading more than knowledge of the social studies content. Should we give children a grade in the social studies that is really related to their reading ability more than, perhaps, their social studies knowledge? Some teachers believe we should try to find out what a child knows about the social studies content. They find that poor readers can respond correctly to the items if they are read aloud with the possible answers.

2. Matching.   Using the process of elimination is a good thinking strategy. Matching items should prompt children to use that strategy. As with all test-item types, children need practice with this kind of item before they are tested using it.

Which of these items is best?

a. You have read about Native Americans, white settlers, and the buffalo. Now, draw lines below connecting the part of the buffalo with the way that part was used by the Plains tribes.

hair	bow strings
hide	food
horns	mattresses
meat	spoons
sinew	bow strings
	mattresses

b. Match the following countries with the continents in which they are located.

Chad	Africa
Chile	Asia
Finland	Europe
India	North America
Mexico	South America

c. Match the best example with its economic categories.

services	skateboard
goods	trip to Disney World
resources	haircut
	gold coins
	farmland
	sleeping
	running a race

The best item is "a", according to testmakers, because it has uneven lists. The child must use process of elimination as well as either direct recall of what has been studied or analysis of what might be possible. Note that in "a", but not "b" or "c", the choices are listed in alphabetical order. This saves the child time when rereading the list. Other pointers for this type of item include not making the list too long and not mixing categories within the lists. Item "c" commits all of these *faux pas.*

3. True–False. This type of item invites guessing with a higher probability of being correct than any other type of test item. For this reason, and the tendency for this type of item to be written at a low level of cognitive difficulty, test-construction experts do not favor true–false items as reliable measures of what children know.

Which of these items is better, a or b, in the following examples?

1.a. _____ Cars are an example of economic goods.
1.b. _____ Cars are goods.

2.a. _____ Henry Hudson was a Spanish explorer.
2.b. _____ Henry Hudson explored the Carribean.

Did you choose "1.a" and "2.b" as better items? (Yes, we know that neither 2.a nor 2.b is a correct statement.) Both are clearer statements of the content. It could be argued, for example, that cars are goods and Henry Hudson was an explorer, albeit not for Spain. Inserting Spanish before explorer tests care in reading possibly more than knowledge about Henry Hudson's exploits. If our objective is related to critical reading, 2.a could be counted as a good item.

Writing true–false items is more difficult than answering them. It is easy to give away the answer to this type of item. All you have to do is use qualifiers such as "all" or "every" that usually signal an incorrect statement. True–false items seem to inspire dispute.

To extend true–false items beyond the level of factual recall, you can ask that children rewrite false items to make them true or tell one more thing they know about true items. The best use of this type of item is as a critical thinking exercise.

4. Multiple Choice.   Testing experts find that this type of item, if well written, is a "better" test of knowledge than other objective-type items. With more answer options, it lessens the chance of getting the correct answer by guessing.

Which of these items is better?

1. Traders from Latin America in the late 1500s brought to Europe:
    a. cloth   b. guns   c. sugar   d. aluminum
2. Which of the following is a product that traders in the late 1500s brought to Europe from Latin America?
    a. cloth   b. sugar   c. both a and b   d. neither a nor b

The first item is straightforward. Items that combine answer choices are tricky and confusing. Also, statements are easier to complete than questions.

Combining multiple choice with map and chart or graph reading is a valuable application of this type of item. The choices, again, should be plausible and not combinations or negations.

5. Essay.   Essays as a technique for assessing a child's knowledge are emerging from a long period of eclipse. Previously, we were persuaded that a more objective assessment of children's knowledge was one that could be counted and quantified, permitting us to compare individuals and groups. We now recognize the centrality of written expression in all curricular areas for assessing higher levels of thinking. Children who can talk about or write about facts and ideas show that they have structured new information. They not only recall and classify information as an objective-type test item would require, but they also can put the information into a context.

Children need frequent practice and instruction in organization of ideas before this type of testing can be legitimately used. Essays should not be used to test factual recall but to have children relate ideas by combining, differentiating, sequencing, juxtaposing, and extending logically. How these thinking tasks are prompted should be developed carefully.

Which of the following essay items is better?

1. Tell about the Constitutional Convention.
2. Describe two reasons why the Constitutional Convention was important to Americans in 1877.

Essay items for elementary students need to include an outline for the response. The second item could be further improved by suggesting the kinds of problems—between states and with other nations—the Constitution resolved.

What parts of these test items are most useful to a middle-grade student?

1. Compare a desert and a woodland forest region in terms of climate and resources.
2. Compare the Sahara and the Appalachian regions.

Both items can be criticized. Whereas the first item helps the student begin an answer outline by supplying "climate" and "resources," it does not supply a specific example of the regional types for the student. The result may be that the student spends all of his or her time trying to recall the name of a desert and a woodland forest. Or the student may write in a general way about the two regions, which may not be what the teacher would consider correct given the difficulty of generalizing about regions as disparate as the Gobi, the Sonora, and the Sahara. The second item specified two regions without giving the student a clue about the criteria on which to compare them.

Self-evaluations

Taking responsibility for independent learning is one of the major, overarching goals of schooling. You can assist children toward this goal by providing frequent occasions for self-evaluation. This technique is appropriate in all of the major social studies areas. Ask children to assess their knowledge and skills through questions such as :

What do you need to spend more time on?
What areas of this topic do you feel you know?
What did you learn today in your research reading?

This can lead them to formulate plans for themselves based on what they see as significant.

My Work Habits and Study Skills

Name:

	Poor	Fair	Good	Comment
Turn in work on time				
Plan my work before the last minute				
Seek help when I do not understand				
Use my time to get work done first				
Help others in my work group				
Know where my supplies are				
Help keep the room clean				
Take my turn doing chores				

Figure 10.4 Self-evaluation form.

Teachers find that self-reports about study habits and citizenship skills are useful data to collect periodically (Figure 10.4).

Self-evaluation reports can also be tied to specific units in which tasks and choices have been specified. Often known as a "contract," this kind of listing helps some students keep focused on what they need to do (Figure 10.5). Forms such as this give an overview of a topic to the student that may have the effect of making a unit more coherent and cohesive to children. The hope is that by lengthening their view of school tasks from the period or day to the week or unit, children will begin to take more responsibility for completing their work.

Conferences

Talking individually with children about how they are doing is a powerful evaluation technique. It will enable you to bridge the distance between the child and his or her paper and pencil efforts. Initially, many children are timid about discussing their work with teachers in a conference setting, but by the second round, children usually take this kind of scrutiny in stride. Individual conferences should focus on work samples and self-evaluations and any observational data that you may have collected. Leading children to see their work in terms of the instructional objectives often sheds a new light on the "why" of school assignments.

Contract for Desert Study

Name: agrees to complete this work

Task:

	DATE	DONE	COMMENTS
Read my text section and teach my group.			
View group filmstrip and contribute to summary.			
Write safari card on desert animal.			
Complete desert map and identify major deserts.			
Contribute 2 items to Desert Trivia.			

Figure 10.5 Contract for desert study.

ORGANIZING EVALUATION

Planning for instruction includes planning for evaluation. Once we have instructional objectives selected for a unit topic, or for the year, it is time to plan how and what data to collect on individual progress toward these objectives. Categories from the taxonomies of educational goals can help you sharpen your thinking about both the content and the method of your evaluation plans.

Relating Objectives and Process Levels

Checking your objectives against a sequence of processes ordered by level of difficulty will assist you in thinking about evaluation. The higher categories of the taxonomies require more practice and greater emphasis on projects that students organize and present. Evaluation of higher levels of thinking need to be supported by instruction and practice on equivalent levels as well as on the cognitive levels that precede them. For example, asking children to interpret weather information on an outline map of the United States requires that they (1) know the locational geography of the United States and (2) recognize the weather symbols and their meanings.

Knowledge

Recall: Names, locates, repeats, lists, describes
   Example: Pledge of Allegiance
Comprehension: Gives examples, tells meaning of, interprets
   Example: Defines family in own words
Application: Explains sequence or process, solves problem, demonstrates
   Example: Shows how to find east in morning
Analysis: Outlines, categorizes, relates events or causes
   Example: Puts clothes and shelter into climate groups
Synthesis: Investigates, revises, creates, presents
   Example: Presents a play about homesteading in Oklahoma
Evaluation: Ranks, judges, compares, using criteria
   Example: After listing basic needs, chooses items to keep for a survival hike in desert

Values

Receiving: Listens, observes
Responding: Participates, complies
Valuing: Initiates[2]

Cross-checking objectives with these taxonomies can alert you to instructional gaps. If your objective requires that children create shoebox dioramas of pioneer life, which is a synthesis-level task, you must prepare them for it. For diorama making to be a meaningful, not a copying, task children must first gather information about the activities, for example, that were performed inside a settler's cabin. They must see pictures and hear and read stories about candle making; wool spinning; root cellar; dry, brine, and larded food preservation; and hearthside cooking.

Cross-checking or analyzing what children must know or be able to do before they can complete an activity is known as *task analysis.* Planning for evaluation should include this step. It is an essential way to examine unit and lesson objectives. Once you are aware of the prerequisite knowledge and skills children need to perform an assignment, you can design a more realistic, meaningful, and successful sequence of instruction. A further benefit is that this exercise produces a structure that you can use to make your objectives clearer to students.

Relating Objectives and Instruction

Another indication of what kinds of data you need to collect comes from the instructional objectives themselves. If children are to learn the names of local landmarks and their

---

[2] Partial list adapted from Benjamin Bloom (ed.) et al., *Taxonomy of Educational Goals. Handbook I—Cognitive Domain* (New York: McKay, 1956); David R. Krathwohl, ed., *Taxomomy of Educational Objectives: The Classification of Goals. Handbook II—Affective Domain* (New York: McKay, 1964).

locations, opportunities to practice with blank maps, map puzzles, and spelling drills are needed. Pencil and paper techniques for mastery may be indicated. If the instructional objective is that children are to work productively in a group, they need to be taught appropriate group behaviors and to be given practice in working in group situations. Teacher observation complemented by group and self-evaluation and conferences may be necessary. If the objective is that children be able to distinguish between valid and invalid conclusions, instruction in supporting conclusions with data and argument must be given, followed by guided practice with appropriate reading exercises. Teacher observation of student discussions and writing samples that support or argue against conclusions is appropriate.

Scheduling Data Collection

Deciding when to collect evaluative data is a third element of the organizing task. Benjamin Bloom's ideas are useful for this task as well. He distinguished between formative and summative evaluation.[3] *Formative evaluation*, the collection of data about how the child is doing as he or she works through an instructional sequence, is crucial if you are to strive for mastery learning by every child. Formative evaluation gives you information about what needs to be retaught for which individuals. This approach to evaluation places the burden of the child's learning progress in your hands. It suggests that you should revise their instruction as they go according to the progress your students make.

Data on what children know about a topic should be collected at the beginning of a unit. For middle grades, this may be done using a pencil and paper pretest or an attitudinal technique. For primary students, teacher observation and group discussions are the more indicated sources of data. Use these data to select students for cooperative-learning groups, placing some of the more informed students with each group. These data may indicate that more direct-teaching time should be spent teaching vocabulary items and providing more concrete and visual experiences.

Data collected during the unit are also useful. Individual worksheets and projects need to be monitored and returned for improvement or some small-group reteaching time. Group efforts need to be evaluated in terms of work habits and cooperation on an almost daily basis.

Formative evaluation pays off for both group and individual efforts. By coaching and monitoring group projects you can guarantee better final projects and presentations. The same is true for individual efforts. Formative evaluation of both content and process objectives serves to keep the unit dynamics intact and flowing.

Summative evaluation is the point in instruction when there is a collective pause to add up and reflect upon what has been learned. It is the moment when projects are presented or when tests are taken. It should be the moment when individual children are asked to

---

[3] Benjamin S. Bloom, George F. Madaus, and Thomas Hastings, *Evaluation to Improve Learning* (New York: McGraw-Hill, 1981).

compare what they now know or can do or feel to what they knew or could do or felt at the beginning of the unit. This is the point at which a cumulative grade is given.

We have seen that organizing evaluation means finding a match between our objectives and our instruction and student activity as well as planning when and what kind of student data to collect to help them progress toward the objectives. How does that get translated in a real situation?

Exercise 10.1   *PLANNING UNIT EVALUATION*

This is a two-step exercise. First, match each activity with the unit objectives it might be used to evaluate. Second, try to match the appropriate evaluation techniques with the objectives of these two units.

Evaluation Techniques

Pretest	Group evaluation
Posttest	Work sample
Individual project	Conference
Group project	Self-evaluation
Observation	

SAMPLE UNIT PLAN 10.1
Second Grade: "Putting Food on the Table"

Objectives	Step 1: Activities	Step 2: Evaluation Techniques
1. Student categorizes food items as plant, animal, or both.	_____	_____
2. Student sequences pictures of food production.	_____	_____
3. Student describes jobs related to food production.	_____	_____
4. Student names ways to preserve food.	_____	_____
5. Student works productively in small group.	_____	_____
6. Student works independently at project centers.	_____	_____

Activities

    a. Story of "Little Red Hen" and discussion of how we take food for granted followed by drawing of favorite foods.

    b. Begin favorite food research books.

    c. Filmstrips and sequence pictures at centers on food production.

    d. Flannel board story on ways to preserve food.

    e. Research at home about food sources; add to books.

    f. Trip to supermarket to watch delivery trucks arrive.

    g. Visit from local truck farmer.

    h. More work on favorite food research books.

    i. Small groups prepare food histories pictures.

    j. Finish favorite food books.

    k. Small groups present pictures to another class.

SAMPLE UNIT PLAN 10.2
Fifth Grade: "Slavery"

Objectives	**Step 1:** Activities	**Step 2:** Evaluation Techniques
1. Student describes slave trade of colonial and early Republic America and social mentality that fostered it.	_____	_____
2. Student describes how blacks responded to slavery.	_____	_____
3. Student works productively in small-group study.	_____	_____
4. Student uses two library sources for individual profile.	_____	_____

Activities

    a. Role play in small groups using slave-auction documents.

    b. Begin reading *Uncle Tom's Cabin* aloud to class.

    c. Student choice of person to research biographical profile.

    d. Text assignment on plantation life read individually.

    e. Research questions for small-group research and discussion.

    f. Television segments of "Roots" shown to class.

g. Small-group discussion and study.

h. Black music of slavery period presentation and singing.

i. Small groups edit members' profiles.

Thinking about the Exercise

The second-grade food unit offers several opportunities for collecting data on children's progress toward the stated objectives. The child's work on sequencing pictures of food production at the centers could be observed and recorded, or a cut-and-paste worksheet that followed the child's session at the center could provide a work sample that would give us some data. Which would be a better measure of what the child knows? Which would be more possible to organize in a busy classroom? For the objectives about categorizing food items and describing jobs and ways of preserving foods, you also have several choices about how to collect data. Most obvious are individual worksheets. However, avoid using that technique too often. Another variation on this same theme is to have small groups compose collages from magazine pictures or to record, for example, a group story about jobs in food production to an aide or a tape recorder that children can then illustrate with a large group picture.

Teacher observation and self-evaluation recommend themselves as techniques for the work-habit and group-skills objectives. The group food-history pictures and presentations will also provide observational data about these objectives. The individual favorite food research books will tell you about the child's ability to ask questions at home and put his or her information into another form. Through teacher questioning, these books could be used at sharing times to work on the categorizing, food-production jobs, and food-preservation objectives. Again, the data are observational. Perhaps using a clipboard form would help you to recall children's oral responses.

Evaluation options for fifth graders are perhaps easier to organize. Completing "I learned . . ." or "What I don't understand . . ." statements could serve as a beginning point following the slave-market role play. The research questions that the small groups discuss should prepare them to respond to the content objectives about the slave trade, the social mentality fostering it, and the black responses to it. But how will you know something about each child's progress in these areas? Clearly, some kind of paper–pencil technique would seem appropriate. Short essays or multiple-choice items about these topics would be well suited.

The individual profiles of significant personages of the slavery period are easily judged for the research objective. Editing them in the small groups would give observational data on productive group study as would the discussion of the research questions.

More mileage could be gained from these projects than is indicated in the activity sequence. It would be profitable to form groups around writing about people in similar categories—slaves, plantation owners, government leaders, abolitionists, freedmen—and pool their stories and present the compilation to the class, which could then record the data on a retrieval chart and discuss it as a large group. Generalizations could be made as a result of this sharing process that would better prepare students to describe the social mentality fostering slavery and the responses to it.

Comparing the statements made after the role play at the beginning of the unit to their feelings and knowledge at the conclusion of the unit would be a powerful self-evaluation technique.

USING EVALUATION DATA

Data collected from evaluation techniques should be used for two main purposes: to monitor individual progress and to gauge teaching effectiveness. Both are essential to building learning experiences that meet children's needs.

Communicating about Individual Progress

Informing students and parents about instructional objectives helps set expectations for learning. Often, the long-range, or year's, objectives are set by the school or the district.

SAMPLE OBJECTIVES 10.1
Third-Grade Social Studies

Objectives

> Work on a project with a group.
> Respect others and value self.
> Assume class and school responsibilities

Knowledge

> Learn about community geography and history.
> Learn about community services and resources.

Study Skills

> Work on a project independently.
> Read for information from several sources.
> Organize and make reports.
> Interview to gather information.

These objectives, and additional ones you diagnose as essential for the class or individuals, should be clear to everyone involved. Many of the long-range objectives will have only tangential relation to the social studies. For parents, seeing the subject matter designation is probably less important than getting a global picture of the year's expectations. You could communicate these objectives through a letter sent home with the students or during the Back to School Night sessions usually held near the beginning of the school year. Unit objectives are communicated by letter at the beginning of each new unit.

Communication about objectives should take place throughout the year, not just at officially designated reporting periods. Periodic checklists or work samples can be sent home to keep parents informed. Individual conferences with students are essential means of keeping students focused on where they are and what they need to accomplish.

Conferences with both children and parents should begin by clarifying areas of growth toward the specified objectives. Sharing your grade book does little to illuminate the child's work to a parent. Explaining the evaluation conventions used at the school may also be necessary, but sharing work samples, such as stories or reports that have been collected over time, provide concrete data about which to meet. Child and parent suggestions on how to plan for further growth should be encouraged. One of the most potent life-molding abilities that you can help children develop is goal setting.

Evaluating Instruction

Using student data to evaluate instruction illuminates both what should happen next with individual students and the entire class in addition to the longer-range reflection about future ways of organizing instruction. There are several ways of reflecting upon student data resulting from instruction.

Examining the class trends in paper and pencil evaluations will enable you to check for flaws in instruction or item construction. If a majority of the class missed certain items, you should examine your own instruction. Did you spend enough time, with enough clarity on the content involved? Is the item ambiguous or tricky? On the other hand, if test results are uniformly tops or poor, you need to consider the congruency between variables such as cognitive level of instruction, density of content, amount of time devoted to content, and the general readiness of the students.

Another perspective on the appropriateness of instruction is examining the consistency between the amount of work assigned and the amount of work children actually complete. A poor rate of project completion may mean that aspects of classroom management such as reward systems and motivation need to be reconsidered. Social rewards, such as being part of a group that is supportive and sharing results with others in a nonthreatening manner are relevant considerations. Typically, children will complete a task that has personal significance.

When children do not complete individual projects, a task analysis to find out which skills the children need more instruction on will help you to carry out similar projects in the future. Report writing from various sources is a classic obstacle for middle-grade children. Consider a fifth-grade assignment in which children are to choose an explorer of the Americas and write about him. To do this, a child needs to combine several skills.

Task Analysis of Report Writing

1. Locate topic using index and table of contents.
2. Prepare questions or main topics to research.
3. Read for main ideas and supporting details.
4. Take notes in own words to answer research questions.
5. Review notes and organize for first draft.
6. Write first draft using notes.
7. Edit first draft for topic flow and organization.
8. Rewrite first draft.
9. Edit for spelling, grammar, and mechanics.
10. Prepare final draft.

Each skill listed requires mastery of the preceding skills. Often we assume that children will figure out how to handle the dynamic of report writing as most of us did, by trial and error and intuition. Commonly, steps two through five are not taught directly to the class, or they are taught for one report and assumed to be mastered for use in all succeeding reports. Looking at the report quality of completed reports and the rate of report completion can indicate which of the skills may need to be emphasized in future instruction.

Exercise 10.2 *TASK ANALYSIS PRACTICE*

Imagine that you teach the third grade and want the class to make a map of the county that shows how people get to their local government offices. Make a list of the things they would have to know about the county and the map before they could do this project. Share your list with a colleague. Do you both agree? Isn't it daunting to become aware of how much we assume when we ask children to do projects? Given this list, how would you build to this project?

SUMMARY

Evaluation of instruction serves purposes of charting individual student progress and providing clues for instructional improvement. It is a continuous process, an integral part of planning. Good evaluation is unobtrusive and instructionally integrated. Yet there must be enough evidence to use so that you can communicate about a child's progress toward specified objectives. It is our hope that evaluation can be made meaningful to children. The results of evaluation should help them recognize their accomplishments and want to strive for further growth.

SUGGESTED READINGS

Cervone, B., and O'Leary, K. "A Conceptual Framework for Parent Involvement." *Educational Leadership* 40, no. 2 (October 1982): 48–49. Suggestions for involving parents in school learning.

Doremus, Vivian P. "Forcing Works for Flowers, but Not for Children," *Educational Leadership* 44, no. 3 (November 1986): 32–35. Represents argument against excessive testing of children's achievement and reliance on academic achievement to exclusion of other developmental areas.

Eisner, Elliot. *The Educational Imagination.* New York: Macmillan, 1985. Classic text on evaluation written from a broad perspective.

Moles, O. "Synthesis of Recent Research on Parent Participation in Children's Education." *Educational Leadership* 40 (October 1982): 44–47. Reviews importance of parental involvement.

Postscript

You have now "covered" the basics of elementary social studies teaching. Hopefully, you are now more aware of the many opportunities for building effective social studies programs. As we come to the close of the experience we've shared through this text, we would like to leave you with these thoughts.

1. Build on your own strengths and interests. All of us have particular talents whether they are in music or in leading good discussions. While you should not be afraid to try new ideas and techniques, try also to give your students the best of your teaching assets.
2. Expect that every child in your class can and will learn. But keep in mind that most significant learning is not apparent after a short period. Learning takes time and multiple exposures. The diversity of children in your class will require you to diversify your methods for meeting their needs. We hope you see this diversity as a valuable resource and treat it as a human blessing in your classroom.
3. Teaching is a wonderful way to learn. Challenge yourself to keep your social studies teaching fresh by traveling, experimenting, learning from further professional exposure and reading, reading, reading. However, you cannot do everything you would like during your first year or years. Becoming a master teacher is a goal you will work toward all your teaching life.
4. See social studies instruction as an important vehicle for learning inside and outside the classroom. It can be the highlight of your teaching day. It was for us when we were teaching the elementary and junior high level.

We have enjoyed working on this textbook. It helped so sharpen our own thinking about the social studies. We hope the experience you had with this book makes you enthusiastic about teaching social studies.

We wish you the rewards of teaching.

June R. Chapin
Rosemary G. Messick

Index